Reporter Anonymous

By the same author

Time and Place
The R.C.s

Reporter Anonymous
The Story of the Press Association

GEORGE SCOTT

HUTCHINSON OF LONDON

HUTCHINSON & CO (*Publishers*) LTD
178–202 Great Portland Street, London W1

London Melbourne Sydney
Auckland Bombay Toronto
Johannesburg New York

First published 1968

© George Scott and the Press Association Ltd. 1968

This book has been set in Plantin, printed in Great Britain on Antique Wove paper by Anchor Press, and bound by Wm. Brendon, both of Tiptree, Essex

09 087560 5

'Because the work you do is so valuable, the responsibilities of the Press Association are heavy. Without your help the public would be uninformed, and without your integrity they would be misled and defrauded.

'You have since the war had to exercise a discrimination never previously forced upon a national press. Many will feel you strike a fair balance, and I believe you will continue to resist temptations to diminish fact for the sake of sensation or to twist truth and to serve partisanship.

'That is the great thing, the great feature, and I think I may speak for all political parties, that we discern and admire in the work of the Press Association.'

Winston Churchill at the annual members' luncheon of the Press Association, 11 June 1952

Acknowledgements

It is impossible to acknowledge by name all those past and present members of the staff of the Press Association whose reminiscences have contributed richly to this book. I must record my particular gratitude, however, to Edward Davies for the unselfish way in which he allowed me to draw upon his own large experience of the P.A.

Many people have helped to provide me with the basic material for this story, but, above all, I do want to thank L. C. J. McNae and Brian Robins, not least for their enthusiasm which prompted several profitable lines of inquiry.

I should also like to express my appreciation to those senior executives, directors and member-newspapers of the P.A., and to the Newspaper Society, for answering my questions so readily and for placing material from their own libraries so freely at my disposal.

I am grateful to the following authors and publishers for permission to use extracts from their books: John Durham and The Golden Head Press Ltd., *Telegraphs in Victorian London;* G. M. Trevelyan and Longmans, Green & Co. Ltd., *English Social History;* Anthony Gibbs, *The Journalist's London* by Philip Gibbs; William Collins, Sons & Co. Ltd., *The Decline and Fall of Lloyd George* by Lord Beaverbrook; David Butler and the Cambridge University Press, *British Parliamentary General Election Results in 1950–64;* and Lord Reith for allowing me to quote from an article he wrote for *The Quarterly Review* in October 1924.

Among the books I have consulted and to which I want to acknowledge my debt are *Dangerous Estate* by Francis Williams; *Reuters' Century* by Graham Storey; *A Life in Reuters* by Sir Roderick Jones; *The Manchester Guardian—A Century of History* by W. Haslam Mills.

Contents

Introductory	Born 1868	13
One	Appointments and rehearsals	31
Two	Weathering the storm	48
Three	Conflict and compromise	56
Four	Mr. Gladstone's Fat Reporter	75
Five	The paternal touch	86
Six	The perils of the law	104
Seven	No holds barred	114
Eight	Struggles with the censor	135
Nine	Private wires for all	147
Ten	New men for a new world	156
Eleven	A losing battle	170
Twelve	Squaring the circle	184
Thirteen	A mysterious resignation	205
Fourteen	In war as in peace	232
Fifteen	'A monopoly news service'	251
Sixteen	The second hundred	275
Appendix 1	Chairmen of the Press Association	279
Appendix 2	Persons present at inaugural meeting, 29 June 1868	284
Appendix 3	Member newspapers, October 1967	287
Appendix 4	Extracts from *The Times* of 20 May 1880	292
Index		299

Illustrations

	facing page
The Palatine Hotel, Manchester	52
The sign in Fleet Street pointing to the first permanent home of the P.A.	52
John Edward Taylor	53
John Lovell	53
Sir Edmund Robbins	53
H. C. Robbins	53
Edward Davies	60
A. L. Cranfield	60
Henry Martin	60
Charles Jervis	60
From the official record of the first A.G.M.	61
Walter Cattermole	61
Samuel Storey (now Lord Buckton)	112
Sir Roderick Jones (*Cecil Beaton*)	112
Chamberlain on his return from Munich (*Topix*)	112
The editorial floor of the P.A.	113
Punched tape carrying news to Britain's provincial newspapers	113
Monitoring incoming and outgoing wire pictures	128
Telegraph mechanics at work in the backroom	128
Battery of copy takers typing telephoned reports	129

Illustrations *facing page*

Main editorial floor on General Election night 1966	129
The 1965 Derby with P.A. man first on the spot	176
Sports picture of the year 1956	176
Winston Churchill speaking at the P.A. annual luncheon 1952	177
Duke of Edinburgh leaving the Press Association	177
The board and officers of the P.A. 1967–8	192
The headquarters of the P.A.	192
Comings and goings at No. 10	
R. A. Butler arriving for a Cabinet meeting	193
The Queen leaves after dinner with Sir Winston Churchill	193
Princess Elizabeth and Prince Philip leaving Westminster Abbey after their wedding	240
A comment by Giles on the affair of the Duke and the photographers	241
News-gathering in the electronic age (*Topix*)	241
The P.A. serves radio and television	
P.A. copy being received at Broadcasting House	256
The author conducts a radio interview	256
The old and new methods of communication	
A Wheatstone morse set	257
Present-day equipment (*Coventry Evening Telegraph*)	257

In Appendix 3

The distribution of newspaper-member subscribers of the P.A.	*page* 286
The main London subscribers	291

Introductory / Born 1868

At half past eight on the evening of Friday, the 4th of February 1870, some 500 boys assembled in Telegraph Street in the City of London. From there they were marched through the gas-lit streets to the General Post Office, in St. Martin's-le-Grand, where they were received by a guard of honour composed of a company of the 49th Foot, the Royal Berkshires. The boys, who were aged from ten to fifteen, had been well drilled by the sergeants of Colonel Du Plat Taylor's volunteer corps, the Post Office Rifles, and they put on an impressive display. The buttons of their new uniforms shone and they wore their square-peaked caps with a jaunty air. The occasion for all this ceremony was the eve of the taking-over of the telegraphs by the Post Office from the private telegraph companies, an historic act of State socialism to which both Conservative and Liberal administrations had contributed. The boys were the first members of the metropolitan corps of telegraph messenger boys. They were drawn up in line before Colonel Taylor for inspection. Then they were addressed upon their duties and responsibilities by Frank Ives Scudamore, the Post Office official who had been the architect of the take-over and was now the head of the new Postal Telegraphs Department.

According to an eyewitness account,[1] Scudamore addressed them 'at considerable length'. He cautioned them that 'the public themselves would act as inspectors over them, and that if they were seen idling, "overing" posts [laughter], or playing with marbles in a sly corner or a blind alley [renewed laughter], they would most assuredly be reported'. On the other hand, Scuda-

[1] Quoted by John Durham, writing in *Telegraphs in Victorian London*.

Introductory

more told them, 'if they proved themselves reliable and trustworthy, they would be rewarded accordingly [cheers] . . . There was no reason whatever why a telegraphic messenger should not rise to be a letter carrier, a stamper, a sorter, or even a telegraphic clerk [loud cheers] . . .' The boys, said this account, 'were afterwards regaled with a substantial supper. The band of the corps played some excellent music and cheers for Mr. Scudamore and Colonel Du Plat Taylor brought the proceedings to a close.'

It was a little after ten o'clock when the guests who had attended the ceremony—and had taken refreshments in the former registered letter department—climbed into their carriages. That same night over 2000 boys were put through their paces at similar ceremonies in all the large towns of the kingdom and instructed in their duties by the local postmasters.

At five o'clock the next morning, Saturday, the 5th of February, as the doors of the Post Office opened for business, the first press telegram to be transmitted over the Government wires was handed across the counter. It had been prepared by a twenty-two-year-old sub-editor on the staff of the Press Association, Edmund Robbins, and with that message the Press Association, which had been founded nearly two years before, had really started out on its career of supplying a news service to the British press. The *Birmingham Daily Post* for Monday, the 7th of February 1870, carried the following:

GENERAL NEWS
(Press Association Telegrams)
The Telegraphs
London, Saturday

The telegraphs were transferred today at 8 a.m. The first message was from Edinburgh, congratulating Mr. Scudamore. All hands were waiting, from the secretary downwards—Bright's bell instruments ringing merry peals.

First 'Press Association' messages:

'Wind and weather reports from all ports.'

'Rumoured in military circles that Sir Henry Storks has tendered his resignation of the Control Department.'

Introductory

'Admiral Sir H. Leeke is lying dangerously ill.'

'An order has been issued raising the standard of the Royal Marine Corps half an inch.'

The press the P.A. (as it was later to be known) was created to serve grew rapidly during the second half of the nineteenth century, especially the provincial press. There is no single explanation for this. It is true, of course, that the abolition of stamp duty and the advertisement tax was an essential prerequisite to progress. These taxes on knowledge, as they have been called, performed a dual function. They were a useful source of revenue as well as an effective impediment to newspaper publication—both desirable objectives from the politicians' point of view, who resented journalistic criticism. It was in spite of these taxes that *The Times* flourished, even though, when they were at their worst, there was a tax of 3*s*. 6*d*. on each advertisement and a duty of fourpence on each published sheet, and the cost of the newspaper rose to sevenpence. It was also because of these taxes, which crippled any potential competitors and at the same time assured *The Times* of an avid circulation among men of rank and influence, that the newspaper enjoyed an almost tyrannical power unknown to any other newspaper before or since. The prospect of reducing that power, of cutting down the stature of the editor of *The Times* to something nearer to manageable size, was an argument that contributed, at least, to Parliament's ultimate decision, in 1855, to abolish the stamp duty, which had been by far the most formidable of the newspaper taxes. For obvious reasons *The Times* was less than wholehearted in welcoming a measure that would, and did, bring very real competition. There were many others who saw the publication of cheap newspapers and the extension of newspaper readership to a much wider slice of the population as being likely to lead to a general debasement of standards. At first sight it is surprising to find the Provincial Newspaper Society (later to become the Newspaper Society), representing 135 country newspaper proprietors, among the most determined opponents of the abolition of stamp duty. But it is clear that its attitude sprang in part at least from fear of the competition which would ensue.

Introductory

In his *English Social History* G. M. Trevelyan makes a melancholy comparison between what had been and what was to come. '. . . the higher culture of nineteenth-century England', he wrote, 'was varied, solid, and widespread over a large proportion of the community. The world is not likely to see again so fine and broad a culture for many centuries to come.' 'Industrial change', said Trevelyan, 'was creating the mass-vulgarity which was destined to swamp that high standard of literary culture with the advent of the new journalism, the decay of the countryside, and the mechanisation of life.' It is hard to appreciate Trevelyan's use of the phrase 'a large proportion of the community' when the mass of the people received virtually no education. The cultivated tastes of the minority had been acquired at the expense of the social degradation, the intellectual starvation and the physical near-slavery of their compatriots. Industrialisation brought hideous evils to Britain, but, ultimately, it also released those forces and impelled those changes which were to crumble social barriers and to admit the many to the kinds of pleasure and opportunity which for so long had been the privilege of the few. It is easy enough to deplore some of the products of mid-twentieth-century mass-culture and to forget or ignore the achievements, material and humane, of the revolution which began in the nineteenth century. At all events, it is a luxurious irrelevance to lament the passing of an age in which England was a largely rural society in which every man, or so it is often alleged, knew his station in life and was happy to accept it.

By the middle of the nineteenth century the English people were well on the way to being transformed into a nation of townies. The boundaries of our great provincial cities were being rapidly overrun and expanded. After the abolition of the stamp duty, newspapers were created, or existing ones extended, to serve a new audience. Newspapers had been published before, of course, and many had survived despite the formidable discouragements of taxation, of libel laws which were framed on the assumption that newspapers and journalists were villains until proved otherwise, and of inadequate means of getting the news or of printing it. Among them were papers like the *Manchester Guardian*, the *Birmingham Post*, the *Yorkshire Post*, the *Liverpool Post*, the *Scotsman*, the *Glasgow Herald*, and the *Cork Examiner*—or their forerunners. What the men who founded

Introductory

them and ran them—and their contemporaries—had in common was courage. Frequently they had high principles, too. Certainly no man went sanely into newspaper production to make money. Outside London a daily paper was virtually unknown; the provincial papers were published once a week, twice a week, or, exceptionally, three times a week. It was not until the stamp tax went that there were dailies, twopenny and penny, and even halfpenny dailies. It was only then that daily newspaper production became an economic proposition.

Because many publishers had successfully evaded paying taxation by smuggling their unstamped papers into circulation, statistics about the number of newspapers before 1855 are not reliable. (As far back as 1743, the trade in unstamped papers was so large and successful that a deterrent Act was passed by which hawkers selling them were liable to three months' imprisonment.) That must be remembered when citing the official figures provided by the Stamp Office for 1836 showing the existence in the United Kingdom of a total of 277 newspapers. By 1856 there were 795. Another gauge of the flowering of the press is to compare the number of actual copies of all provincial newspapers circulating in 1836—about 18,000,000 in the whole year—with the number delivered *by post alone* in 1857, which was 71,000,000. Before the abolition of stamp duty only the biggest of provincial papers could hope to sell 10,000 copies of a single issue.

The newspapers owed their release from the fetters of taxation to the relentless campaign waged by radicals and reformers of all classes and spearheaded by such crusaders as Cobden and Bright. Cheaper and better-quality paper on which to print them came after the removal of the duty on paper in 1861 which in turn made possible a major development in newspaper production. The paper manufacturers produced a paper strong enough to be fed to a rotary press in a continuous roll; before then it had had to be fed sheet by sheet. The means of fast newspaper production and, therefore, of much bigger circulations had been created.

This would have meant little, however, without the railways and the electric telegraph. It was to them that the newspapers owed their ability to exploit the opportunity presented by the abolition of taxation. The railways not only provided quick,

Introductory

efficient links between town and town. They were not only the arteries of the Industrial Revolution. They were also the means by which the telegraphs were first put into use in Britain and by which they spread all over the country. The telegraphs followed the railway lines and in the 1840s, the same decade that saw the astonishing promotion of the railway, some 2000 miles of track were accompanied by telegraph wires carrying service messages for the railway companies and any public traffic they could attract. Here was the practical harnessing of the invention which was to transform the reporting of news from a long, uncertain, frustrating process into the almost simultaneous translation of events into publication that we take for granted today. The first submarine cable was laid, between Dover and Calais, in 1851 and on the 13th of November that year stock-market reports were telegraphed between London and Paris for the first time. No other invention, perhaps not even television, not even the simultaneous transmission of pictures by means of space satellite, has had so revolutionary an effect on the newspaper press.

As with any other development which promotes such radical change, retrospect brings, momentarily, a romantic regret for the past. The ways by which journalists and newspapers gathered and communicated news before the telegraph were more colourful and more adventurous. Before the railways and the telegraphs, newspapers had had to wait upon news carried across seas by sailing ships and on land on horseback, stage-coach or pony-trap or donkey-cart or by pigeon. Even by dogs. In those days, as now, there was great anxiety to hear the racing results as quickly as possible. The Manchester newspapers often did not receive the results of the big races until a day, perhaps two days, later. The gap between a race being run and the result being known allowed betting to go on long after the horses had finished running. The bookmakers thought themselves safe enough. One, however, an enterprising individual, who arranged for a team of dogs to carry the St. Leger result from Doncaster to Manchester, knew the result hours before anyone else. He laid his bets and stood to make a fortune, but many bookmakers refused to pay.

It would be wrong, despite its ultimate significance, to suggest that the coming of the electric telegraph immediately solved all communication problems or displaced old methods. It was not until about 1917, for instance, that the *Bolton Evening News*

Introductory

pensioned off the homing pigeons which their football reporter used on Saturday afternoons to tell his office the score: one pigeon at half-time, one at full-time. (Sometimes, instead of returning to their cote on the flat roof of the Mealhouse Lane premises, they landed on a building nearby and had to be coaxed down with offers of food.)

In the early days the telegraph wires linked only the towns; parts of the country were many miles away from the nearest telegraph office, which was often at a railway station. Also, while the speed at which cables were laid across oceans was indeed remarkable, it did not and could not happen overnight. There was still much scope for individual enterprise and resource, like that displayed by Thomas Crosbie of the *Cork Examiner*. This Thomas Crosbie, the first of the family which has owned the *Examiner* for nearly 100 years—and for most of its existence—was, like so many of those pioneers, an editor who believed in getting his own news. He used to go out in a small boat from Cork Harbour to pick up news from the ships calling there. It was in this way that he heard from an American ship of the surrender of the Confederates in the American Civil War. He telegraphed the news to *The Times*, giving it a scoop over its rivals. (*The Times*, recognising Crosbie's enterprise as well as his brilliance as a writer, offered him a job as a leader-writer in London at the splendid salary of 700 golden sovereigns a year, an offer the paper regretfully withdrew when it learned that Crosbie was a Roman Catholic.)

The appetite for news in town and country alike was a ravenous one and it fed on whatever scraps were thrown to it. Much of the news was, by modern standards, intolerably stale. But news is still news, even if three days or three weeks or three months old, if you have not heard it before. Or so, at any rate, thought the readers of the British press in the middle of the last century. To buy a paper for personal consumption was uncommon and newspaper readership was vastly greater than circulation figures of the time suggest. Newspapers were read in clubs, pubs, financial and commercial exchanges, mechanics' institutes, coffee-houses and newsrooms. Until 1855 and the abolition of the stamp duty the provincial papers, with few exceptions, were a hotch-potch of news and advertisements, presented with a total lack of concern for the appearance of the printed page. The advertisements

Introductory

were mainly local. Most of the news, however, came from London—copied, as was the custom throughout the country, from the London papers. (One of the benefits the railways brought to provincial journalism was the speedier delivery of the metropolitan papers; the practice of 'lifting' material from them went on well into the latter half of the nineteenth century.) Local news items derived mostly from the courts.

The owners and editors of those provincial papers—many of them printers—must have been conscious of the inadequacy of their news supplies. But so long as they were publishing only once or twice a week the majority probably did not care too much. With the emancipation of the press in 1855, however, with the birth of new papers and the conversion into dailies of existing ones, and with a much sharper awareness of competition, they began to recognise that their old sources of news were not good enough and could no longer be tolerated. Their discontent focused upon the private enterprise telegraph companies, like the Electric and International, and the British and Irish Magnetic, which had carried out the development of the electric telegraph in Britain.

The potential value of the telegraph as an instrument for transmitting news had been demonstrated. In November 1847, for example, only four years after the first public telegraph line had linked Paddington and Slough, the text of the Queen's Speech, at the opening of Parliament, was transmitted by telegraph to the chief towns of Britain at the rate of 430 words an hour. As the whole speech consisted of 730 words, this meant that it could be sent over the wires in less than two hours—much quicker than the train could bring a copy from London to, say, Leeds. In theory, anyway. The inefficiency of the telegraphs is a recurrent motif of this story. As the *Yorkshire Post* historian has observed, the transmission of the Queen's Speech in 1847 from London to Leeds struck a hitch or two: '. . . its reception at Leeds was not an unqualified success. The first word was received at 1.5 p.m., but the last not till 6.5 p.m. The human instruments were very fallible and there were two intermediate stations, at Derby and Normanton, the latter the earliest centre for the North.'

The technical imperfections of the telegraphs, though, were not the only cause for complaint by the newspapers against the telegraph companies. In the early days of the telegraph only the

Introductory

bigger provincial newspapers used it for transmitting their own messages. It was not until later that the press was given preferential rates and it would have been hard for a weekly paper, for instance, to justify the cost of telephoned news. But the telegraph companies themselves, seeing the newspapers as a promising market and with their wires idle for much of the night, began themselves to collect and transmit news to the larger towns, operating at first as separate agencies. At the outbreak of the Paris revolution in 1848 the *Manchester Guardian* made use of news supplied in this way to bring out several special editions of the paper on a day which was not a normal publication day.

After a few years of operating independently the Electric and Magnetic companies combined to offer a single supply of news and it was then that the troubles really began. The news-gathering organisation of the telegraph companies was known as their Intelligence Department. It had its own editorial and reporting staffs—not all of them journalists—and it offered a service of up to 4000 words a day: a Parliamentary summary, Court and Society gossip, general, commercial and sporting news, law reports and the weather. Put like that, the service sounds admirable, but the quality of the news was, to say the least, erratic, its accuracy questionable and its transmission unpredictable. The annual subscription for this supply seems to have varied between £150 and £250, the terms varying according to what the companies thought they could get out of a paper. Furthermore, many newspapers complained that the newsrooms and hotels often received a better supply than they did, and as the practice of the newsrooms was to placard the 'intelligence' as soon as they received it, the newspapers felt they were having the ground cut from under them.

The general feeling of grievance and dissatisfaction mounted only gradually, however. True, in 1856, the *Manchester Guardian*, which, even before its expansion into a daily the year before, had developed a powerful and influential voice, tried hard to get a better report from Parliament than that supplied by the telegraph companies. Two things stood in the way: there was not enough room in Parliament for separate representatives of the provincial press; and the telegraph companies would not send over their wires any Parliamentary report which had not been prepared by their own staff.

Introductory

Many of the new daily papers flourished to their readers promises of a news service of unprecedented quantity and variety. They looked to the telegraph companies to provide a large part of it; their disappointment with what they received often turned to public anger. On the 2nd of July 1855, two days after Mr. Gladstone had repealed the stamp duty, the *North and South Shields Gazette* offered to subscribers to its weekly edition a daily telegraphic edition issued and delivered free every night. It was to prove a success eventually but its beginnings were inauspicious. Its first issue carried this statement:

'Owing to some yet unexplained blunderings amongst the Telegraphic Authorities themselves, we regret that our first impression should be so late. Every arrangement—both written and oral—was made on our part to give full and early information of all the important events that had transpired during the last twenty-four hours, but the bungling mismanagement of the Telegraph people has neutralised these to some extent for the present publication. This, however, we trust will not occur again, as we have forwarded an energetic remonstrance to headquarters which we trust will prevent a repetition of such gross and culpable negligence...'

In 1860, the year that Devon and Cornwall were linked by rail, the *Western Morning News* was founded in Plymouth as a daily to serve the two counties. The founders, Edward Spender and his brother-in-law William Saunders, also offered their readers at their breakfast-table all the news for which they had previously waited until evening and the arrival of *The Times* from London. Again, to do this meant dependence on the telegraph companies and their Intelligence Department. But it is clear that Spender and Saunders, too, were soon dissatisfied with the service. They founded their own news agency, the Central Press, which from the 1st of January 1863 offered a daily service of eight columns of general and foreign news and, in addition, leading articles, Parliamentary sketches, a London letter, late reports of the 'corn trade and agricultural markets', law cases, meetings, and articles which included 'a careful compilation of literary and religious intelligence'. This service was sent not over the telegraph wires but by trains leaving London in the evening for the big towns and cities of the Kingdom.

One other indication of the poverty of the service supplied by

Introductory

the telegraph companies is given by H. R. G. Whates, the historian of the *Birmingham Post*. 'At any time from 1860 onwards', he has written, 'the conductors of the *Post* would willingly have disowned their earliest papers, for they were sadly lacking in gravity. News, the life-blood of a newspaper, was a desperately scarce commodity until the Telegraph Act of 1869 authorised the Postmaster-General to buy up the several telegraph undertakings. Until then, provincial newspapers had to bargain with the competing companies; charges were high and the appliances for transmission were extremely primitive. Telegraphic news in the *Post* and other provincial papers amounted to no more than a column or so. A supply that was scarcely adequate for a weekly newspaper was wholly insufficient for a paper publishing on five or six days a week. It had to be supplemented by local news gathered by a small staff of reporters, by news articles sent through the post and by wholesale clippings from small weekly newspapers from all over the country.'

As the new daily papers in the big towns grew more confident, as their sales increased and their front pages became more and more packed with advertisements—to the point where a page one with nothing *but* advertisements became the accepted, respectable form—so their ambitions grew. Their editors and owners were, almost invariably, men of pugnacious political convictions seeking to inform and persuade the literate within their community, at a time when politics were made of stern stuff and newspaper readers would look forward with relish to the verbatim report of a speech by the likes of Gladstone or Disraeli. These provincial newspapermen of the mid-nineteenth century were also, very frequently, men of reforming zeal who were among the leaders of campaigns to clean up the squalor and ameliorate the misery of the industrial towns in which they lived. Their capacity to influence their communities, to induce passionate indignation, to impel the authorities to action, was very real. They wanted their newspapers to be worthy of the power and responsibility beckoning to them. They wanted to produce papers which could be compared with any produced in London, even *The Times* itself.

One by one, they set up offices in London. At first, this usually meant a single editorial representative who would give them a personal service of news, but it showed their growing impatience with the second-hand and the second-rate. Their impatience with

23

Introductory

the telegraph companies became even more difficult to control—though, it must be remembered, it was still only a minority of newspapers which felt this concern to any degree. To those who could perceive the potential of the telegraph, the actual performance was an agony. Among those newspapers which suffered was the *Scotsman*:

'Errors and delays were endless, and to the enterprising conductors of newspapers they became intolerable. Obstacles were raised at every step; other papers did not lend much aid or encouragement. But the conductors of the *Scotsman* had reached the conclusion that "it was their business as purveyors of news to supply the public each morning with adequate reports of all that has taken place in the three Kingdoms possessing special or general interest, on the previous day".'

The owners of the *Scotsman* wanted to make their daily paper 'the paper of today, not of yesterday or last week'.

The *Glasgow Herald* was of like mind and in 1866 both these Scottish newspapers decided they must have their own special wire, leased from the telegraph company, a private wire which would carry telegrams from London directly into their own offices and cut out the use of messenger boys. Private wires were adopted in time by all leading provincial papers. But the *Herald* and *Scotsman* did not lease theirs until after they—and other Scottish newspapers—had challenged the power of the telegraph companies and had come off worst.

The Electric and Magnetic Companies held a monopoly control of the supply of news by telegraph and they exploited that power in the traditional way of monopolists. Their attitude towards the newspapers was one of take it or leave it. Any newspaper which, in the eyes of the telegraph companies, complained too loudly and too offensively about the service they were receiving could expect to be sharply corrected. It might well find its name removed from the list of newspapers entitled to receive messages at reduced rate. It then faced the choice of paying the full rate—in effect a heavy fine—or of doing without any telegraphic service at all.

In 1864 the telegraph companies gave notice to the Scottish daily papers that from the following year the price they would have to pay for the supply of news was going up to £200 a year. The reason given was 'the large additional outlay for foreign,

Introductory

colonial and other news'. The Scottish newspapers got together in Glasgow to decide what to do. Apart from the *Scotsman* and the *Glasgow Herald*, there were representatives from the *North British Mail*, the *Glasgow Morning Journal*, the *Edinburgh Courant*, the *Caledonian Mercury*, the *Edinburgh Daily Review*, the *Dundee Advertiser* and the *Dundee Courier and Argus*.

The resolution they passed shows how comprehensive were the criticisms of the telegraph companies:

'That, in the opinion of the meeting, this increase of charge cannot be justified on the grounds stated, in so far as this meeting is quite unaware of any improvement in the character of the foreign and colonial intelligence, and that the said increase is therefore uncalled for. That the joint arrangement recently made between the Electric and Magnetic Companies for the transmission of news must have materially reduced the working expenses of those companies but, notwithstanding, the news itself has not improved in quality nor in earliness of transmission, as the newspaper proprietors were led to expect. On the contrary, well-founded complaints have been made of the loose and unintelligible manner in which the news is not unfrequently received, and of the late hour at which much of it, especially of Parliamentary intelligence during the session, is often received. That from the lavish manner in which the telegraphic news is now forwarded to public reading rooms, clubs, and hotels, the intelligence sent to the newspapers is much depreciated in value, and that this grievance is aggravated by the fact that in many cases the news is sold to these establishments at a much cheaper proportionate rate than that paid by the newspapers. That, for these and other reasons which can be urged if necessary, the meeting respectfully requests that the companies reconsider their demand, as the undersigned are disinclined to accede to it.'

The Scottish newspaper proprietors thought they had a trump card. They were in touch with a new telegraph company, the United Kingdom, and had strong hopes of making an agreement for the supply of news at the price they had been paying the Electric and Magnetic. They were out of luck. The other two companies let the United Kingdom, the new company, into their cosy little combine, and the monopoly continued on its way, the Intelligence Department at the Central Telegraph Station in Telegraph Street in the City of London now operating on behalf

Introductory

of three companies instead of two. The Scottish papers had to pay up.

The following year a small meeting of newspaper proprietors was held in Manchester. Two of them came from Manchester itself, the others from Edinburgh, Dublin, Leeds, Newcastle, Dundee and Halifax. It was an important meeting, not because it had any immediate practical effects but because it established the principle of provincial newspapers acting together, as a cooperative agency, to organise their own collection and supply of news. What they wanted to do was to organise a daily news service, superior in all ways to that provided by the telegraph companies, at no extra cost and as nearly as possible at cost price.

That first meeting—to which several of the proprietors had come on behalf of others in their part of the country to see what was in the air—was held on the 17th of October 1865. Those who attended listened to what Mr. Glynn, a Newcastle solicitor, and Mr. A. J. Holmes, a telegraphic engineer, could tell them about the practical possibilities of setting up their own telegraphic association. A fortnight later a much larger meeting was held at the Palatine Hotel, Manchester, again under the chairmanship of John Edward Taylor, son of the founder and first editor of the *Manchester Guardian* and now himself its proprietor and editor. The outcome was the formation of the Press Association Company Limited. Among its objects was the organising of a system of news-collecting and reporting in London, with correspondents in all towns of importance in the United Kingdom. But first it would be necessary to find a means of transmitting the news, which meant either making an arrangement with one of the existing telegraph companies or through a new company.

The telegraph companies said they were willing to get out of the news-collecting business, so far as newspapers were concerned. However, if John Edward Taylor and his colleagues had imagined they could beat the telegraph companies as easily as that they were quickly disillusioned. The price the Press Association would be charged for the transmission of its news would work out at three or four times what newspapers were paying the telegraph companies for the existing service from the Intelligence Department.

The Press Association Company did not seriously pursue the

Introductory

other courses open to it, either of finding a new telegraph company which would agree to carry its news service or of setting up its own national telegraph system. The reason for not doing so, apart from the difficulties or the capital which would have been involved, can be easily guessed. From the early 1850s the idea of the State taking over the telegraphs had been shuttled around Westminster. The daily newspapers agitated for it with more and more persistence. They were joined in 1865 first by the Edinburgh Chamber of Commerce and then by chambers of commerce all over the country, their prime interest being the adoption of a uniform rate of sixpence for twenty words, irrespective of distance, a system being operated successfully in Belgium and Switzerland. The shortcomings of the telegraph companies as a news agency had been demonstrated to the politicians in a conspicuous way on the occasion of Gladstone's Budget speech of 1860 (when income tax went up from ninepence to tenpence in the pound). The mistakes in the reporting of that speech by the Intelligence Department—and their reproduction in the newspapers—were said to be so numerous that confusion was widespread.

It was in 1865 that the Liberal Postmaster-General, Lord Stanley of Alderley, instructed Frank Ives Scudamore, an assistant secretary of the Post Office, to prepare a report on the pros and cons of a nationalised telegraph system. Scudamore reported in favour. From then on, although there were to be further reports, draft Bills, and a Select Committee of Enquiry (to which John Edward Taylor gave evidence), the State take-over was only a matter of time. The actual Bill empowering the Government to acquire the telegraphs was introduced in Parliament early in 1868 and became an Act on 31 July of the same year. Disraeli was Prime Minister at that time; Gladstone was back in office by the time of the physical transfer of the telegraphs in February 1870. In the interval there had been exhaustive negotiations with the private telegraph companies over compensation. In the end, to the disgust and indignation of many, the shareholders received a very grand total of some £$5\frac{1}{2}$ million.

The introduction of the Telegraph Bill was the cue for which the daily newspaper proprietors had been waiting. They held a meeting on 6 April 1868, in Manchester, again at the Palatine Hotel which stood alongside Victoria Station, overlooking the

Introductory

River Irwell. Once more John Edward Taylor, of the *Manchester Guardian*, took the chair, as he did at a further meeting in London on 29 June. This second one, a decisive one in the story of the Press Association, was held at the United Hotel in Charles Street, Haymarket. To this hotel, with its handsome Nash-Repton façade—which was virtually all that had been left of the old Opera House after the fire the year before—came most of the really big men in provincial journalism, the proprietors of twenty-eight daily papers, from Cork, from Dublin, from Belfast; from Glasgow, Edinburgh, Newcastle, Plymouth.[1] To judge from the minutes, it must also have been a most industrious and business-like meeting at which important, detailed decisions were taken. They agreed to form a new co-operative association to collect and supply news, which would be open to any provincial newspaper proprietor who wanted telegraphic news. None but newspaper proprietors could become shareholders, thus ensuring that the association would always be run by newspapermen in the interest of newspapers. A committee of fifteen, appointed to make arrangements for the formation of the new company, went quickly to work. The meeting at the United Hotel was held on a Monday. By Friday of the same week John Edward Taylor was able to send out to potential members not only a copy of the resolutions taken at that meeting but also a report by the committee which explained the services the association would provide and their estimated cost. It showed that if more than three-quarters of those who subscribed to the service provided by the private telegraph companies were to join the new association it would be possible to cut down on the average rates then being paid. If fewer than three-quarters, then the charges would have to go up. The report stressed a theme which runs right through the story of the P.A.: the value of working together. '. . . the Association is formed on the principle of co-operation', said the committee's report, 'and can never be worked for individual profit, or become exclusive in its character . . .' So it has remained.

An early danger to the new association was overcome. The meetings in Manchester and London had been confined to the proprietors of daily newspapers. This put up the backs of members of the Provincial Newspaper Society who were running weekly papers and who felt they were being snubbed by their big

[1] See Appendix 2.

Introductory

brothers. (Many of the daily paper proprietors also belonged to the Provincial Newspaper Society, which had been founded in 1836, and had on several occasions proved the wisdom of collective action.) The Society had co-operated in the formation of the earlier, 1865, association, and one of its members, Joseph Fisher, of the *Waterford Mail*, had himself drawn up an elaborate scheme for establishing a news-collecting organisation and was to devote a lot of energy to the cause of the State taking over the telegraphs. Taylor had also offended the Yorkshire Newspaper Society, which rebuked him roundly for telling the Parliamentary Committee that the *Yorkshire Gazette* and the *Doncaster Gazette* were not very influential papers.

It was John Edward Taylor's job to soothe the anxieties and the injured feelings of the weekly paper owners and this he did with almost complete success. On the 15th September 1868 another meeting was held under Taylor's chairmanship at the Palatine Hotel in Manchester, at which the new company was formally constituted, and a Consultative Board and a Committee of Management appointed. On the Committee, the executive responsible for the day-to-day operations, was George Harper, of the weekly *Huddersfield Chronicle*, who had succeeded Joseph Fisher as president of the Provincial Newspaper Society.

Everyone seemed pleased with the way things were going—with the exception of Joseph Fisher. He now launched an attack from a new angle. In the *Waterford Mail* he wrote an editorial in which he criticised the new organisation because, he said, in choosing its officers it had passed over every Conservative daily paper and had chosen representatives of the daily press exclusively from Liberal organs.

'There is not upon the Committee of Management ... a single gentleman of Conservative opinions.[1] Such a completely one-sided organisation cannot command the confidence and support either of the press or the public. It may answer for party purposes, but it will fail to reach that higher function which such a body should aim at. Looking at the names upon the directorate, it cannot be said to have a representative character; the members have been selected solely from those of very marked political

---

[1] This seems to ignore George Harper, whose *Chronicle* was described in a supplement to the *Huddersfield Daily Examiner* of 20 April 1966 as speaking for the Tory Party.

29

Introductory

proclivities, but whose leanings are like the handle of a can, all on one side.'

Mr. Fisher notwithstanding, the project progressed. The old 1865 company was wound up. On the 6th of November 1868 the new company, the Press Association Limited, was registered. The P.A. was born.

One / Appointments and rehearsals

At a festival dinner at the Savoy Hotel in 1920—fifty years after the State take-over of the telegraphs—Lord Riddell said that he had been told the story, by 'one of the principal actors', of the inception of the Press Association. 'I believe,' said Lord Riddell, 'it was conceived in a four-wheeled cab on the way to Brixton on a foggy night. I believe that the four founders went to Brixton in a four-wheeled cab and, having been befogged, held most of their deliberations in the cab, and as a result of these deliberations the Press Association was formed.' Was it? Who were the *four* founders? What were they doing making their way to Brixton on a foggy night? Lord Riddell's story leaves us with a pleasingly mysterious and humane picture. Another one, though, is probably more reliable because it was related in 1872, only four years after the founding of the Press Association, and the man who told it was John Edward Taylor of the *Manchester Guardian*.

Taylor was able, he said, to look back with pleasure at the hard work he had put in to induce newspaper proprietors to co-operate for the common good. 'Many of my friends were sceptical,' he recalled. 'Even my friend in the chair,' he said, referring to Frederick Clifford, of the *Sheffield Telegraph*, 'was one of the sceptical ones, and endeavoured one day, when we were walking arm-in-arm, to damp my ardour.' Clifford said to Taylor, 'Do you think you can ever get over the prejudices and the jealousies of the provincial press? 'I answered him,' Taylor went on, 'that I thought there was no prejudice and no jealousy which would interfere with our working harmoniously and in common in a matter of business.'

Two years later Taylor again recalled that 'one of the first persons to whom I mentioned a proposal to form this Association was Mr. Clifford. It was in a walk through a quiet street in Westminster that he and I canvassed the possibility of amalgamating or associating the varied interests which are to be found amongst the newspaper proprietors of England, and of getting them into harmonious action.'

What we do know, then, is that John Edward Taylor was the father of the Press Association, the man all his contemporaries acknowledged and saluted as such. Two men, father and son, bore the name of John Edward Taylor, and both rank among the most important and revered in the history of English journalism. The father founded the *Manchester Guardian* as a weekly in 1821 and he edited the paper until his death in 1844. He was thirty when he went into journalism, a successful Manchester merchant who had committed his political energies to the Reform movement. His eldest son, Russell Scott Taylor, succeeded him as editor. He was evidently a precociously brilliant young man, for he was only eighteen when he took over the editorship. But his reign was brief. At the age of twenty-three he died of typhoid fever. John Edward Taylor the second was not yet ready to enter the *Guardian*; unlike his brother, he was considered too young at eighteen and from Manchester New College went to the University of Bonn. When he came back from Germany he was called to the Bar, but by the time the *Guardian* became a daily in 1855 Taylor, still in his early twenties, was an active force behind the newspaper's progress. It was being edited by Jeremiah Garnett, the founder's junior partner, and when Garnett retired in 1861 John Edward Taylor became editor-proprietor. His journalistic achievements are measured not only in what he contributed directly to the development of the *Guardian*, nor even in his parentage of the Press Association, but also in his choice of an editor to succeed him in 1871. The man he appointed was his cousin, C. P. Scott, who transformed the *Manchester Guardian* from a reputable regional paper into one of powerful national and international influence and who established editorial standards which have survived to this day as criteria by which journalistic conduct may be judged.

Pictures of John Edward Taylor show him as a man of full face, with an enormous beard. Contemporary accounts reveal him as one of commanding presence and formidable zeal. To the

Appointments and rehearsals

end of his life he fought against the arrogant inhumanity of nineteenth-century materialism. He campaigned against drink. He left a negative mark upon the *Guardian* which distinguished it from all other daily newspapers for nearly a century: he gave an order in 1873 that racing tips should no longer be published and it was not until 1967 that, though still blushing in a corner, they showed their face again. All this suggests a man of heroically austere and virtuous character, but he was certainly not a man of unrelieved solemnity. His remarks at Press Association meetings show he was capable of a gentle self-mockery. He also enjoyed living in style and taste. He built up an art collection, including late Italian masters, Turner water-colours and medieval stained glass. When it was sold at Christie's (after his death in 1905) it meant the breaking up of one of the biggest private collections of the day.

John Edward Taylor gave his organising energies to the founding of the Press Association but the burden of carrying out the complicated and arduous work of getting it ready for operations fell largely upon other shoulders. The Committee of Management, of which he was Chairman, held frequent meetings following the formal constitution of the new company on the 15th of September 1868. Vital decisions had to be taken about raising finance, appointing staff and making arrangements for the supply of home and foreign news. Taylor was there at the first meetings, but, because of ill-health, he was absent from them from the end of October until June the following year. He wintered in Rome.

Three other members of the Committee carried on the task of translating the enthusiasm and the sometimes extravagant hopes of their colleagues into an effective machine. Those three men were John Jaffray of the *Birmingham Daily Post*, Frederick Clifford of the *Sheffield Telegraph* and George Harper of the *Huddersfield Chronicle*. The other member of the original five-man Committee of Management was William Saunders of the *Western Morning News*. He did valuable work in the early days, but he dropped out because of the conflict between the interests of his own news agency, the Central Press, and those of the Press Association. Alexander Ireland of the *Manchester Examiner* was elected in his place, but his contribution does not seem to have matched that of his colleagues on the Committee.

John Jaffray was a Scot, of modest background but with the

advantage of having been to Glasgow High School. He came to England to work as a reporter, first at Shrewsbury and later at Birmingham. He was taken on to the *Birmingham Journal*, the forerunner of the *Post*, by its owner, John Frederick Feeney. Jaffray arrived in Birmingham with £20 to his name. When he died fifty-seven years later, at the age of eighty-two, he was a baronet and a rich and successful businessman. Feeney had made him a partner and the daily they founded flourished. When writing of these model examples of Victorian virtue, of their personal talents, their rectitude, their good works, their seemingly indefatigable industry, their robust and idealistic involvement in public life, it is hard to penetrate the legend and discover credible human beings. A picture of John Jaffray in middle age shows a man of handsome bearded Scottish face, the bony structure well (but not over-well) fleshed; a face revealing the expected dignity, that quality of commercial shrewdness with which he was credited, but also a trace of humour lifting the corners of his mouth. Like John Edward Taylor, Jaffray was a Liberal, although when the split came in the Liberal Party over Home Rule for Ireland he went over with Joseph Chamberlain and the Unionist faction to the Conservatives. Like Taylor, he made just one unsuccessful effort to get into Parliament; Jaffray fought as a Liberal candidate in 1875, Taylor the following year. Like Taylor, he developed an appreciation of art, which he employed to his own pleasure and profit as well as that of the Birmingham City Art Gallery. John Jaffray deputised for Taylor while he was out of the country and succeeded him as chairman of the Press Association.

Frederick Clifford was a well-known barrister, a Q.C. who later became a knight. He was a member of the family which for many years owned the *Sheffield Telegraph*. Generations of provincial newspaper proprietors (including his own descendants) at Press Association gatherings were to praise Clifford for the skill and foresight he showed when he drew up the P.A.'s first memorandum and Articles of Association; it was remarkable how long they were to last without any important revision. Frederick Clifford's name was the first in the original book for recording attendances at Press Association annual meetings.

By coincidence, George Harper served an apprenticeship in Shrewsbury, where Jaffray also started his career in England; but

Appointments and rehearsals

Harper was a native of the town. He joined the *Huddersfield Chronicle* in 1850, soon after its birth, acquired a joint proprietorial interest in it, and then, in 1868—the year the P.A. was founded—became the sole owner on the death of his partner. (The story of the *Chronicle*'s conversion into a daily three years later offers a glimpse of just how fierce the competition was between newspapers. Another weekly paper, the *Huddersfield Examiner*, had been going since 1851. It seems that both papers decided, at much the same time, to launch out as dailies, the *Chronicle* as a morning and the *Examiner* as an evening. According to the *Examiner* version of the story there was some kind of gentleman's agreement between George Harper and Joseph Woodhead, who owned the *Examiner*, that they should both become dailies on the same day. But in the early hours of Saturday, 28th January 1871, when his *Weekly Examiner* had been 'put to bed', Woodhead heard that the *Chronicle* was going to jump the gun and bring out its first daily paper on the following Monday morning. He ordered a knocker-up to get his compositors out of their beds and report back to the printing shop. He had them working throughout that morning and afternoon to produce the first number of the *Daily Examiner*. By the early evening copies of the new paper, still damp from the press, were being sold at a halfpenny in the streets of Huddersfield—and the men selling them were the same compositors who had produced them. The *Chronicle* duly appeared as a daily but, unlike the *Examiner*, it has not survived.)

George Harper, as we saw in the previous chapter, was the man who, as president of the Provincial Newspaper Society, ensured the co-operation of the weeklies in the setting-up of the P.A. It is also clear from the correspondence which has been handed down that he was very much involved in the detail of organising the new agency. Only three days after the Manchester meeting at which he was appointed to the Committee of Management, John Edward Taylor was writing to him with a list of 'papers, news rooms etc.' in the Huddersfield area which were on the subscription lists of the Intelligence Department of the telegraph companies. It was obviously important that the Press Association should hold on to as many of the customers of the old service as possible. Taylor asked Harper to find out how much these subscribers had been paying and 'should you have any influence with any of the managers of the Institutions or individuals entered in the list I should be obliged if you would use it in favour of the Press Association'. To Taylor's own list of subscribers in Bradford, Huddersfield, Halifax and York, pencil additions have been added, presumably by George Harper himself:

'Mr. Westlake, Sun Inn; Mr. Geo Clarke, George & Dragon; Mr. Dufton, Spotted Cow; Mr. Pinder and Thompson, Ball & Mouth.'

The Committee's first staff appointment was that of a company secretary, and they chose badly. This was not immediately apparent and the first sign of trouble did not come until July 1869, more than six months after W. A. Irvine had started work in the temporary offices at 112 Strand. (By this time Irvine had also been appointed Secretary of the Provincial Newspaper Society, for which he had been recommended as being in every way suitable.) There was a fuss over a cheque for £15 which the Salisbury Hotel—an hotel just behind Fleet Street which was much used by provincial newspaper proprietors—had cashed for Irvine and which was dishonoured. Because both Jaffray and Clifford were away at the time, George Harper was left to try to sort it out. The dishonoured cheque had not been one of Irvine's own and he appealed to Harper not to bring the matter before the Committee or Management, 'as it would materially injure me altho' the innocent victim of doing a kindness to a friend'.

The letter in which W. A. Irvine made his successful appeal to George Harper was dated the 14th of August 1869. Three days later, on the 17th, another man was appointed to the staff of the P.A. This was an appointment the Committee never had cause to regret. The man was John Lovell, who now became manager at a salary of £450 a year. Lovell had been among 145 applicants for the job. Another who reached the short-list of four from which the final choice was made was J. M. Le Sage, a famous contemporary journalist, who was to be the *Daily Telegraph*'s correspondent in the Franco-Prussian War and later the paper's editor. That Le Sage should have applied shows that newspapermen were well aware of just how important the job was going to be. The manager of the Press Association would have to be a man who was intimate with the needs of newspapers, who could organise and administer an editorial staff in London

Appointments and rehearsals

and a country-wide corps of correspondents and would not feel lost in the commercial world.

John Lovell was thirty-four when he was appointed. His story, again, is one of prodigious energy and resource. He was the son of a Guildford shoemaker, 'a man of solid sense and immovable honesty'. John Lovell was the eldest of a family of seven and he had to go out to work at a very early age; he had virtually no formal schooling but he had learned to read. As a boy of fifteen, Lovell was rummaging through a load of waste paper his employer had bought from a London publisher. He came across fragments of Dickens, including some from *David Copperfield*, in which he read how Copperfield learned shorthand. Lovell decided to learn it, too. From one of his uncles, a stationer in Guildford, he bought the *Pitman Teacher*, price sixpence. When he had learned all he could from that he wanted to advance to the next stage of the course. But he could not afford the 1s. 6d. for the second textbook on top of the cost of the candles he needed for reading and working at night. His solution was to give flute lessons to the boys of the town for a penny a time. That got him his second Pitman manual. To buy the third one, at half a crown, John Lovell constructed what was described as 'an iron harmonicum' from bits of metal supplied by a local blacksmith. Then, in the best tycoon tradition, he raffled the instrument among all the boys he knew. Eventually he landed his first job in journalism, as a district reporter on a weekly paper, the *Surrey Standard*. His wages were five shillings a week. His perseverance is deservedly legendary, but credulity falters before the story of how, having heeded advice to read Addison and Steele's *Spectator*, he copied into shorthand each of the 555 issues they published and then transcribed his shorthand back into longhand. Lovell moved on to the *West Surrey Times*, thence to the *Sheffield Times* and the *Birmingham Daily Post*. In 1868 he took the editorial chair of *Cassell's Magazine*, but he soon left there for his appointment at the Press Association.

Twenty years later an appreciation of him described him as 'a faithful and generous friend, a great collector of books, an immense smoker, but his chief beverage is tea. In social life he is a brilliant talker, and there is not a sturdier democrat in the country.' He probably did not have much time for social life in the early part of his career at the P.A., however. As a contemporary account put it, 'the establishment of this Association was a tremendous piece of work, and ran into mountains of figures and details'.

The appointment of a manager had been the first of 'three matters gravely affecting the working of the Association' on which the Committee of Management had reported to the first annual meeting of the P.A. on the 3rd of March 1869. (With John Edward Taylor still in Rome, John Jaffray took the chair.) The other two had been arrangements for the supply of foreign telegrams and for setting up a department to handle sporting news.

The telegraph companies were already buying a service of foreign news from Julius Reuter, probably the most famous of all names in the history of the world's news agencies. Reuter, a German Jew, had been among the first to see the possibilities of the electric telegraph and in the late 1840s he had operated on the Continent a primitive service of commercial and financial news. Many places were still not connected by telegraph and he had bridged the gaps by using the railways, carrier-pigeons and relays of horses. In 1851 he came to England and set up his first telegraphic office in two rented rooms in the City of London. Reuters grew and prospered and by the time the Press Association was formed, the agency was supplying foreign news which now included political news, directly to the London papers and, through the telegraph companies, to the provincial press of Britain. The P.A. Committee of Management looked at other possible sources of foreign news; they received some 'very favourable' proposals; but it did not take them long to decide that the best thing they could do was make a deal with Reuter. The telegraph companies were paying £3000 a year for his telegrams. Julius Reuter thought the P.A. ought to pay him more, but the Committee stuck out and on the 21st of December 1868, only three months after the formation of the new company, Irvine, the Secretary, was able to send telegrams to the members of the Committee: 'R. has come down to the £3000. Copy of letter by post tonight.' Reuter retained the right to supply his news direct to subscribers within a fifteen-mile radius of Charing Cross. The P.A. had the exclusive right to circulate his telegrams to newspapers, newsrooms, hotels, clubs and institutions elsewhere in the United Kingdom. In turn, the P.A. had to accept that it should not obtain overseas news from any other source—

Appointments and rehearsals

with the exception of occasional items from private informants. When that agreement was finally signed with Julius Reuter, soon after the first annual meeting of the P.A., an association began between the two agencies, which was to grow closer and closer over the years and which has survived to this day, to the great profit not only of the British press but of the British people as well.

When the Press Association began, sporting news meant little else but horse-racing because other sports were not yet organised enough to make them newsworthy on a regular, national basis. A Mr. C. H. Ashley had been supplying the telegraph companies with racing results and other information collected by his own men at all recognised race meetings. Now he offered the same service to the P.A. for a fee of £1100 a year. He accepted the P.A.'s counter-proposal of £1000 a year (excluding the cost of telegrams). There was also William Wright, a gentleman who, as the *Sporting Times*, had been supplying London's West End clubs with their sporting news. When the Press Association tried to interest the clubs in a new service many of them said they would rather stick to Mr. Wright. So the P.A. bought his business 'for a moderate sum'.

In the early months provincial newspapers were in no great hurry to buy shares and become members of the new Association. This was due partly to uncertainty about when the telegraphs would be transferred to the State and indeed whether the transfer would take place at all. But it was only a temporary hesitation. By the time of the second annual meeting, in May 1870, three months after the P.A. had started its operations, the Committee were able to report that 'with a few trifling exceptions, the proprietors of all the daily morning and evening papers in the three kingdoms out of London' were members as well as 130 proprietors of tri-weekly, bi-weekly and weekly papers. (Those papers which did not take shares had to pay more for the news supplied by the Association.) What was no less important, many more newspapers, newsrooms, sporting houses and London clubs were buying the Press Association services than had subscribed to the old private telegraph companies. The only drop, an insignificant one, was in the number of hotels subscribing.

One of the Committee's main anxieties was the complicated business of drawing up a tariff, of deciding how much to charge for the agency's supplies of news. The Committee waited and

Reporter Anonymous

waited for the Post Office to decide how it was going to charge the Press Association for sending its telegrams, but, because there was still no answer as the time of the State take-over grew imminent, they had to go ahead and issue a tariff, not knowing whether their charges would mean a profit or a loss to the Association. Even at the second annual meeting, when the Post Office had been operating the telegraphs for three whole months, the Committee had to report that they still did not know. The general principle of charging cheaper rates to the press than to the public had already been accepted by the Government. The press were to pay a shilling for seventy-five words during the daytime and a shilling a hundred at night—after 6 p.m.—when the wires would not be so busy. (A member of the public was to pay one shilling for twenty words.) Because the same P.A. message might be going to hundreds of different addresses, a charge of twopence for each duplicate message was laid down. But one detail had not been settled and from the Press Association point of view it was a very important detail. What the Committee wanted to know from Frank Ives Scudamore, the Post Office official in charge of the telegraphs, was how the wordage of the P.A. messages was going to be computed—separately or cumulatively? Many of the telegrams, those from a race meeting or a provincial stock exchange, for example, might well be no more than twenty, thirty or forty words long. Was each message to cost a shilling, no matter how short? Again, it might well be that in the course of a day five Reuter telegrams might be sent out whose total wordage came to no more than 150 words. Were these to be charged for as five messages or as two of seventy-five words each? Would all the words transmitted during the course of the day be added up and divided by seventy-five to work out the bill for the day's telegrams? The answers to questions like these were going to have a profound effect on the P.A.'s finances. The Committee assembled all their arguments and put them in a memorandum for Scudamore of the Post Office. It was the kind of problem upon which the mind of a senior civil servant might dilate with relish. Unfortunately, at that time he was 'too heavily oppressed with the business of preparing for the transfer [of the telegraphs] to give it his immediate attention'.

The task of drawing up a tariff would have been headache enough without the complication of not knowing how the Post

Appointments and rehearsals

Office was going to assess its charges. The aim of the P.A. was to give the newspapers—and other subscribers—the kind of news they wanted, when they wanted it, at the length they wanted it and at a congenial price. It was impossible, of course, ever to do all these things to everyone's satisfaction. The needs and tastes of the newspapers, some mornings, some evenings, some published daily, some only once a week, some appealing to a big city audience, some to a small country community, were bound to cover a vast range.

The way John Lovell and his Committee tackled it was to divide the news into sections: General, Reuter, Parliamentary, Stock Exchange, Racing and so on. Each of these sections was subdivided into services of differing lengths, sent either by day or night. From this catalogue of choices the subscriber picked out the bits and pieces he wanted. At the top of each message from the P.A. there was a description of the service—Reuter Two, for example. From lists provided, the Post Office knew which subscribers wanted a particular service.

For anyone unfamiliar with the ways of news agencies, it sounds an extremely complex operation. So it was and so it had to be in those early days. Those Victorian newspaper proprietors were hard men to please. The Manchester papers, for instance, had made it known they were in favour of longer Parliamentary coverage than they had been getting from the private telegraph companies. (It was several years before the provincial papers succeeded in their campaign to get their own representatives into the Parliamentary press gallery.) At the first annual meeting Alex Ritchie, of the *Leeds Mercury*, said his paper 'would rather not have long Parliamentary reports, except on very special occasions, such as that on which Mr. Gladstone introduced his Irish Church Bill. It would, as a rule, be a great inconvenience to me,' he said, 'to give more than two columns of a debate; and I do not believe that the generality of readers care for more. Gentlemen like to peruse their newspapers at breakfast-time, and they will not always care to wade through four or five columns of Parliamentary matter.'

To a certain extent it was possible to resolve disagreements of this kind simply by offering both a short and a long version of a report. Even so, there had to be limits to the number of news categories and subdivisions of categories. In the words of the

Reporter Anonymous

Committee: 'With the daily morning papers, there was no great embarrassment. With the daily evening papers it was otherwise. Published at different hours, in different towns; issuing sometimes one, sometimes two, and sometimes three editions daily; requiring, according as they were more or less remote from London, either a careful summary of the contents of the metropolitan journals or no news whatever from those journals.'

These evening papers, the Committee said, also wanted news 'during the most barren period of the day; and often, in cases where they were the offspring of a weekly paper, requiring, in addition to their ordinary news, a special supply during the whole of the twenty-four hours on Fridays, and perhaps no news at all on Saturdays. It was no easy task to devise subdivisions which should meet their varied wants, without descending to a minuteness which would have loaded the tariff with detail, and rendered the instructions to the Post Office too complicated to be understood and carried out without a long period of probation. The weekly papers, again, published at all hours, and issuing second and sometimes third editions at intervals which almost constituted them bi-weekly journals, presented difficulties which, if less serious in degree, were equally embarrassing in kind; while the complication was still further increased by the necessity that existed for providing both for the special requirements of the press of Ireland and Scotland, where remoteness from London and local circumstances were productive of an entirely new set of wants, and also for the even more special and peculiar wants of the commercial newsrooms, mechanics' institutions, and other public institutions scattered up and down the whole of the three kingdoms.'

The hopes and expectations with which some newspaper proprietors joined the new association were impossible of fulfilment. They wanted, quite simply, more for less, a bigger, better supply of news than they had been receiving from the telegraph companies at a lower price. There were, in fact, some shocks in store for certain papers. Although the Press Association charges were in strict proportion to the amount of news a customer ordered—the first year's annual subscriptions varied from 14*s*. 6*d*. to £400 —there were those who must have felt they were being badly stung. The trouble arose out of the discriminatory practices of the telegraph companies, whereby newspapers were being

Appointments and rehearsals

charged different rates for the same service. When the Press Association introduced a strictly equitable tariff, those who had previously been enjoying what was, in effect, a subsidy from their fellow-proprietors were bound to feel hurt. One of them, Frederick Spark, of the *Leeds Express*, reckoned the P.A. services were going to cost him twice as much as he had been paying to the telegraph companies, but he stayed loyal to the Association and ultimately became chairman of the Committee of Management.

Framing a sound and acceptable tariff was only one aspect of the massive burden which fell chiefly upon John Lovell, the Manager, in the months preceding the transfer of the telegraphs. The complaints about the quality of the news supplied by the private companies may well have been justified, but now Lovell had the job of making sure the Press Association could do better. That meant organising a network of correspondents to feed in the news from all parts of the British Isles.

Outside London, he made arrangements with correspondents to send messages of important general news and of commercial news from the big exchanges and markets, such as Manchester, Liverpool, Glasgow and Cork. Most of these correspondents were journalists employed by the provincial papers, but they also included clergymen, solicitors, town clerks, businessmen, schoolmasters, anyone, in fact, who could be trusted to supply reliable information. They were paid 'linage'—on the basis of how much of their 'copy' was used. (The founders of the P.A. do not seem to have considered calling upon member-newspapers to supply their own news agency with news from their areas, although this practice has been adopted by national news agencies in some other countries.) The Committee reckoned that when the P.A. went into action 'no corner of the three kingdoms' was 'unwatched by their representatives'.

In London itself, having fixed up the foreign and sporting news, the Parliamentary and City departments had to be manned and reporters and sub-editors were needed to collect and put into shape the supply of general news. The telegraph companies had had two men covering Parliament. The Committee took them over—appointing George Moir Bussy, 'a gentleman of lengthened experience in the gallery', the first chief of the Press Association Parliamentary staff; he was to be paid five guineas

43

Reporter Anonymous

a week. With the death of the *Morning Star*, a third gallery seat became available. The Press Association took it and appointed a third man to their Parliamentary staff. Then a City editor, a T. W. Green, 'a gentleman highly recommended by leading City firms, and possessing the advantage of having occupied a similar post on two London papers', was placed in 'suitable offices' in Old Broad Street 'with a competent staff'. (The Committee's descriptions of the arrangements to make the P.A. an efficient working machine have a suspiciously euphoric flourish about them. 'A competent staff' to assist the City editor may have been no more than one messenger boy; we do not know.)

There was another service which the Press Association had to discharge—the supply of Parliamentary news to the London clubs, then, so much more so than now, the home of political discussion and activity. The telegraph companies had set up at Westminster a small printing office where running reports of Parliamentary debates were set up in type, printed off in slips, and delivered to the clubs by hand. The Government bought this outfit as part of the telegraph system but saw no further use for it, so the P.A. took over the office and the services of one compositor and three messengers.

On the 1st of January 1870 the Press Association moved from its temporary offices in the Strand into new, permanent headquarters in Wine Office Court, a narrow alleyway off Fleet Street, containing the famous Johnsonian pub, Ye Olde Cheshire Cheese. These offices may have been adequate for the small staff with which the Press Association started its life—or the Committee may have thought them adequate—but twenty-two years later the then chairman, Robert Eadon Leader, of the *Sheffield Independent*, referred to the conditions in which the admittedly bigger staff of the time had to work: ' . . . the insanitary arrangements, the want of ventilation, and the heated atmosphere . . . are such as no body of proprietors, with any conscience or heart, ought to allow to continue . . .'

The Committee had taken a lease on these offices—for which they had authorised £30 to buy furniture—after 'much anxious consideration'. What, they had asked themselves, would be the most suitable site for the Press Association? Offices nearer Telegraph Street, the Post Office H.Q. for the new State telegraphs system, might have seemed more convenient. But getting news

Appointments and rehearsals

was just as important as despatching it and by establishing the P.A. midway between Westminster and Telegraph Street, amid the cluster of newspaper offices which then lay on either side of the Ludgate Hill end of Fleet Street, the agency would be in the most advantageous position of all. The Committee had also been persuaded by the promise that a pneumatic tube would be laid between the Houses of Parliament and Telegraph Street, with a telegraph station within a few hundred yards of Wine Office Court, through which the P.A. messages would be sent out. They understood, too, that there would be a special wire connecting Wine Office Court with the centre of the telegraph system. Lastly, they bore in mind that when the Metropolitan Railway system had been completed the Press Association offices in Wine Office Court would be within three or four minutes' ride of all the great railway termini, of the Houses of Parliament, and of the commercial centre of the City.

When the Press Association established itself in Wine Office Court there was little more than a month to go before the big day when the State would take over the telegraphs. Head office had to be staffed. A junior clerk 'with knowledge of shorthand' was engaged at eight shillings a week. There was an obvious need, one would have thought, for a corps of messengers, but, surprisingly, the first messenger was not taken on until a week after the P.A. had gone into action; he was paid seven shillings a week. By the end of 1870 there were eight messengers, each getting the same wage. The time was to come when these boys, in their blue uniforms with red piping, under the command (no lesser word will do) of sergeants and corporals, were to become a familiar and respected sight in Fleet Street. Their beginnings were more humble, however. They had to wear their own clothes. It was not until 1872 that they were supplied with boots and the uniforms came a year later.

On the journalistic side just one man was hired to look after the reporting of events in London. It is important here to remember that, for the most part, his job must have consisted of 'lifting' interesting items from the London papers for the provincial press. There were also 'spacemen'—free-lance journalists—who would take on reporting jobs as and when required. Lastly, to carry out the sub-editorial work, which meant collating all the 'copy' coming in and shaping it into the various lengths required to meet the prescriptions of the P.A.'s many subdivided categories, the Committee took on three men, 'all of whom had had considerable experience in metropolitan journalism, and two of whom had the additional qualification of experience in provincial journalism'. Such experience was undoubtedly necessary, for, as the Committee acknowledged, the work these three men were to do was 'of a highly responsible character', and 'by the exigencies of the services had to be spread over twenty-two hours out of the twenty-four, and to include Sunday in its scope'.

One of these three was to be paid at the rate of £4 10s. a week, a good wage for those days. He was Edmund Robbins, who was to become distinguished both in the history of the Press Association and that of British journalism. Edmund Robbins had started his newspaper career at the age of eleven as an apprentice on a weekly paper in his native town of Launceston in Cornwall. At the age of eighteen he went off to London and for three years worked as a compositor on the Central Press, the news agency which William Saunders had set up. In 1868 Saunders made Robbins a junior sub-editor, then permanent sub-editor, then night editor (which included taking charge of the telegraph service), all this editorial promotion in a period of less than two years. Edmund Robbins joined the Press Association on the first day of January 1870, the day the new agency moved into Wine Office Court. Three weeks later another young man, Henry Whorlow, then aged twenty-two, and six months younger than Robbins, joined the P.A. and also began a long and honourable career.

In the last months before the transfer of the telegraphs the P.A.'s preparations became so intense that the Committee of Management sometimes had to meet twice a week in London. This must have imposed a considerable strain on men like John Jaffray and George Harper who had their own newspapers to look after in Birmingham and Huddersfield. In January John Edward Taylor, who was now living in London and controlling the *Manchester Guardian* from there, and Frederick Clifford were appointed as a two-man sub-committee to advise John Lovell on 'pressing business'.

For a fortnight before the actual day when the Press Association went into action each member of its newly recruited staff was at his post rehearsing the precise work he would have to perform

Appointments and rehearsals

when the telegraphs were transferred to the Government. And before that day arrived Edmund Robbins and Henry Whorlow had an interview with the Manager, John Lovell, which Robbins was to recall fifty years later. 'Mr. Lovell,' he said, 'gave us instructions as to the lines upon which the Press Association should be conducted.' There were three cardinal principles to be remembered always, said Lovell. 'First, accuracy, the second, promptitude, the third, absolute impartiality.' One hundred years later they are still the basis of everything the Press Association does.

Two / Weathering the storm

However intense the pressure upon the Committee and staff of the Press Association before the Government took over the telegraph system it was nothing compared with what it was like immediately afterwards. The effect of the State take-over was, in one word, chaos. Within twenty-four hours the system had virtually broken down and had brought the Press Association very close to disaster. It was many weeks before the telegraphs were back to anything like an acceptable standard of efficiency. The major cause of the trouble was simply that the Post Office could not cope with the load imposed upon it. On the first day, the Saturday, the number of private telegrams went up by twenty per cent over the day before. 'A large number of these messages were merely congratulatory', said the *Manchester Guardian*. Then there was the vastly increased traffic in press messages pouring into the telegraph offices. Many of these never reached the newspapers who were paying for them and some were seriously delayed, not arriving until the day after they had been handed in; some, even, were delivered by post. The newspapers had looked forward to great things from the Press Association. The service they received was not merely no better than the old one but in some instances was totally non-existent. They did not know why. It is small wonder that they bombarded Wine Office Court with their complaints. 'Six or eight thousand letters and telegrams', as John Jaffray said, flew at them from all parts of the United Kingdom. The Post Office received its fair measure, too, of course. Newspapers filled up some of the space that should have been taken by Press Association news with tart reflections on the situation. On Tuesday, February 8th, for instance, the *Edinburgh Evening Courant* announced:

Weathering the storm

'Our readers will notice the dearth of telegraphic intelligence in our columns of today. For the want of our usual news per wire, we are quite unable to account, having received only unsatisfactory replies to our applications to the telegraphic department of the Post Office. If, as is just possible, some powerful atmospheric derangement took place last night, we ought at least to have known it; but if, on the other hand, the expensive arrangements made by ourselves and other newspaper offices have been altogether set aside by the authorities for the transmission of private messages, we have a right to complain.'

The reference to the possibility of 'some atmospheric derangement' was justifiable because the weather at that time was appalling. In that same issue of the *Evening Courant* there was an item, under the heading 'Reports from the North', which told of 'accounts of a storm which appears to have exceeded in violence anything which has occurred for some time'. The storms which lashed the whole country during that first week of Government-controlled telegraphs commanded more and more attention from the provincial press. On the Wednesday the *Birmingham Daily Post* reported:

'On Sunday morning a terrific storm raged for several hours on the Caithness coast. The sea as far as could be seen was one sheet of foam; and at Wick the waves "rose to the height of several hundred feet, and drifted inland from the coast like fog". The new harbour works, which were nearly washed away by a great storm last year, were on Monday again damaged to the amount of about £15,000.' Give or take a few hundred feet in the height of the waves, it was clearly some storm.

The following week, on Tuesday, the 15th, the *Sheffield Daily Telegraph* stated: 'The recent heavy gales from the North East have been attended with much damage, and in one case loss of life in the metropolis.'

The same day, the *Edinburgh Evening Courant* was confiding its own troubles again: 'By some mismanagement or misadventure in the telegraphic department, our foreign intelligence is very meagre, and the account of the proceedings in the House of Lords almost nil.'

And the *Manchester Guardian* had this to say:

'There has been another serious breakdown of the telegraphs —due, we are officially informed, to the heavy gale and a fall of snow in various parts of the country. Of the wires connecting London with Manchester, Liverpool, Leeds, Birmingham, Hull, Newcastle and other important towns, two or more were found to be out of order at the busiest part of the day yesterday, and the interruption appears to have continued without material abatement up to a late hour last night. Communication with the continent was also seriously interrupted by the bad weather.'

It would not have been surprising if John Lovell—and with him the Press Association—had gone down under the strain. But he endured. Although they could not have foreseen the demands that were to be made upon him, the Committee had chosen a man with just the temperament and the stamina to see it through. Even so, it must have been a near thing. He stayed in his office for three weeks, day and night, snatching sleep when he could, occasionally taking a nap upon a pile of newspapers. His staff, too, worked eighteen hours a day, seven days a week.

The immediate effect on the Press Association service must have been heart-breaking. John Jaffray said: 'The Association was placed in a position of extreme peril and difficulty. On the one hand, it found itself unable to meet the requirements of its subscribers; on the other hand, it found its plans thwarted and rendered of no effect by the inability of the Department to perform the work it had undertaken to perform. With every desire to assist the Association, the Department was helpless. The telegraphic system was so far deranged that time alone could right it.'

All the P.A. could do was to try to help the Post Office and to accept, for a while at least, the need for drastic compromise. It was that or nothing at all. This meant abandoning the plans which Lovell and his colleagues had worked out with such skill and care during the months before. In order to relieve the wires the Press Association agreed to shelve the scheme for classification of the news—the very keystone of the system they had taken such pains to elaborate. All P.A. telegrams went to all newspapers. Those who were paying only for 'second-class' or 'third-class' news received exactly the same service as those bigger papers which had asked for the full, 'first-class' news service. Far from feeling grateful, the weekly papers cursed as their offices were flooded with supplies of news they had neither the time to edit nor the space to print. To cut down the pressure on the telegraph clerks, the Press Association agreed to give the Post Office twelve to sixteen copies of every sheet of news sent out. This meant the P.A. had to take on extra staff.

There was trouble, too, over the reporting of Parliament, one of the services upon which the big provincial daily papers placed most importance. The trouble was not with the Press Association's newly recruited team of gallery reporters but, once again, with the Post Office. The private telegraph companies had sent their reports by wire direct from Parliament to the provinces. The Post Office had proposed to change this system when it took over and to transmit the P.A. reports from Parliament to the telegraphic centre in Telegraph Street by pneumatic tube. That would have been fine, but the tube could not be laid in time. Then the idea was to send the reports through the wires which connected Wine Office Court both with Parliament and with Telegraph Street. That arrangement also fell through and the Post Office said that, instead, it would send the reports from Westminster to Telegraph Street through its own wires. Parliament was due to reassemble just a few days after the transfer of the telegraphs. On the eve of Parliament's return the Telegraphs Department told the Press Association that because of some damage to the wires, the Parliamentary reports, a dozen or more copies of them, would have to go by messenger to Telegraph Street.

As Jaffray said, 'In this day the idea of riding two miles through crowded streets with every slip of what is called "Telegraphic News" is an anomaly which by-and-by would not be believed to have existed.' But it did exist and the Press Association had to put up with it. It cost another £16 a week for extra staff and there were delays of between three-quarters of an hour and an hour and a quarter in the despatch of Parliamentary reports to the country.

The P.A. Committee were prepared to put up with the curtailment of their services and the extra cost for a while, knowing there was little else they could do and believing these were temporary expedients. A week or two, they thought, to give the Post Office a chance to put their new house in order, and then all would be well. But temporary arrangements often have the habit of becoming permanent ones, especially where the body concerned is a Government department. The Post Office of 1870 was of this mind. Week after week after week went by with no sign of improvement. Indeed, not merely was there no sign of the

Reporter Anonymous

Post Office being able to carry out what had been expected of it but it now came up with a proposal which really alarmed the directors of the Press Association. This latest proposal was a classic example of the reaction of a public authority to its own incompetence. If the telegraph system could not cope with the load, who was to blame? Not the Post Office, of course. Who else but the customers and in particular the news agencies and newspapers? (Apart from the Press Association, press telegrams were also sent by the Central Press, the Lombard News Company, a Mr. W. Lewis and the newspapers themselves; of these, the P.A. was by far the biggest user of the telegraphs.) They must all be sending much the same news, so why not, the Post Office argued, let all the news agencies amalgamate! Alternatively, let them all accept a limit imposed on the number of words they could send by wire each day to their subscribers.

The Press Association would have nothing to do with either of those suggestions and, sensing correctly that this was a situation in which counter-attack would be their best protection, the Committee sent a memorandum to the Telegraphs Department about the business of transmitting Parliamentary reports direct from Westminster and also asked for a conference with Frank Ives Scudamore, the head of the Department, on the whole subject of the delays and omissions in the delivery of their telegrams. At the same time they told him that, so serious did they consider the position, they had decided to call a general meeting of the P.A. members.

Scudamore replied by letter, saying that he was about to visit the large provincial telegraph stations to put things in order and asked them to put off their meeting for ten days or a fortnight. The Committee agreed to postpone the meeting of members to give the Department every opportunity to sort out the mess. Scudamore's letter was written on the 5th of March. Two months later John Jaffray was able to report that from that time forward there had been 'a marked and growing improvement'.

'The service to Ireland, it is true,' Jaffray told the annual meeting of the Press Association, 'is still very defective, and grave complaints of delay continue to reach the Association from towns which are not in direct telegraphic communication with the stations from which the news is despatched. Even where there is little cause to complain of systematic delay in delivery, there is

The Palatine Hotel, Manchester, scene of the earliest meetings of provincial newspaper proprietors to discuss forming the Press Association

The sign in Fleet Street pointing to the first permanent home of the Press Association in Wine Office Court

ABOVE LEFT: *John Edward Taylor, 'father' of the P.A.*

ABOVE: *John Lovell, the first Manager*

Sir Edmund Robbins, Manager 1880–1917

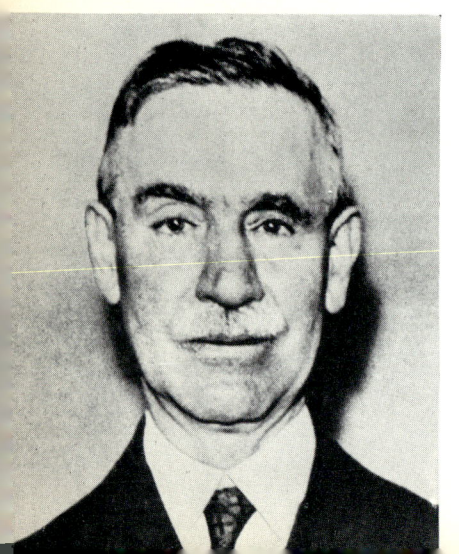

H. C. Robbins, General Manager 1917–38

often a fitfulness and irregularity in the supply which requires amendment.' But the Committee no longer felt it was necessary to ask members to accompany them in a deputation to the Postmaster General, as they had intended to do.

Despite the improvements, however, the P.A. service was still far from what it set out to be. The Post Office still could not cope with the Association's classification system, so that all the papers were still receiving exactly the same amounts of general and foreign news. It was still impossible to consider providing longer Parliamentary reports for those papers which wanted them and, as we saw in the previous chapter, the P.A. still did not know on what basis they were going to be charged for their messages. There were also complaints from individual members that their local post offices were not being kept open to receive telegrams after eight o'clock in the evening—which meant another cause of delay in their news supplies.

Nevertheless, John Jaffray and his colleagues believed the worst was over and that if they kept up the pressure on the Post Office they could hope one day to get the thoroughly efficient telegraph service they all wanted. The way in which John Lovell and the Committee of Management dealt with the Post Office was obviously firm and insistent. But there was nothing rash or intemperate about it. 'We have not shirked either statement or discussion,' said Jaffray. In drawing the Department's attention to the unsatisfactory state of affairs they did so 'as calmly, moderately and inoffensively ... as we possibly could do ... In addition to bearing in mind the propriety of always being moderate in criticisms of public men and departments, we have remembered that this Association and the Post Office will, in all probability, have to work together for years to come, and that it is not wise to quarrel with those to whom you are yoked. Therefore we have never had anything but the most pleasant personal relations between the Committee and Manager and the representatives of the Post Office Department.'

In the early years of the Association the patience and moderation of the founding fathers were to be severely tested. They were encouraged in their attitude right at the start, however, not only by a prudent appreciation of the need to establish goodwill for the future but also by the personality and efforts of Frank Ives Scudamore, the head of the new Telegraphs Department. From the time when he had been instructed to examine the possibility of the State taking over the telegraphs, through the early negotiations with the newspapers over preferential rates and special facilities, Scudamore showed a genuine sympathy with the needs of the press. Because there are numerous occasions in the history of the Press Association when the Post Office and its officials are deserving of stricture, it is only fair to say of Scudamore that he was of the highest calibre of senior civil servant, diligent, perceptive, never less than courteous, never arrogating to himself powers he did not possess nor forgetful of his public responsibilities. He had spent all his working life in the Post Office, where he initiated a number of reforms, including the introduction of women as clerks. He also had some small reputation as a writer and contributed to such papers as the *Standard* and the *Scotsman* and to *Punch* and the *Comic Times*. According to the entry in the *Dictionary of National Biography* one of his happiest efforts was 'a lecture on the fairies' called 'People whom we have never met'.

The leaders of the Press Association respected Scudamore and had confidence in his good intentions, at least. With him in charge, and a gradual improvement in the telegraph system, John Jaffray was able to leave his colleagues, in May 1870, with the impression that it was only a matter of time before all would be well. The mood of that meeting in the Salisbury Hotel might well have been hostile and critical. Many of the provincial newspaper proprietors gathered there had experienced three months of costly disappointment and frustration. Instead, they showed a warm understanding of the difficulties the Committee had encountered and, to some extent, combated on their behalf. When John Jaffray sat down at the end of his often melancholy recital of events the meeting cheered him.

As the years to come were to show, the provincial newspaper owners who made the Press Association were not slow to express their anxiety or dissatisfaction when they felt their interests were suffering. But the vast majority of them were fair-minded men and, as more and more of them gained first-hand experience of what it meant to run the P.A., they were careful in their criticisms of the men they themselves elected year by year to serve them as their directors. In this atmosphere of common regard and common interest there grew up the kind of warmth, which is supposed to exist in families but frequently does not, which generated frank speaking and good-natured raillery. For some men at those early meetings, such as William Frederick Tillotson, of the *Bolton Evening News*, James Alexander Henderson of the *Belfast News Letter*, and Thomas Crosbie, of the *Cork Examiner*, the Press Association was to become literally a family affair, for others bearing their names were to continue their membership of the P.A. for the next hundred years.[1] The Association to which they belonged was made by themselves and for themselves and it was made by men with a conscious grasp of the principles which must guide it. John Jaffray was such a man. As he came to the end of his report to that 1870 meeting he summed up the way the Committee had gone about the P.A. business:

'. . . They have catered for every man alike; there has been no preference given to anybody; the dailies have no preference over the weeklies, but these last, who were fined almost by the old companies for the meagre one day's supply, are now well served and get their news at a moderate and fair cost. Again, there is no taint, so far as I can make out, of party feeling with reference to any news we send out and there never will be if, from time to time, the Committee to which the management of the affairs of the Association is entrusted come before a body of gentlemen like that I see before me—for no man will be able to stand up and bear the rebuke which he would richly deserve if he allowed any partisan feelings to interfere with the due and fair discharge of his duty as a member of this Committee.'

---

[1] Both Tillotson and Henderson were founder-members of the Press Association, their names appearing in the first register of members filed at the Office of the Registrar of Public Companies on 16th March 1869. It was not until the following year, 1870, that the name of Thomas Crosbie, proprietor of the *Cork Examiner*, was registered as a member. On the other hand, Crosbie, unlike Tillotson and Henderson, had attended the decisive meeting in London in June 1868, which led to the formation of the P.A. (Appendix 2) and although Thomas Crosbie did not attend an annual meeting of the Association until 1883, the Crosbies, along with the Tillotsons and Hendersons, can fairly claim today to be the only newspaper owners with direct descent from the founders. The membership of all three families has been unbroken.

Three / Conflict and compromise

In the ten years John Lovell was Manager of the Press Association—the first ten years during which the P.A. was actually operating—he had to fight 'the world, the flesh, and the devil'. This was how Dr. Cameron, of the *Glasgow Daily Mail*, one of the original members of the Consultative Board, saw it. Lovell had to contend with the inevitable criticisms from subscribers; he had to try to pacify those who felt that others were getting a better deal than they were; he had to fight rough competition; most of all, he had to defend the Press Association against both the inefficiencies of the Post Office and its recurrent attempts to extract more money from the newspapers and the news agencies.

John Jaffray's early optimism about improvements in the telegraph system was never justified. From time to time there were senior officials and politicians who listened sympathetically to representations from the press and tried to remedy the shortcomings of the system, but right up to the first world war, and even beyond it, the Press Association and individual newspapers had reason, good reason, to complain of delays in the transmission and delivery of telegrams. To be charitable, let it be said that the press may have desired and expected more from the Government-controlled telegraph system, more urgency, more priority to the needs of newspapers, than it could ever have given. There were times, however, when not even a saint could have viewed the shortcomings of the Post Office with charity.

There was, for instance, this heart-cry from poor George Harper, at the *Huddersfield Chronicle*, in a letter he wrote directly to Frank Ives Scudamore:

'... Of course my position as one of the Board of Management of the Press Association familiarised me with the very defective state of the service generally, but I had no idea that a town like Huddersfield, situated in the midst of a complete network of large towns, could, by any possibility, be placed at such a serious disadvantage.

'The supply to this office is so wretchedly performed as to place me at a most serious disadvantage with contemporaries in the neighbouring towns of Manchester and Leeds, the papers from each of those places being regularly on their way to Huddersfield, and frequently actually in the town, before I can get my paper to press.

'I possess every advantage which eligible premises and a large and efficient staff can supply, but when I have invariably to wait until three, and very often four o'clock in the morning for important news, it is impossible I can run the race of legitimate competition with my more favoured neighbours.

'To an old established daily paper such delays would be a serious blow, but for one which has its way to make it is disastrous. Had I supposed such a state of thing possible I should never have changed from a weekly to a daily.

'I have before me as I write envelopes bearing on the face of them such hours as 3-12, 3-35, and 4-5 [presumably the a.m. times of delivery]. Last night the marriage of Princess Louise was commenced to be telegraphed about eight o'clock, and it continued at intervals up to half past three o'clock this morning.

'The editor was so satisfied that we should be sacrificed if we waited for the telegraphing of the ceremony that he cut the report, which you will find in today's paper (a copy of which I send you) from the evening edition of the *Pall Mall Gazette*, the *Globe*, and *Evg. Standard*. These papers were purchased in London in the afternoon, sent down by train at five o'clock (a distance of two hundred miles) and their report was available to us hours before we received the Press Association report through the wire. . . . The Parliamentary, too, is very unsatisfactorily supplied. We rarely get the close of debates until two or three hours after the rising of the House. All this entails a very large and unnecessary outlay and prevents me making any use of it for editorial or sub-editorial purposes. It is impossible to write summaries at three or four o'clock in the morning and the consequence is a very interesting portion of a daily newspaper has, in my case, to be frequently omitted altogether.'

Harper's letter was written in March 1871, and it typifies the distress of many Press Association members. Under the pressure, as he put it, 'of repeated and well-founded complaints', John Jaffray, as Chairman, wrote to Scudamore about the 'great and unnecessary delay' in transmitting Parliamentary reports. No one could say that Scudamore dealt summarily with the complaints that landed on his desk. He replied to this one with a letter some 2500 words long, but, as Jaffray said, 'without undervaluing that gentleman's labours, I may say that a great deal of the letter is wide of the point'. One passage in it, however, did show that, whatever the strains and recriminations, the relations between Scudamore and the Press Association were still good enough for him to permit himself a little wry wit. Jaffray had said in his letter that 'a very strong feeling is growing up that the time for the exercise of patience and forbearance towards a new and difficult enterprise is fast passing away'.

'If', wrote Scudamore, '. . . you allude to the invariable courtesy and good humour which you have displayed in transacting business with me, I can only say that I do not think any circumstances have arisen, or are likely to arise, which should or will alter our relations in this respect. If, however, you point to some exercise of patience and forbearance elsewhere, I must own that I am just a little puzzled. When I look at my collection of leading articles and paragraphs, sarcastic, personal, abusive, and angry, with which the judicious kindness of my friends has kept me constantly supplied, although the supply, I am happy to say, has greatly fallen off of late, I am inclined to ask if these be instances of patience and forbearance, what will wrath amount to? If they do these things in the green tree, what will they do in the dry?'

Although the telegraph system was always the cause of complaint, it did get better and newspaper proprietors knew that so long as Scudamore was there their complaints would be properly investigated and, where possible, remedied. In May 1874 he wrote to John Lovell about a complaint by a P.A. subscriber in Morpeth, Northumberland, to whom the Post Office had failed to deliver sporting messages. Scudamore told Lovell a special inquiry had been made; it was found that the clerk at Morpeth

Conflict and compromise

'had neglected to read off the messages from the instrument as they were sent to him', and that 'for this and other irregularities' he had been sacked. Frank Ives Scudamore warned the Morpeth postmaster that if any similar irregularity should occur somebody else would get his job. Clerks were also dismissed that year at Leeds and Edinburgh for negligence in the handling of Press Association telegrams.

In 1875 Scudamore resigned and accepted an offer from the Ottoman Government to go to Constantinople to organise the Turkish international post office. It was the view of Edmund Robbins, as he recalled later, that Scudamore was pushed out of the Post Office because he 'was supposed to have given the game away too much to the press, and subtle influences began to work for the purpose of undoing what Mr. Scudamore had done. He was spirited away to Constantinople and given a good berth there. So he was got rid of.'

After Scudamore had gone, relations between the Post Office and the P.A. deteriorated. The Post Office, indeed, was under fire from many sides. The preamble to the 1868 Act described its object as 'a cheaper, more widely extended, and more expeditious system of telegraphy'. Only five years after the transfer of the telegraphs a Treasury Committee was appointed to investigate 'the causes of the increased cost of the Telegraph Service since the acquisition of the Telegraphs by the State'. That 1875 Committee quoted figures to show that in the first two months' working there was a surplus of £27,726. But then the service began to lose money and at the end of the first twelve months it revealed a deficit of £49,493. In 1872–3 this had increased to £204,955, although the traffic it was handling had greatly expanded.

'It was expected', the Committee's report stated, 'that the Post Office would employ only 1528 clerks and 1283 messengers, whereas . . . six months after the date of the transfer there were at that time employed in the Telegraph Branch no less than 4913 clerks . . . and 3116 messengers . . .' In the year 1874–5 the number of inland and press telegrams which the Post Office was handling was over 19,000,000, very nearly three times as many as the private telegraph companies had carried in their last year of operation. But—should one say inevitably?—the expenditure on the service had gone up even more rapidly. The Committee admitted it was difficult for the Government to work as cheaply as the private companies but thought that the proportion of working expenses to income ought to be kept within 70 to 75 per cent. In fact, for 1874–5 the proportion had risen to 97 per cent compared with 57 per cent in the first year or so of operations.

The Post Office was stung by the report and its senior officials looked outside themselves for someone to blame. They chose the press. From the moment the Department had begun to show deficits, the idea had grown until it had become fixed that the cheaper rates enjoyed by the press were uneconomic. The Post Office struck the first hard blow at the Press Association in 1875 by removing hotels and taverns from the lists of P.A. subscribers entitled to receive telegrams at press rates. Very few of these customers were prepared to pay for news to be telegraphed to them at the full public rate and the P.A. lost more than £4500 a year in revenue. But much worse was to come when in January 1876 the Postmaster General, Lord John Manners, heeding the insistent theme of his officials that all the Department's troubles could be traced to the preferential rates for press telegrams, said that these rates must be revised. The 'revision', of course, could mean only one thing—an increase.

The Post Office assertion that it was making a loss on press telegrams was one which was to be made time and again, decade after decade, and was to be rejected, just as resolutely, by the representatives of the news agencies and the newspapers. It has to be admitted, though, that, at the start at least, the Post Office really did get very little in return for what was a lot of hard work. It had finally committed itself in 1870 to a method of charging for Press Association telegrams which was, without question, very favourable to the P.A. Broadly speaking, charges were based on the total wordage of all telegrams, not on the length or content of individual ones. The total number of words wired during the day between 9 a.m. and 6 p.m. was divided by seventy-five and the answer was the number of 'messages' to be charged for at one shilling a time. The same method was used to arrive at a number of 'messages' sent from 6 p.m. onwards except that the total wordage was divided by 100. The basic charge, then, was one shilling for each 'message' to one subscriber, plus a 'duplicate' rate of twopence for each additional address to which the same message was sent at the same time. This meant, for example, that when a message was despatched to thirty subscribers at the same

Edward Davies, General Manager 1938–62

A. L. Cranfield, first Editor-in-Chief 1926–27

Henry Martin, Editor-in-Chief 1928–54

Charles Jervis, Editor-in-Chief 1954–65

correspondents and reporters.

"The supply of Foreign news has been the subject of grave consideration by the Committee. Hitherto the provincial press has been supplied by the Telegraph Company, with whom Mr Reuter contracted for the exclusive use of his telegrams. The Committee have been at great pains to test the possibility of obtaining this news more fully and economically through various agencies, but, although they have now before them several proposals of a very favorable kind, they have for various reasons considered it prudent to negotiate with Mr Reuter's Company for the exclusive right to supply his telegrams to the newspapers, news-rooms, hotels, &c. in the provinces. The contract price will be the same as that paid by the Telegraph Company. Besides securing this valuable news for the provincial press, it will be obvious to the Shareholders, that the practical monopoly of the earliest foreign telegrams will, of necessity, make the News-Rooms, Clubs, &c., the customers of the Association. The negotiation is not yet completed, but the Committee believe that they will be enabled to announce completion very shortly.

To meet the wants of the chief newspapers, and news Rooms and Clubs, it is necessary to have an efficient department for the supply of Sporting news. It is true, that individual activity would, no doubt, supply the means of meeting this requirement, even if the Association did not combine this amongst its other news purveying departments; but

From the official record of the first annual general meeting of the P.A.

Walter Cattermole, Superintendent of the P.A. messengers (1930)

Conflict and compromise

time the Post Office would get only twopence halfpenny for each telegram delivered. The return could be much less because there might be two or three deliveries to a number of subscribers before the number of words added up to the total of a single full message. There was one instance where the Post Office delivered 1640 telegrams for which they were paid, in all, £1 15s. 2d., which works out at about a farthing a telegram.

So, while the Press Association naturally resisted any argument which could lead to a rise in costs, it can be conceded nearly a century later that some changes to bring the Post Office a more adequate return for its services might have been justified. But the way Lord John Manners set about it provoked in the press a reaction of real and understandable alarm. He proposed, among other things, to charge for each news despatch as a separate message. He also proposed to abolish the duplicate rate except where the message was sent to more than one subscriber in the same postal district. The Press Association made estimates of how much more these and other proposals could cost; they ranged from an increase of 6 per cent to one of $500\tfrac{3}{8}$ per cent! The language in which members of the P.A. expressed their feelings at the 1876 annual meeting showed how deeply they felt.

The chairman that year was John Archibald Willox, of the *Liverpool Courier,* a young man still in his early thirties who, starting with the paper in his teens as a reporter, had worked his way up until he had become the *Courier*'s principal proprietor. In presenting one of the longest reports in Press Association history, almost wholly taken up with a detailed résumé of the crisis over the Post Office, Willox managed to keep his indignation just within bounds.

'When the State proposed to acquire the telegraphs,' he recalled, 'it was thought necessary to secure the co-operation of the Press, and this was done by the concession of terms, which, though liberal, were no more than fair and equitable. . . . The arrangement then made was a distinct covenant between the Government and the press—entered into with deliberation and with open eyes—and I think I am justified in saying that, if there had been any suspicion of bad faith or insincerity on the part of the Government, the press would not have acquiesced in the transfer as it did. It would be too strong, perhaps, to say that we have been deceived and betrayed; but there can be no doubt that the policy of the Government—almost from the outset—has been marked by disloyalty to the spirit of the compact . . . At first no facility in the use of the wires was deemed too great; every point of controversy was adjusted in a liberal spirit; and one almost began to think it was safe to put faith in princes, or at least Telegraph Departments. But the officials were only taking time to get accustomed to their new position, and when they had gained confidence, their policy quite changed. They first began to lop off the outer edges of the agreement, cutting away one privilege and then another, until now they propose to destroy it altogether. This innovation involves a serious injury to newspaper proprietors and the public, and is an open violation of the agreement, not yet ten years old.' (It is easy to hear there the tones of the man who was later to become a Conservative Member of Parliament.)

H. L. Carr, of the *Western Daily Mail*, Cardiff, spoke with a naive melancholy. He was afraid, he said, that the Government people did not care about the provincial press as they ought to. It was a very difficult matter to stir the public mind on a question of this sort. 'The public generally do not care how newspapers get their news, or where they get money from in order to pay for it. As long as they get their paper for a penny it is sufficient for them.'

The Press Association and the Provincial Newspaper Society came out loudly and strongly against the Postmaster General's proposals. When the matter came before the House of Commons, it was decided to set up a Select Committee 'to inquire into the organisation and financial system of the Telegraphs Department' Among the witnesses who gave evidence to that Committee were John Edward Taylor and John Lovell for the Press Association. The view of the press expressed in evidence was that the loss alleged by the Post Office on press telegrams was in fact the result of over-staffing and extravagant administration. The Select Committee reported that they had not had enough evidence to sustain the Post Office argument. Not long afterwards, the Post Office decided that the old method of counting of messages must end and, instead, a separate charge would be made for each message of 75 or 100 words. The Press Association took the first steps towards contesting the legality of this change, regarding it as a breach of the 1868 Act. But, as a compromise, the Post Office did agree that a series of messages dealing with the same subject

Conflict and compromise

could be considered as 'continuous' and be charged according to the total number of words; the P.A., without much regret, shelved the idea of litigation. The change in the system of charging was an important one and would add several hundred pounds a year to the Press Association bill. The effect inside the P.A. was a much stricter attitude towards the length of news messages.

The report of the Select Committee and the new ways of charging for press telegrams which were introduced did not mean an end to hostilities between the Post Office and the Press Association. At the head of the Telegraphs Department now was a Mr. C. H. B. Patey. While the P.A continued to declare that it had no wish to have anything at the expense of the State, he, by his conduct and his letters, clearly believed it was setting it. At any rate, contemporary records suggest a situation of something like single combat between Patey and John Lovell. There was no likelihood now of humour illuminating the formal exchanges; Patey never unbent from the stiff, official posture: he was never more nor less than proper. In dealing with the Post Office, however, the men at the head of the Press Association were realists. Their colleagues congratulated the Committee on the 'very wise compromise' they had made with the Post Office over press rates. 'That the Press Association had been badly treated was indubitable,' said one of them. 'But it is always better to make a compromise than to fight, especially with a powerful Government department.'

It would be possible to multiply the instances and elaborate the detail of the brushes and full-scale battles between the Post Office and the Press Association. There were many points at which their interests were not compatible and where their interpretations of the law were bound to conflict. But, having dealt with those basic disagreements which led to the 1876 Select Committee, enough has been said to establish the pattern of the relationship which was never to change significantly in the P.A.'s first fifty years, even though there were to be periods when, at a personal level, it was wholly amiable.

It must not be pretended that all was sweet harmony within the Press Association, either. The achievement of the provincial newspaper proprietors in banding together to produce a cooperative news service was real enough but no organisation could have pleased all of them all of the time. There were complaints by evening newspaper owners that they were suffering at the expense of the dailies and from weekly papers that the Association concerned itself too much with the needs of their big brothers. As William Pollard Byles, of the *Bradford Observer*, speaking as chairman in 1878, reminded his colleagues, 'we have something like 400 customers . . . distributed throughout the three Kingdoms, some inland, some in seaports, some in capitals, some in manufacturing, and others in agricultural districts; some publish daily papers, some weekly, some morning, some evening, and some are committees of newsrooms and clubs . . . to please and satisfy such a varying clientele with the news of all domestic events arising throughout the three kingdoms is a task of no ordinary difficulty, and one we cannot expect to perform without some imperfections and consequent complaints.' But very few complaints were either substantial enough or left unremedied to cause any permanent disaffection.

Nor, at the 1871 annual meeting, did a charge of political bias by the Association in its reporting seem to bear much investigation. The only specific instances cited carried little weight. The first was to draw a comparison between the reporting at length of a Liberation Society meeting about the disestablishment of the Church of England which was to be the subject of a Commons motion a few days later and the failure to report the Middlesex Conservative Banquet the same evening. The other was the P.A.'s failure to send a single line about the presentation at Beverley of a testimonial to the Conservative Sir Henry Edwards, whilst sending a report of a testimonial to a provincial editor at Cardiff for his exertions during the last general election on behalf of the Liberal candidate. The meeting was not impressed. Even Conservative members of the Association testified to their confidence in the political integrity of the P.A. The man who had been foremost in pressing the charges, Robert Redpath, of the *Newcastle Journal*, withdrew them. Thirteen years later, he was to become chairman of the Association.

There was one other piece of internal trouble which could not be despatched so easily and the memories of which lingered painfully for some time after. This is the moment for the brief reappearance of W. A. Irvine, the Press Association Secretary who had protested his injured innocence over the dishonoured cheque. Some nine months after that incident he was given the sack. In the words of the official record, 'his business habits were not satisfactory'. But the P.A. directors did not realise at that time just how unsatisfactory they had been. There had been many complaints about errors in the accounts sent to members. These accounts, involving minute calculations, were Irvine's responsibility and the Board decided they must get a Secretary who was also a bookkeeper. Irvine took a month's salary in lieu of notice and bought a single ticket to Belgium. Only after he was safely out of reach was it discovered that he had been forging cheques, embezzling funds and 'cooking' the books.

Irvine owed the P.A. £710 and, as it transpired, the Provincial Newspaper Society, which had also lost his 'services', was short of some of its funds as well. The P.A. Management Committee were all for prosecuting him, but, discovering he was in Belgium, did not think it worth the expense of having him followed. On his part, he proposed that, if given protection from prosecution, he would return to England and repay his debt by instalments. The directors refused. They never heard from him again. They waived the fees of £400 which had been voted to them for their year's services and so kept down the actual loss to the Association to £310. They required the new Secretary, J. Thompson Bidder, who had been with one of the telegraph companies, to give a security for £1000. The auditor lost his appointment.

In financial terms the P.A.'s beginnings were very small. For a time, indeed, two of the directors, John Edward Taylor and John Jaffray, had to give a guarantee for £2000 to the Association's bankers. From the beginning, shareholdings in the P.A. were restricted to provincial newspaper proprietors.[1] When they

---

[1] The number of £10 shares a newspaper had to hold to qualify for membership of the Press Association varied according to what kind of paper it was. At the start, a daily morning paper had to hold twelve shares; a daily evening, six; a morning published not more than three times a week also had to hold six; a morning published twice a week, four; an evening published not more than three times a week, three; and a weekly paper had to hold two shares. Although the number of qualifying shares was raised more than once and the active shareholders became more and more confined to the daily morning and evening papers, the classifications remained the same for more than fifty years. A daily morning newspaper,

had first banded together in 1865 their primary object had been to get better facilities for telegraphing news, mainly from London to the provinces. It could well have been in the interest of the London papers to have joined in the company formed in 1868, for they, too, must have appreciated the need for a good home news agency. (This was demonstrated by the fact that by the end of the first year of operations, all the London morning and evening papers, as well as several London weekly and sporting papers, were buying news services from the P.A.) But there is no evidence either that the London newspapers were approached to take part in setting up the new agency or that they made any overtures themselves.

The P.A. was working on narrow margins and it may have been shortage of cash which explained why an order was given in January 1879 that a cheque for £400 to pay directors' fees must not be presented for a month. Nevertheless, although there were small losses in the early years, by 1880 it was possible to begin to accumulate a reserve fund. What is more, even though its resources were so limited, it did manage to provide members—and subscribers—with a supply of news which was incomparably better than the one they had received from the old telegraph companies.

It was also more reliable than that provided by certain competitors. John Jaffray, in 1871, defended the Association against complaints of its being beaten in the race to supply the news. He mentioned 'an agent in Birmingham' who had advertised his ability to provide a report of the Birmingham Corn Market at 2 p.m. The P.A. report of the same market was not handed in to the Post Office for despatch until three o'clock. Why so much later? The explanation, according to Jaffray, was that you had to choose between speed and accuracy and the Press Association chose accuracy. The Corn Market, he said, did not open until two o'clock and 'no reliable report worth the paper upon which

then, had to put up twice as much share capital as a daily evening, a distinction which gives a fair idea of their relative status in 1868. Despite the way in which the evenings grew in importance, it was only in recent years that the distinction was abolished. For early shareholders, only £7 was called up in respect of each £10 share. By 3rd March 1869, 431 shares had been allotted. By the tenth annual general meeting in 1878, 182 newspaper shareholders had subscribed £7343 for 1049 shares.

it is written can be obtained until three o'clock'.

'What,' asked John Jaffray rhetorically, 'can be more delusive and misleading than this affectation of speed at the expense of truth and accuracy? . . . In all our commercial reports, from the London Stock Exchange downwards, we refuse, and shall continue to refuse, to send out statements until we receive them from authoritative sources and are assured of their accuracy.' Jaffray said that, unlike some of its competitors, the P.A. would never send out a report until the event had occurred.

The editorial staff were not paid glamorous wages. We have already seen the terms—good terms for those days—on which the top men were hired; the wages paid to the less exalted were much more modest. In the early days a wage of between £1 10s. and £2 10s. was the range for most P.A. journalists until they had served for several years. As late as 1894, H. C. Robbins—another member of the famous P.A. family—was taken on at £2 10s. a week, although he had already had some newspaper experience. But, in order to keep good staff, the P.A. had to follow the lead given by Fleet Street. In 1875, for instance, the P.A. chairman reported that when all the London papers raised the salaries paid to their reporters and sub-editors, 'applications flocked in to the Committee from members of our own staff and we were compelled to succumb and follow the example of the London offices'. He described the Press Association staff as 'thoroughly efficient and respectable'. In fact, as an organisation set up to supply members with their news services as cheaply as possible, the P.A. administration has always been economy-minded but it has never been mean and from its earliest days it showed towards its staff a paternalistic concern which was certainly not a characteristic of all newspaper ownership at that time. They also expected and got their money's worth from the staff. From time to time sub-committees were appointed to examine the state of the staff and in 1877 one such sub-committee decided that reporters were not doing enough work and, for a time, control of reporting and sub-editing was given to the Secretary. The P.A. directors were stern disciplinarians as well. In 1881 a Parliamentary journalist was dismissed because he had been refused admission to the Lobby 'in consequence of certain remarks made by him in the hearing of the Officers of the House of Commons'. Unfortunately, there is no record of what he had said. In the same year two reporters were reduced in salary for 'misconducting' themselves when reporting speeches in Yorkshire. A little later still, a chief sub-editor was required—and he agreed —to become a teetotaller after he had made a bad error of judgement one night.

The number of P.A. journalists who slacked and got away with it must have been few indeed. Many of them worked very long hours to make a bit more money. There were men employed by the P.A. on a retainer at the Law Courts who, when the Courts rose at 4 p.m., would rush to the House of Commons to do a Parliamentary 'turn'. Some of the staff, including non-journalists, also earned a little extra by taking on sports reporting at nights and weekends. Being a P.A. reporter was also physically laborious. Copies of stories had to be made for delivery by hand to the London newspapers and it was the reporters who had to make them, using metal-backed pads of flimsy paper and carbons and a stylo pen. It was not until 1906 that duplicating machines were installed to do that job, but even after that, until well after the first world war, reporters covering outside engagements, such as London dinners, still had to carry their pads of paper and carbons and their stylos aound with them. The carbons made a mess of dress-shirt cuffs. One distinguished P.A. reporter confessed years afterwards that he had deliberately pressed so lightly on his stylo that he produced only six readable copies— not nearly enough. He pleaded that he could not press any harder because of a war injury to his wrist and so managed to get himself taken off that kind of job.

Although there were moments when the Press Association wondered whether it should send its own special correspondent to cover an important foreign news story, throughout its history it has depended upon Reuters for overseas coverage. From the start, its service proved its value to P.A. subscribers. It was only five months after the Press Association had begun to operate that the Franco-Prussian war broke out. Then there was the Paris Commune and the Carlist Insurrection in Spain. The P.A. was able to send out extensive Reuter reports. Coverage of these 'emergencies' meant spending more on transmitting longer telegrams—but the P.A. directors reckoned it was well worth while.

John Lovell has left a description of the work involved during

Conflict and compromise

a typical Press Association day in 1880. He took a Friday—the busiest day of the week—in February when Parliament was sitting. 'On that day,' he said, 'as many as 436 separate messages, varying in length from the brief racing result or market report of a single line to the speech of four columns in length, and consisting in the aggregate of 39,000 words, passed into the hands of the Press Association staff to be dealt with. A considerable number of those messages poured in from all parts of the world through Reuters' Agency. An equal number poured in from all parts of the United Kingdom from the Association's correspondents. Some were distributed from race meetings, others from the great commercial centres in different parts of the country. A large number originated in the City Office in Copthall Court, Threadneedle Street, and a still larger number in the gallery of the House of Commons and its annexes. The work of the Association, however, did not end in receiving those messages. Its business was to manipulate them into classes, and to multiply and distribute them to the newspapers and newsrooms of Great Britain; and when it had done its work it had multiplied the 436 messages into 7897 addresses, while the 39,000 words had become 262,000 . . .'

The first ten years of the Press Association's active life were dominated by the figure of John Lovell. But under him Edmund Robbins grew in stature and importance. One of the first tasks Lovell unloaded upon him was that of negotiating an agreement with Lloyd's for the supply of shipping news. What was much more difficult and which took him very many years to achieve was the breaking down of what seemed to him the 'impassable barrier' between Government departments and the Press Association. The P.A. was not alone in suffering from the practice of Ministers of giving just as much information as they felt was desirable to one or two favoured newspapers. In official quarters the idea persisted that when *The Times* had been told duty had been done—a tribute to the status of that newspaper but infuriating for everyone else. Edmund Robbins went to every Government department in turn but he made slow progress. Years later the Prime Minister's Office was still capable of releasing only to 'Party' newspapers the news of the date on which Parliament would convene. The P.A. protested to the Prime Minister, Lord Salisbury, but received an 'evasive' reply from his secretary. Robbins was also much involved in trying to sort out the many troubles with the Post Office. It is clear that he was given more and more responsibility and in 1874 he was appointed Secretary and Assistant Manager. (He had already taken on the additional job of Secretary of the Provincial Newspaper Society.)

Of the four directors who had done the hefty spade-work at the beginning, just one, Frederick Clifford, of the *Sheffield Daily Telegraph*, continued to serve on the Committee of Management, with a break of only one year, throughout the 1870s. He was chairman for two years from 1871 to 1873 and he was elected to the chair again in 1878. Clifford was a man of many qualities. Apart from his legal expertise as a Queen's Counsel, which had been so valuable to the P.A. when he drew up the original articles of association, he was very much a practical newspaperman, a one-time assistant editor of *The Times* as well as a newspaper proprietor. He was a man of developed artistic taste and he had been a prominent member of the Council of the Guild of Literature and Art. He had one other virtue from the point of view of the Press Association—he lived in London. This was of no small importance, for, even after the P.A. had got over its teething troubles, its directors still had to give a good deal of time to its affairs. It was time they could not easily afford, for they were almost all working journalists; proprietors they might be, but they were still in the process of building up their papers and few of them were in a position to run them by remote control. It was, then, no merely formal tribute that John Edward Taylor paid to Clifford when he retired from the Committee of Management in 1874.

The reason for Clifford's retirement, like that of George Harper three years earlier, was a provision which, on Taylor's insistence, had been written into the Association's rules at the start, that one director should retire from the Committee of Management and one member from the Consultative Board at each annual general meeting. This ensured a constant supply of 'new blood' and it meant that every kind of newspaper, large or small, morning, evening or weekly, from every part of Britain, was represented on the Management Committee at one time or another. It meant, too, over the years, a widespread knowledge and appreciation of the practical difficulties of the Association which, if it could not always remedy complaints, could modify them: it did much to contribute to the 'family' atmosphere which prevailed at P.A. meetings. One other consequence of this system was that normally the chairman of the Association—the director elected as chairman by his colleagues—held office for only one year. Frederick Clifford was an exception—though by no means the only one in P.A. history.

A ballot held among the five directors forming the original Committee of Management resulted in George Harper being the first to retire. John Edward Taylor followed him in 1872 and John Jaffray the year after that. Like Clifford, Jaffray had held the full title and responsibilities of chairman for two years as well as deputising for Taylor during the winter of 1869-70. The last annual meeting of the P.A. which Jaffray attended was the 1872 one. Taylor turned up only once after 1875—and that was seven years later; but he was much involved in the arguments with the Post Office. Harper continued to attend year after year and in 1885 he was elected once more to the Management Committee and became its chairman three years later.

Jaffray and Taylor had taken back seats but soon there were new men to take their places whose own names were to become distinguished as newspapermen and who were to build up the strength of the Press Association. Men like Peter Stewart Macliver, of the *Western Daily Press*, Bristol; John Willox, of the *Liverpool Courier*; Frederick Spark, of the *Leeds Express*; George Toulmin, of the *Guardian*, Preston; John Jevons, of the *Nottingham Daily Express*; Joseph Glover, of the *Leamington Spa Courier*, and James Lancelot Foster, of the *Yorkshire Gazette*, who first went into newspapers in 1823 and who lived to hear himself described in 1881, upon his retirement from the Management Committee, as 'not only the father of the Yorkshire press but the father of the provincial press of this country'. These were men of independent principle, of stubborn resolution, whom none could soft-soap but who recognised in their private and public dealings the need for restraint and courtesy. They respected gods which have been depreciated; some of the virtues they valued and exemplified have become tarnished; but they had a vigour and an assurance about their purposes which the modern world may well envy.

Foster was a man who believed in looking after the pennies. When he was elected to the Committee of Management in 1876 the Association was owing £3746. When, as Chairman, he presided over the 1880 annual meeting he was able to report that the debt had been wiped out, that a credit of over £1000 had been achieved and that £3000 had been deposited with the P.A.'s bankers to establish a reserve fund 'for any contingencies'. 'We very well know,' he said, 'what newspaper proprietors are liable to under the law of libel, and that there are plenty of wolves prowling about ready to devour anyone making a false step. It is therefore necessary that an institution like ours should have a reserve fund to fall back upon in an emergency.'

The Press Association now had firm ground underneath its feet. Of all who had contributed to that achievement, of all the directors and all the members of the staff, none had contributed so much as the Manager, John Lovell, and it was by coincidence that at that same 1880 meeting where Foster looked forward to 'a great and brilliant future' for the P.A., John Lovell's resignation was announced. He was leaving to become editor of the *Liverpool Mercury*, one of the plums of provincial journalism. The tributes to him were numerous and obviously sincere. The meeting agreed to spend not more than 100 guineas—an inadequate sum, it was admitted—upon a testimonial to him.

John Lovell took the opportunity to restate the code by which he had conducted the affairs of the P.A.

'In the first place,' he said, echoing Jaffray's words nine years earlier, 'while we have always aimed at the greatest degree of promptitude we have never sacrificed accuracy to speed. It is easy enough, for instance, by discounting the transactions of the commercial and of the betting world, to send away quotations before the market is ripe, and nine times out or ten the guesses of an experienced observer will turn out to be right. It is, however, the constant recurrence of the one blunder in ten which eventually prevents the acquisition of a reputation for accuracy. [Cheers.] The slower process is the surer, and in the long run it is the paying one. [Hear, hear.] We have lived to see the time when commercial men and betting men with earlier news in their hands refuse to act upon it until it is confirmed or otherwise by the arrival of the later Press Association telegram. [Cheers.]

'Another principle upon which we have consistently acted,' Lovell continued, assured of an appreciative audience, 'has been never to sacrifice quality to price. As an instance, we always send

Conflict and compromise

a staff of our own from London to report the speeches of eminent men delivered in various parts of the country, instead of entrusting the work to local correspondents who, to say the least of it, are at such times too much employed in their own business to give proper attention to the interests of the Association.' (This was the opposite of the complaint that had been voiced years earlier by a Cardiff member about local reporters putting the P.A. before their own papers.)

The visible evidence of the value of the Press Association was in the provincial newspapers themselves. The success of the P.A. liberated the provincial papers from their old dependence upon the metropolitan press. Although the P.A. itself still 'lifted' items from the London papers, sometimes quoting them, sometimes not, their subscribers no longer had to wait for those papers to arrive in their own towns and cities. Furthermore, the Press Association supplied a regular and abundant service of first-hand reports, factual and objective reports, extensive coverage of Parliament, verbatim reports of all major speeches and a vast miscellany of news items as well as the regular reports from the City, the commercial markets and the like. The provincial press grew numerically—at the end of the first decade of Press Association operations there were some 300 more provincial newspapers being published than in 1870—and it grew enormously in stature. In the quality of their content and production and in the extent of their political influence, both local and national, the leading provincial papers could now claim equality with the best that London could offer. The big provincials had to take on large staffs of sub-editors to choose, cut, shape and assemble the news that flowed in from the P.A. Many of them also leased private wires from the Post Office so that messages from their London offices to their head offices in the provincial cities should not be impeded or delayed. The P.A. did not allow them to send P.A. services over these private wires because it would have given the bigger, wealthier papers an unfair advantage over their competitors. But their London editorial staffs gathered enough material of their own to justify the cost of the private wires.

These papers were published in towns and cities which were still spreading and booming. Their readerships expanded rapidly, the public appetite for news and information seeming almost insatiable. They reflected the intense political passions and argu-

Reporter Anonymous

ments of their day and, very frequently and most honourably, they acted as the social conscience of a callous and grossly materialistic society. In all this the Press Association was their indispensable servant.

Four / Mr. Gladstone's Fat Reporter

On the 19th of May 1880 the Press Association either achieved a most remarkable political scoop or perpetrated what would have to be admired as a very skilful and imaginative piece of fictitious reporting. To this day it is impossible to be absolutely sure which it was.

In the General Election of April 1880 the Conservatives, after six years in power (during which time Disraeli had become the Earl of Beaconsfield), were defeated. A few days later Beaconsfield called a meeting of leading Conservatives to discuss the future of the Party in Opposition. The meeting was held in private at the Earl of Ellesmere's London house and servants from both Houses of Parliament were employed to make sure that no unauthorised person—in other words, no journalist—could get into the meeting.[1] Nevertheless the following morning, the 20th of May, the London and many provincial dailies carried a most

[1] Edmund Robbins has left on record a surprising comparison from the year 1894. It was in March of that year that Gladstone retired from the leadership of the Liberal Party and a meeting was called at the Reform Club to choose his successor. 'It struck me,' Robbins recalled later, 'that a party meeting of that kind would be of a great deal of interest and I made bold to go and see Mr. P. Adams, chief Liberal Whip, for the purpose of suggesting that reporters should be allowed in to report this party meeting. I thought his hair would stand on end, but after we had talked the matter over he said that the idea that the meeting should be reported was a good one. The only difficulty would be who should report it. An independent reporter took a full note and that was, I believe, the first party meeting reported.'

What a pity that the meetings and 'processes' by which in recent years Sir Alec Douglas-Home, Harold Wilson and Jeremy Thorpe became leaders of their respective parties were not also open to the press!

Reporter Anonymous

detailed and circumstantial account of what was said at the meetings, including a long report of Beaconsfield's own speech.[1]

It read like a 'leak' on a scale to make even the most able of modern Lobby correspondents envious. But was it a leak? The next day Lord Rowton, Beaconsfield's private secretary, requested the Central News—the Press Association's main competitor—to announce that the report was absolutely fictitious. That same morning all the London morning papers, with the exception of *The Times*, published a letter from Sir William Hart Dyke describing the report as purely imaginary. On Saturday, 22nd May, *The Times* published a letter from Lord Beaconsfield to the Editor:

Sir,
The liberty of the press is one of the most precious privileges of Englishmen and, therefore, it is their interest that it should not be abused.

I have never been apt to complain of the reports of anything that I may have said in public if they only contained inaccuracies, which pressure, or even some little malice, might occasion or inspire. But when an elaborate declaration of policy is placed in my mouth, as in the report of the proceedings at Bridgewater-house in your issue on Thursday, not one single word of which was delivered by me, and which conveys, in every sense, the reverse of what I expressed, I think it a duty to request that you will make this disclaimer on my part as public as the statement which you have circulated.

I remain, Sir,
Yours faithfully,
Beaconsfield

The Press Association defended the report by stating that the substance of it was obtained from an M.P. who was at the meeting. Presumably the *bona fides* of the story was accepted by the P.A. Committee of Management because no reference to the incident appears in the minutes of their meetings. It would seem, too, that the provincial press accepted it as a piece of good and

[1] The text of the report as published in *The Times*, with minor omissions, is to be found in Appendix 4. It is worth the attention on any student of politics.

Mr. Gladstone's Fat Reporter

fair reporting because it is not mentioned in the monthly circulars of the Provincial Newspaper Society in the months that followed. Political news was a vital part of the P.A. service, and the provincial papers, in particular, placed a high value on it. For their part, the politicians quickly appreciated the worth and utility of a news agency which would pass on their words of wisdom to what was virtually the whole of the British press. The status of the Press Association was reflected in the regard with which individual P.A. reporters were held by leading politicians. This was especially true of Walter Hepburn, the P.A.'s first chief reporter. Hepburn became known as 'Mr. Gladstone's Fat Reporter'. Hepburn was, by modern standards at any rate, a huge man, weighing about twenty stone; he had an appropriately dignified manner to go with it.

It was Walter Hepburn who accompanied Gladstone on his famous Midlothian campaign in the north of England and southern Scotland in November 1879 and March 1880, denouncing the Beaconsfield Government with lofty, sonorous eloquence. Gladstone conducted a whistle-stop campaign, and crowds gathered, wherever his train halted, to hear him deliver a speech from the steps of his railway coach. Gladstone had an affection for Hepburn, but, in according him the privilege of travelling in his own railway coach, he was also making sure the P.A. reporter was always at hand and able to hear each word he spoke. If, for any reason, Hepburn was not in sight, ready to take a verbatim note of the Liberal Leader's speech, Gladstone would say, 'Where's my reporter?' and wait until the P.A. man was there. Similarly, he would delay making his speech at a meeting until he saw that Walter Hepburn was comfortably seated at the press table below the platform. On one occasion a deputation met Gladstone at a railway station and presented an address to him. The guard blew his whistle and the train started again before Gladstone had had a chance to reply. It took more than that to prevent him from making a speech. As the train rattled along Gladstone dictated to Hepburn what he would have said. 'Gentlemen,' he began. The morning papers published it and the 'gentlemen' of the deputation were no doubt surprised to read it.

One other story will illustrate not only the extent to which Gladstone appreciated the value of the Press Association but also his understanding of the mechanics of news-agency reporting. He

Reporter Anonymous

had planned to make an important speech at a wayside station from which it would have been impossible to send a wire. So he dictated it to Hepburn in advance and the P.A. man despatched it with a suitable warning about the time at which it was to be released. Unfortunately, the train did not stop as it had been scheduled to do; Gladstone did not make his speech; but the report of it was published just the same.

Mr. Gladstone also had his own very special value to the Press Association. In 1895 the then chairman of the P.A., Alexander Jeans, of the *Liverpool Daily Post,* reported a loss on the year's working and explained the reasons for it. 'All those who have been connected with newspapers know,' he said, 'that we have passed through a period of very great calm. I have had a good many years' experience myself of newspaper life, and I think that last year was probably the dullest we have had for many years. The most serious loss we had was, no doubt, the withdrawal of Mr. Gladstone from public life. Probably,' said Jeans, 'two-thirds of the falling off in the revenue has been due to that cause; for not only did Mr. Gladstone make a large number of speeches himself, which almost every newspaper in the country reported, but he also provoked a large number of replies, which were also reported.'

Speeches made outside Parliament by the likes of Gladstone were reported by the P.A. as 'offered specials' and newspapers paid extra for them, at the rate of ten shillings for a column of 2000 words. In London special reports were sent direct from the place where the meeting was being held, the reporters, with their special stylos, having to make as many as sixteen carbon copies; messengers took some of them to the Post Office for transmission to the provinces and the others were delivered by hand to the London papers. If the meeting was in the country it could mean as many as half a dozen reporters being sent on the job with travelling and hotel expenses involved. The reputation of these teams of P.A. reporters was so high, however, that many London papers no longer sent their own men to cover big out-of-town political meetings but preferred to buy a P.A. 'offered special'. Only a very limited number of statesmen were considered 'big' enough to merit verbatim reporting by the P.A. In the late nineteenth century they included, apart from Gladstone, Lord Salisbury, Lord Rosebery, A. J. Balfour, Joseph Chamberlain, Sir Henry Campbell-

Mr. Gladstone's Fat Reporter

Bannerman, John Morley and Sir William Harcourt. For such men the P.A. would offer a verbatim or a column report.

Although, after a long struggle, provincial papers won the right to have their own men in the Gallery and the Lobby in Parliament[1] they still looked largely to the Press Association to provide the solid coverage; their own writers developed the Parliamentary sketch. Newspapers today still lean heavily on the P.A. report of Parliament, leaving their staff men to portray the atmosphere of the House, the character of the Members and the flavour of their exchanges.

Newspapers, as well as radio and television, still rely heavily on the P.A. for a service of General Election results. But in the nineteenth century the need was even more apparent. Polling then did not take place on the same day throughout the country and nearly a fortnight could elapse before the final result was declared. Partisan excitement ran high throughout the period of the Election and, because the results were staggered, each one received much more attention than now. Local post offices stayed open to receive news agency messages of results declared overnight. As soon as the Fleet Street newspapers received them from the P.A. they displayed the results for the benefit of the crowds gathered in front of their windows. The P.A. sold the results, charging 1s. 6d. for a twenty-word message, to shopkeepers—chemists, newsagents, tobacconists—who also exhibited them in their windows. A Stroud Green newsagent, W. R. Cummins, who ran a jobbing printer's business as well, and founded the *Muswell Hill Record*, had a fleet of cyclists waiting outside the Press Association offices to bring back the results. In its usual economical way

---

[1] Provincial morning papers were admitted to the Commons and Lords Galleries in 1881 and to the Lobby soon afterwards. Provincial evening papers, however, were not allowed Lobby representation until 1950 when the rebuilt premises were first occupied. Another indication of how the provincial press—and the Press Association—had to fight against a traditional metropolitan bias among politicians was given in January 1874, when Gladstone decided on the dissolution of Parliament. Instructions were given that his manifesto was to be sent only to the London papers. Edmund Robbins went to the Treasury the next day, demanding to know why the P.A. had been ignored in this way. The Secretary of the Treasury justified his action on the curious grounds that as Gladstone was the Member for Greenwich, and Greenwich was a metropolitan borough, it was only necessary to send the information to metropolitan papers.

the P.A. relied upon its small editorial staff, only very slightly enlarged, to organise and handle a General Election.

For a co-operative news agency, representing papers of all shades of political opinion, the reporting of politics, especially behind-the-scenes politics, must always be a delicate business. One editor or proprietor will see as a first-class piece of journalism what another will regard as tendentious reporting. Accusations of political bias erupted from time to time and at the 1889 annual meeting they provoked a long discussion. It was never bad-tempered; there were spasms of laughter when one or two speakers—among them John Lovell, now a member of the Management Committee—ridiculed the critics; but the talk was serious enough.

The man who started it was Henry Byron Reed, of the *North Star*, Darlington, who was also Conservative M.P. for East Bradford. He spoke of a feeling of disquiet among certain P.A. subscribers and 'somewhat widespread outside' about its political news.

'I understand,' he said, 'that the Association was embodied for the purpose of sending to its subscribers items of news, that with political bias or opinion it has nothing to do, and that with rumours, speculations, or contingencies it has no concern.' At this there were shouts of 'No, no' from other members. 'The moment the Association embarks in the region of speculation or opinion,' he went on, 'it embarks upon very doubtful waters indeed, which might one day upset the Association. Now, it seems to me that the Press Association has often laid itself open to the charge of having sundry of its inspired reports tinged with the suspicion of partiality to one political party.' This time more cries of 'No, no' were countered by others calling 'Hear, hear'. Byron Reed cited what he considered an example of bias, an item sent by the P.A. on the 29th of April. He read it to the meeting:

'The Press Association learns that there is some difference in the Ministry [Lord Salisbury's Conservative Government] on the question of Local Government for Ireland, mainly in consequence of the Liberal Unionist leaders. The subject has been discussed at considerable length at recent Cabinet Councils. Mr. Chamberlain's scheme, formulated towards the close of last year, was carefully examined last month, and certain other propositions bearing on the matter have been submitted to the Government.

But whilst the general view of the Cabinet is in favour of placing Ireland on the same footing as England and Scotland with reference to local government, on condition that the land question be first dealt with, Lord Salisbury and Mr. Balfour are reported to be opposed to the concession, their contention being that in the present condition of affairs it would be imperilling the welfare of the loyal minority to hand over to the localities in the Sister Isle the management of their own parochial and district affairs. In conference with the members of the Cabinet Mr. Chamberlain has more than once during the present Session insisted on the importance of Local Government being dealt with in the near future, and it is an open secret that several prominent members of the Conservative Party have acquiesced in the contention of the member for West Birmingham. The present condition of affairs, therefore, is regarded with some anxiety by the friends of the Government, there being a strong desire to avoid any rupture with the Liberal Unionists at this juncture.'

Byron Reed was clearly a very serious young man—he was only thirty-four at the time—and prominent in the national organisation of the Conservative Party. He was also a sturdy churchman who, at the age of twenty, had written *An Appeal to the Wesleyans on Behalf of the Established Church*. Now, as he finished reading and looked up, he obviously thought his charge was proved beyond question. 'Reading that paragraph closely and carefully and critically,' he said, 'there can be no doubt that it conveys'—he added a typical Parliamentary parenthesis—'I do not say it was intended to convey—but it does convey to the critical reader an opinion adverse to the present Govenment.' Again the meeting was divided into those who thought it conveyed no such thing and those who agreed with him.

'In the first place,' said Reed, betraying his ignorance of the ways of Cabinet Ministers, ' . . . no representative of the Press Association could have the least means of knowing what transpired at Cabinet Councils. What is more,' he added, 'I am able to say, having made some inquiry into the subject, that the statements are not in themselves in accordance with the facts.'

'How do you know?' someone called out.

'I know from putting the question plainly to members of the Government themselves.' That naive reply was received with the laughter it deserved, but Byron Reed was not to be put off: he pressed home his accusation. 'Moreover,' he said, 'the whole spirit and tenor of the paragraph implies an acquaintance on the part of the gentleman who wrote it with the mind of members of the Cabinet, that those members of the Cabinet confidentially gave to him their intentions and disruptions, and that the Press Association has a kind of seat behind the curtains of Cabinet meetings from which it is able to learn the business of the State.' He made his protest against the P.A. circulating as news what was really nothing but 'rumours, surmises or speculations'.

The man who might well have written the item of which Reed was complaining was at the meeting in his capacity as managing editor of the *Nottingham Daily Express*—James Dods Shaw. Shaw was a man of many parts, each of which he played with distinction and style. He had worked on the literary staffs of the *Liverpool Daily Post*, the *Leeds Mercury* and the *Manchester Guardian*. He wrote prolifically—of his holiday travels in Canada, Egypt, Siberia, Japan, China, Malaya and Ceylon; on antiquarian subjects as well as social and political ones. For many years he acted as the political correspondent of the Press Association.[1] So respected was he that when in 1908 it was decided that there should be a verbatim record of all speeches in Parliament, and an official staff of reporters, Shaw was put in charge and became the first editor of *Hansard*. He was knighted in 1913. A man of considerable presence, he was always most meticulous in his dress. A colleague said of him that 'he would as soon have been seen walking the streets in his night-shirt as he would have been seen without his glittering top hat and spats; we often wondered if he slept in them'. Although in 1889 the peak of Shaw's career was still a long way off, he was already a man of reputation and one well experienced in the practices of Parliament and politicians. He was well equipped to read a little lesson to Byron Reed, who had been elected to the Commons three years before.

[1] The P.A.'s first Lobby Correspondent was Edmund Robbins. Many years later he told how it came about. 'In 1873,' he said, 'there was a Ministerial crisis. Mr. Gladstone had been defeated by a majority of three on the Irish University Bill. I was a most rampant politician at the time and I suggested that it would be of interest if I went to the House of Commons to obtain more information of what was going on in political circles. The idea was thought to be a good one and the next morning I went and so I became the first Lobby Correspondent of the Press Association.' He held that title for the next six years.

Mr. Gladstone's Fat Reporter

'I have had a large and intimate acquaintance,' said Shaw, 'with the manner in which the political news of the Press Association is obtained and circulated ... I have had constant opportunities of conferring with those who represent both political parties. It has been my business to make myself acquainted with them and I have found that both Liberals and Conservatives ... recognise fully the impartiality and the fairness of the Press Association and are willing to confide to me those facts, rumours, opinions and possibilities which Mr. Byron Reed regards as outside the province of the Association. It might, perhaps, surprise Mr. Reed,' he continued, with gentle sarcasm, 'to learn that I have on many occasions had an opportunity of obtaining from members of the Cabinet precise information as to what has taken place at Cabinet meetings. It is desirable that the press should know that the news and rumours and the political intelligence which is obtained by the Press Association from the lobby of the House of Commons is not due to the imagination of the reporter but is based upon actual information which is obtained as the result of authentic inquiries.' Shaw said there had been some special occasions when members of the Cabinet had told him what had happened and what had been done because they felt it was desirable that certain facts should be made public.

'I have never heard it imputed that the Press Association is a Liberal agency,' said Shaw. 'I have never heard it suggested from either side that because I represented the Press Association information should be withheld from me or that there was the smallest fear of its being coloured.'

John Lovell sought to kill the accusation with ridicule. As he stood up to speak, his manner was one of suppressed amusement. 'Several gentlemen,' he said, 'have spoken of the Liberal bias of the Press Association reports, but I have heard nothing quite so strong said today as was said in a paper which I hold in my hands.' He began to read from the paper. 'The two great news agencies, the Central News and the Press Association, which supply the press of this country with the bulk of their telegraphic matter, are worked entirely in the interests of the Unionists and Tories.' This quotation was received with laughter and cheers. 'That is strong,' said Lovell, 'but it did not seem strong enough to satisfy the gentleman who wrote it.' He read a further extract. 'From the Presidents and Directors down to the humblest penny-a-liner, both the Central News and the Press Association are manned by Unionists and Tories, or else by mercenaries'—there was loud laughter here—'without such a thing as a political conscience, who have been subsidised by the Unionist and Tory Party.' It is doubtful whether Byron Reed joined in the roars of laughter which went up as John Lovell finished reading and laid the paper on the table. But Lovell was not to get away with it quite as easily as that.

'Name the paper.' 'Name it.' Lovell picked up the paper again, glanced at it and said solemnly, 'The name of the paper is *United Ireland*.' There was more laughter and it is unlikely that Lovell's final remarks on the subject of political bias were accepted by all those present. 'You have, therefore, the testimony of both sides. The chances are that if neither the plaintiff nor the defendant is satisfied with the impartiality of the judge, the judge has been fairly impartial.'

This certainly did not wash with Charles Pebody, the editor of the *Yorkshire Post,* and a redoubtable defender of the Conservative cause. He not only thanked Byron Reed for raising the matter but delivered a stern reproof to those who dared to treat it frivolously. Because of the way the Press Association was composed, and the functions it had to perform, 'the Directors,' he said, 'should not laugh at the suggestions, but they should take them into their candid and serious consideration'. Pebody made a sweeping assertion. 'Conservatives are in a very lamentable minority,' he said, 'both in the room and on the Board, and they are clearly in a very lamentable minority among the representatives of the Press Association, not only in the gallery but in the lobby too.'

Serious the accusations were because no news agency could hope to preserve its reputation if there was evidence of political bias in its reporting. But John Duncan, of the Cardiff *South Wales Daily News* and a member of the Committee of Management, probably satisfied most of the critics. 'The complaints today,' he said, 'have come from Conservatives. But nearly all the complaints made this year have been that the Association is a great deal too Unionist and Conservative. All these complaints,' he emphasised, 'have been investigated by the Board, consisting of three Liberals and two Conservatives [the Chairman, George Harper, was a Conservative—or Tory, as he preferred to be called], and they have come to the unanimous conclusion that in every case there was no justification for the charge.' With that the matter was dropped and, while there were murmurings from time to time, the charges of political partiality were never again seriously pursued.

Five / The paternal touch

Anyone in the vicinity of Wine Office Court on a Saturday night just before Christmas, 1882, would have heard a voice booming out a rousing Victorian ballad called 'The Midshipmite'.[1]

> 'Twas in fifty five on a winter's night
> Cheerily my lads, yo ho!
> We'd got the Rooshan lines in sight,
> When up comes a little Midshipmite,
> Cheerily, my lads, yo ho!
> 'Who'll go ashore tonight,' says he,
> 'an' spike their guns along wi' me?'
> 'Why bless 'ee, sir, come along!' says we,
> Cheerily my lads, yo ho!
> Cheerily my lads, yo ho!

The singer was Gladstone's Fat Reporter, Walter Hepburn. He was providing the last item of home-made entertainment at a dinner in Ye Olde Cheshire Cheese opposite the Press Association offices. The menu—'Ye Bylle of Fayre'—was simple but substantial:

> Course Ye Firste
>
> Ye 'Old Cheshire Cheese' Puddynge
>   Consystynge of
>   Ye Rumpe Steake,
>   Ye Sheepe's Kydneys,

[1] Taken from *The Franklin Square Song Collection*, published by Harper and Brothers, New York, 1892.

The paternal touch

Ye Plumpe Larkes,
Ye Native Oysters,
Ye Edible Mushroome,
and
Ye other ingredients
Envelloped in a goodlie cruste

Course Ye Seconde

Ye Ripe Stilton,
Ye Celerie Crispe,
Ye Kynge Pippins,
Ye Oranges from Ye Foreigne Partes,
Ye Nuttes.

Drynkes

Ye Fyne Browne Beere,
Ye Punch

Ye Cygares,
Ye Sundries.

The occasion was a complimentary dinner given by the members of the P.A. staff to the Manager, Mr. Edmund Robbins. Robbins had succeeded as Manager after John Lovell's retirement in 1880. There was to be a Robbins occupying the managerial chair for the next fifty-eight years: Edmund until 1917, his son Harry from then until 1938. For the first eighty-five years of its existence the Press Association always had at least one Robbins on its staff; at one stage there were four. To an important degree the character of the agency was the character imposed on it by the Robbins family and, above all, by Edmund Robbins.

Whatever the other virtues of the system by which the P.A.'s Board of Directors was constantly changing, one inevitable consequence was that the Manager enjoyed a position of continuing power. There is no doubt that Edmund Robbins enjoyed it to the full and, as the years went by and the walrus moustache turned white, he claimed the privileges owing to him. He performed the role of a personal proprietor, a law unto himself, master of his own house, a stern authoritarian, but a paternalist in the best tradition. The Committee of Management, just as much as the staff, came under his rule. Towards the end of his career, particularly, he was their servant very much in name only. Matters had to be dealt with in his way and to his convenience. It was his habit, for example, to leave the office at precisely 5 p.m. and it would need to be something of a most urgent and important kind to cause him to stay a minute longer. It is said that on one occasion a meeting of the Management Committee seemed to be going on and on but at 4.58 p.m. Edmund Robbins rose from his chair. 'Gentlemen,' he said, 'the meeting is adjourned,' and he left the room. Though a social reformer in public life, his attitude of mind towards some kinds of change and 'progress' could be very conservative. He hated the telephone and, it is alleged, until the day he died in 1922 he refused to answer it or speak on it. Once, when alone in his office, the telephone rang so insistently that Robbins became quite desperate. He went outside into the corridor and called to a messenger named Sims to answer it. Robbins then carried on a conversation with the caller by using Sims as a go-between.

One innovation of the early days of the present century which the Manager did welcome was a speaking tube by which he could get in touch quickly with any department. Robbins liked to demonstrate to visitors how useful it was. This he did when his Chairman dropped in to see him on a casual visit. Robbins, switching on to the despatch department in the basement, invited him to test the tube. The Chairman put the tube to his ear and, as he listened, a smile lit up his face. What he had heard was a terrible din and then a voice shouting, 'Stop your bloody row—that's the guv'ner on the toob.' The Chairman handed the tube back to Robbins. 'Yes,' he said, 'it seems to work very well.'

No member of the Press Association could ever have complained of laxity on the Manager's part in watching how the money was spent. Any sub-editor, for instance, who was careless enough, when composing a news item, to let it run over the 75- or 100-word multiple upon which the Post Office charges were based was given a full-scale sermon upon his irresponsibility. 'Do you realise,' was the theme of the Manager's reprimand, 'that negligent behaviour such as yours could bring to ruin this great institution which has been built with such labour and such devotion?'

The paternal touch

But there was the other side of Edmund Robbins, that side which cared conscientiously for the welfare of the men working under him. He never forgot, even at the height of his career, how he himself had started work at the age of eleven and the importance of a helping hand at the right moment. During his time as Manager the staff of the Press Association, though much bigger than in Lovell's time, was still small enough for him to know each member of it personally. (In 1908, when he was celebrating his own journalistic half-century, there were about 150 in all on the staff of the news agency.) Edmund Robbins knew about the private lives of his staff. He knew when one of them had a new baby to look after and he would try to give him a bit of extra work to earn another ten shillings a week. Throughout his career he impressed on his directors the need to provide the staff with some security. The dinner which the staff gave him in Ye Olde Cheshire Cheese in 1882 was to celebrate the setting up of the first insurance and endowment scheme, which had been very much the result of his work. So were the improved schemes for their welfare which followed in later years. Robbins had been shocked by the effects of the 'bohemian' life of Fleet Street, seeing so many journalists die young, some not even reaching thirty and only a relatively few surviving until forty. This was just as true of men on the staff of the P.A. in the early days as of those on newspapers. And they left their widows and children destitute.

Edmund Robbins was always at pains to make sure his paternal benevolence was not mistaken for softness. Early in 1914 the engagement was announced between two members of the Press Association staff, Fred Mace, a messenger (who rose to be deputy editor-in-chief), and Miss Elizabeth Lowing, who was one of the first women to be employed by the P.A. Edmund Robbins induced the Committee of Management to vote a sum of money to buy a wedding present for the young couple—a dining-room suite and a massive sideboard. At the presentation the Manager beamed upon all benignly. He lavished his good wishes upon the couple (he also, just before their wedding day, called them into his office and gave them a short lecture on the facts of life). But, lest there should be any misunderstanding, he did not forget to add that if there were any more such romances in the P.A. no one should regard the wedding gift presented that day as establishing a precedent. Robbins adopted a stern attitude towards any man who was importunate enough, having asked for a rise and having been turned down, to keep on asking. The Manager would send for him and deliver himself of a homily on the corruptive qualities of money and the virtues of a contented mind, free from materialistic ambition. The sermon would always end with a reminder of the need for loyalty to the Press Association, a loyalty which the staff could express by showing self-restraint and an understanding of the necessity for economy in every aspect of their work. 'We must keep the flag flying,' said Edmund Robbins before sending the man away empty-handed.

The Manager must have been as pleased as his staff when at the end of 1892 the directors decided it was time the Press Association moved into offices more in keeping with its status in the country. The premises at 7 Wine Office Court seem picturesque when viewed from a distance of more than seventy years. There was, for instance, the gas lamp at the entrance to the Court from Fleet Street bearing the information that the P.A. was never closed. But 'picturesque' can be a euphemism for squalid and uncomfortable. Hanging over the front windows of the P.A. building were large patent reflectors: they were necessary in order to get a little daylight into the rooms. And the rooms themselves, however adequate they may have seemed when the news agency was in its infancy, were, twenty years later, most unpleasantly cramped. In 1884 the office furniture was valued in the accounts at only £150, and while it was admitted it was worth very much more it does not suggest that the furnishings were other than basic. As early as 1879 the directors were discussing the creation of a special reserve fund to buy freeholds for the building of a fine headquarters for the P.A., but it was another sixty years before the present one was built. Meanwhile, when it proved impossible to arrange a satisfactory extension in Wine Office Court, a move had to be made. (Not before time, the cashier may have thought, for in 1887 part of a chimney had fallen into his office, injuring him slightly.)

Even the new premises at 14 New Bridge Street were not wholly suitable as offices, but there was plenty of room in them and the regret at leaving Wine Office Court must have been small. Number 14 was a substantial old-fashioned building. The P.A. leased it from the Trustees of the Bridewell Royal Hospital (which controlled the Bedlam Lunatic Asylum). It was within two minutes' walk of the Ludgate Circus post office and very close to most of the important newspaper offices. At the first annual meeting of the Association held in the new headquarters on the 9th of May 1893 the Chairman, Francis Hewitt, of the *Leicester Daily Post*, did not try to restrain his pride. Standing in the boardroom, with its large stained-glass window, he treated his colleagues to a magniloquent discourse upon the history of the 'mansion' they were now occupying.

'The place upon which we stand,' he said, 'is historic ground. Here the Norman Kings held their Court, and on this site were important buildings, which, from the Norman era, were of service in the history of London and England. Here for several centuries was an edifice which served as prison and poorhouse, and where, for many generations, London's refractory apprentices were confined and punished after the fashion of those times.' The six cells were still there when the P.A. moved in. Hewitt went on to recall how, for the past hundred years, the part of the building now occupied by the P.A. had been the official residence of the Treasurer of the Bridewell Trust.

'How the stately gents and dames of that olden time, who,' Hewitt mused, 'in these very rooms, read their small, dear, and meagre newspapers, and gossiped over the news a fortnight old from Scotland and Ireland, three months old from Austria, America and Russia, and a year old from our distant Colonies, if they could revisit their former abode, and witness a busy hive of workmen day and night all the year round, sending and receiving instantaneous news to and from all parts of the world—how surprised they would be at the changes which had taken place in the occupants and the rooms of their old home.'

As Hewitt had hoped, the meeting was not a long one and at the end of it the members of the Press Association trooped off to inspect their own offices. The ground floor had a fine entrance hall and a big manager's waiting-room which were a source of joy to Edmund Robbins. His own room was a huge one, running from the front to the back of the first floor, with oak-panelled walls and a carved ceiling. A large mirror hung over the marble mantelpiece. Now, at last, Robbins had accommodation fitting for a man of his public reputation and he reigned over an establishment which was also much more in tune with the organisation he had done so much to create and with the quality of the men who worked for it.

Henry Whorlow had his office nearby on the same floor. Whorlow, always a man of sober dignity and competence, served the P.A. in a way surpassed only by Edmund Robbins himself. He had been on the staff since the very beginning, of course, joining only three weeks after Robbins. When Robbins succeeded Lovell as Manager, Whorlow moved up from Chief Accountant to become Secretary. He also took over from Robbins as Secretary of the Provincial Newspaper Society. The first typewriter to be used in the P.A. was a Remington which Whorlow received in exchange for an advertisement inserted in the Newspaper Society's Monthly Circular. For a long time it stood idle in his office, regarded with suspicion by the older men. But then Whorlow's amanuensis started to use it for particularly long letters. At first, when he put them before Henry Whorlow, he did so with some little anxiety, but Whorlow signed them without comment. When the machine became decrepit, Edmund Robbins agreed that the P.A. should invest in a new Underwood. He ruled, however, that while the P.A. had used the old Newspaper Society machine, the new one must be kept for Press Association business only.

The Financial Room—the Cashier's Department—was also on the first floor. The Cashier was Joseph Bowskill, who had joined the P.A. as a compositor to set up in type Parliamentary reports in an office near Trafalgar Square. These were for the London clubs. 'Copy' was brought to him by a boy on horseback, down Whitehall from Parliament, and the printed sheets were taken round to the clubs. With the coming of the tape machine, Bowskill was no longer needed, but he was found a job in the Financial Department and rose to be Cashier. He was an ardent spiritualist and it was easy to lead him on to his favourite topic, a tactic successfully employed by reporters, already in the red on expenses but in need of a further sub. Joseph Bowskill attributed his physical health to Mother Seigel's Syrup, which he recommended to any member of the staff complaining of illness, be it a cold, backache, varicose veins or chilblains. It was Bowskill's practice to go alone to the bank in Chancery Lane. He distributed the gold and silver coins in the many capacious pockets of his cutaway coat; he put fivers in his breast pocket. Once, when crossing Fleet Street, a man shouted 'Mind the bus' and threw his arm across Bowskill's chest. When the Cashier got to the other side of the street he found he no longer had the fivers—amounting to £120. The Committee of Management passed a resolution of sympathy with him and thereafter he made the journey to and from the bank in an ancient 'growler' and he was always accompanied.

His companion was Walter Cattermole, another man who believed in allowing his figure to grow and grow as Nature intended. When he heaved his bulk into the 'growler' it swayed unhappily on its springs. Walter Joseph Cattermole was superintendent of the small army of P.A. messenger boys. He had the manner of a regimental sergeant-major and sought to instil a military sense of discipline and smartness into the boys. The messengers wore dark blue uniforms with red piping around the cuffs and down the trousers; each had his number in blue on his red collar. The words 'Press Association' were embroidered in blue on a flat military-type cap. Senior to the messengers were the despatch clerks, who were ranked as sergeants, corporals and lance-corporals, and carried out a daily inspection of brass buttons, boots, hair, face, hands, fingernails.

Most of the boys came from the poorest parts of London and as they set off from home in the uniforms they were often followed by the cry of 'Pick-a-narny', the Cockney corruption of 'Pig in harness', a nineteenth-century term of abuse for men who disgraced their families by enlisting in the regular army.

The first messenger was appointed on 12th February 1870, a week after the P.A. had transmitted its first message. Between then and 30th May 1881, 334 boys were employed as messengers, many of them for short periods only. The 'Boys' Admission and Discharge Book' explains why some of them left. One, it says, left 'to go to America'. Another quit the P.A. 'to go as messenger in G.P.O.' One left to 'go for a page'; another 'to go to school again'; yet another because 'his father did not like him being out so late at night'. The reasons why some were sacked give a clear impression of the kind of lads they were and the discipline which their seniors tried to impose on them. 'Was ordered', runs one entry, 'to take letters to the G.P.O. but did not do so—he gave the letters to another boy to post, consequently the letters did not get there in time and several were returned ... Discharged at a minute's notice.' 'For smoking in the kitchen', runs another record of dismissal. 'For being forty minutes going to Temple Bar and back' . . . 'For using bad language and threatening to throw the Mallett and Bowl at Mr. Bowskill at the West End Office' . . . 'For pilfering—was ordered to take a cab from Westminster to the Association with important copy concerning the Mordaunt case—he had a shilling given to him to pay the cab, instead of which he took the train from Westminster Bridge to the Temple station and kept the 10*d*. change, at the same time delaying the copy' . . . 'Discharged for throwing a live dog out of the first-floor landing window' . . . 'Discharged for refusing to do his work and also for calling Mr. Cuthbert a b—— Scotch Haddock' . . . 'Discharged for gambling in the kitchen, after being repeatedly told that he was not to do so—also for being continually late and over his time with messages' . . . 'Discharged for tearing up message instead of delivering it at the Turf Club' . . . 'Destroying and burning seats in the kitchen.' Apart from those dismissed for such misconduct, others had complaints listed against their names: 'Making unnecessary noise by running up the stairs, also throwing shoe brushes around' . . . 'Tossing for beer in Reporting Room' . . . '17 minutes before he opened the door for Mr. Cuthbert' . . . 'Did not go for *The Times* until 8 minutes after 5 a.m., delaying Mr. Cuthbert's work' . . . 'Making a noise in Editorial Room' . . . 'This boy ran home, after being told to stay on overtime till 2 a.m.'

The messengers worked an eight-hour day, six days a week. Their wages started at five shillings a week with threepence an hour overtime and an extra shilling for those on the all-night turn. (The first eight boys who were taken on were paid seven shillings a week, but from 1871 onwards this was reduced to five shillings.) The boys were supposed to get a shilling rise every six months for the first two years, but it did not work out that way. A boy had to apply for the increase. He would put in his application at the end of the first six months, but he might have to wait from four to six weeks for it to be approved. His next increase would not then be due for another six months from then.

It was not an easy life, but many of the boys rose a long way in the P.A.—to editorial jobs, to senior posts in the Manager's and Secretary's Departments—and elsewhere in Fleet Street. Two of these boys who started together when they were fourteen were Jack Baker and Joe Moore. Baker, who was with the P.A. for

The paternal touch

fifty-five years, ultimately became Chief Cashier, while Moore became managing director of his own engineering works. They joined the Press Association 'Militia' in the nineties. One of the jobs given to Moore, a strong lad, was to carry two scuttles of coal at a time from the basement up to the Cattermole flat on the top floor. A boy was allowed twopence for his fare to the Houses of Parliament and back. Joe Moore used to run it all the way, across Blackfriars Bridge, along Stamford Street, and back over Westminster Bridge before others using public transport had arrived. He lived in Hackney and walked daily to and from work. He left home with sandwiches but he had usually finished these off well before dinner-time, so he went to Pearce and Plenty in Farringdon Street where he had 'a baby's head'—a steak-and-kidney pudding—and two veg for fourpence. This he could afford only by saving his fares.

This was the kind of boy who came under Walter Cattermole's command. To any who dared to give him 'lip', Cattermole would threaten, 'I'll send you about your business altogether.' But he knew what it meant to them to have a steady job and a boy had to step a long way out of line before he would actually sack him. One member of the Press Association staff of those days before the first world war—Fred Pearce—has left some vivid notes. One of them recalls how, around the late 1900s, the *Daily Graphic*, during the winter months, was running a free soup kitchen for the homeless, many of whom also used to come into the P.A. Despatch Department, in the basement at New Bridge Street, asking for any stale bread or scraps of food not eaten by the messengers. When the manager of the *Graphic* heard about this he sent Pearce a big bundle of tickets for free soup and bread and asked him to give them to any hungry men and women who came in. The word soon got around and after two or three nights a big queue of down-and-outs gathered outside the P.A. building. Police had to control them and Edmund Robbins received a complaint about it. Robbins stopped the distribution but at the same time he praised what Pearce had been doing.

At the turn of the century Fleet Street itself was a turbulent, gregarious place, bustling with horse-drawn carts, carriages and buses. There was a grocer's shop, a greengrocer's, an old-fashioned coffee-shop and a sausage shop where fried onions sizzled in the pans just inside the window. There was an abundance of eating-houses and the pubs were open all night. Hard work and long hours were not accompanied by the strains of modern journalism. The atmosphere on the second floor—the editorial floor—of the Press Association, for instance, was not one of sound and fury. From the memories which have been handed down the picture is one of leisure, gentility and quiet. The sub-editors wore top-hats and frock-coats and waited in armchairs for 'telegrams to drift in, some many hours late'. Only the squeak of a pencil or a stylus was heard. One chief sub-editor bought canvas shoes for the messengers to preserve the calm of the evening. If the clerk-in-charge said the telephone was ringing, the chief sub, enjoying his cigar, would say, 'See what it is, old man. If it's not important, tell the caller to put it on the wire.' This might well be the same chief sub whom legend credits with hurling his phone frequently into the wastepaper basket. But it probably was not quite as tranquil and easy-going as all that. Until the first Roneo machine was introduced around 1905 the sub-editors had to write everything by hand on flimsies, 'punching out' as many as twenty copies. If, as often happened, the last three or four copies were too faint for the despatching clerk in the basement to read, more copies had to be made. Even after the arrival of the Roneo the messages still had to be written, though now on wax stencils; the stencils tore easily and those which the subs did not spoil were probably ripped by the man operating the machine.

The second floor at New Bridge Street housed what were called the Day and the Night Editorials. They were divided by the Instrument Room, in which were three Morse telegraph machines, two of which provided direct lines to the Post Office; these were used for sending short, important service messages and for receiving paragraphs from P.A. correspondents. A third Morse machine gave New Bridge Street a direct link with the P.A. room at the Houses of Parliament. Also in the Instrument Room was a tape transmitting machine which had a keyboard which was the replica of that of a small piano with black and white 'notes'. It was used for sending messages to the London papers. This seems to have been a temperamental machine, quite liable, when there was important news to transmit, to catch fire or blow all its fuses. Another tape machine connected the P.A. with Reuter's head office in Old Jewry.

The paternal touch

Before the first world war—and for years afterwards—ultimate editorial responsibility rested with the Manager, but from day to day the chief sub-editor was practically in charge. In 1900 there were six men in the Day Editorial and nine on the evening and all-night duty. Then there were the reporters. Apart from the specialists, like the men reporting Parliament or the Law Courts, there were five general reporters and a chief reporter, Walter Hepburn. Each of them had to be capable of taking a sustained verbatim shorthand note. They also had to be able to play solo whist because Hepburn insisted on a 'school' every afternoon in his room. Or so the unlikely story goes. In fact, these were the men who covered all major stories for the Press Association, political leaders on tour, important trials, Royal visits, national disasters. Their reputations were high both in Fleet Street and in the provinces. Their status, as well as their calibre, may be judged from a story about one of them, Sam Perks. He was a short, stout man with an explosive temper; erudite, fluent, a fine raconteur. He was also very jealous of his profession. At a meeting he was covering in the provinces, the speaker, a front-bench politician, used the word 'ingenuous'. 'I will repeat that word—*ingenuous*,' he said, 'because reporters invariably confuse it with *ingenious*.' Perks jumped to his feet at the press table, his chair scraping harshly on the floor. He was trembling with anger and indignation. He accused the speaker of a gross insult to members of the Fourth Estate and ended his outburst with a demand for an apology. The politician made a faltering apology and brought his speech to a premature end.

Like journalists of any era, the P.A. reporters had to be men of resource. Jack Howe, who had graduated from the Financial Department to become a staff reporter, was rushed off on a fast train north to cover the railway disaster at Aisgill Moor in which twelve people were killed on Christmas Eve, 1910. He was among the earliest reporters from London on the spot. After spending most of Christmas Day morning collecting his story he set off in a cab for the nearest post office, writing his 'copy' on the way. The post office was closed, but he hammered on the door until the postmistress opened it. He pushed his way in, handing her a press telegram, some 3000 words long.

'I can't accept this,' she said. 'I won't accept it.' Howe tried to persuade her, first using charm, then reason. Still she firmly refused. 'Besides,' she said, 'it's Christmas Day and we're having a party.'

Howe took a telegraph form from the counter, wrote a short message on it.

'Could you please send that?' he asked her. Merely glancing at the length of it, she said she would. Then she read it. It was addressed to the Postmaster General. It said: 'Postmistress here refuses to accept P.A. story of Aisgill Moor disaster. Please direct her to despatch message.' She was shocked. After thinking it over she agreed to accept the message. Howe dictated it to her as she hammered it out. It took them a few hours to do the job, by which time they were on the best of terms and Howe stayed to join her Christmas party.

What was probably the biggest P.A. scoop of this period was achieved by the chief of the Parliamentary staff, James McCallum, though the story had nothing to do with Parliament or politics. It happened during a Parliamentary recess when McCallum became available for general reporting. He was chosen as one of two reporters, representing the British press, who were to watch the exhumation of a body in Highgate cemetery. This was the climax to a most extraordinary story about the Duke of Portland. The coffin which was to be opened was that of a man called Thomas Charles Druce. But did it contain Druce's body or was it filled with lead? That was the great mystery. There was a rumour which had persisted since the day Druce had been buried forty-three years before that the Duke of Portland had chosen from time to time, when it suited his convenience, whatever that might have been, to masquerade as a Mr. Druce, the owner of a flourishing furniture shop in Baker Street. Then, the story went, having tired of the game, the Duke decided to put an end to Druce by pretending to have him buried, the funeral rites being performed over a coffin full of lead. The exhumation was considered necessary to prove the succession to the dukedom of Portland, which was being claimed by one of Druce's sons.

The Home Office agreed that two reporters, one from the P.A. and one from the Central News, could attend the exhumation which was to be performed in a wooden shed surrounding the tomb and vault of the Druce family. The news agencies had to agree to certain conditions to prevent one trying to beat the other with the news; they also had to accept official censorship of their reports.

The paternal touch

The story in the *Star* on the day of the exhumation, 30th December 1907, tells just how the P.A. managed to beat the Central News and the Home Office.

THE BODY OF DRUCE

SECRET OF THE HIGHGATE TOMB REVEALED THIS AFTERNOON

LEADED COFFIN THEORY COLLAPSES

'An aged, bearded man': Thomas Charles Druce found in the grave where he was laid 43 years ago.

The Druce coffin contains a body.
This is the message conveyed first by the Press Association. It settles definitely once and for all the allegation that the coffin in the Highgate vault was filled with lead.
The announcement came over the tape at 12.30.
A few minutes later the official statement was issued . . .
'At 12.30', says our reporter, 'the gates of the wooden shed opened, and everyone held his breath in the sharp morning air.
'Thence came the representatives—one each—of the Press Association and the Central News. They were arm-in-arm!
'Those who had expected an undignified sprint between the rival agency men were disappointed.
'It appeared that the cemetery authorities, in their desire to avoid anything not in accordance with the strictest decorum, had given the pressmen within their gates implicit instructions, hence these unusual amenities.
'But a change came over the peaceful scene when the gates were reached. There are some steps, and for a moment the Men Who Knew the secret disappeared from view.
'When they emerged into view again one man was blowing his nose vigorously on a bright red handkerchief.
'Simultaneously, as if by magic, a long line of men who stretched right along the road, and who had been suspiciously inactive, were quickened into alertness.
'Directly the bright red bandana made a spot of colour in the air the first man waved a flag . . .

'The next man waved a flag ...
'The third man waved a flag ...
'And so all along the line—a vista of flags.
'At the end of the line was a special telephone ...
'Another line of communication was as follows:
'At the top of a long road leading from the cemetery, standing on a wall about a quarter of a mile from the cemetery, was a pressman with a pair of glasses.

'Half a mile away, on the roof of a building in High Street, Highgate, was a second man with a telescope.

'He took a message and sent it direct by a telephone which had been engaged all day.

'The most stringent precautions were taken to prevent uncensored news coming out of the gate.

'After their first appearance the privileged agency reporters had to walk into the superintendent's office at the gate.

'Ten minutes later both came out, each in charge of two policemen, and handed the official report through the gate to their colleagues outside.'

All that needs to be added is that the red handkerchief was the agreed signal for 'body'; McCallum would have blown his nose with a green one if the coffin had contained lead. The plan had been devised after McCallum and a colleague, Andrew Gray, had made a reconnaissance of Highgate cemetery a few days before.

One of the measures taken by the P.A. to cope with the increased work which followed the outbreak of the Boer War in 1899 was the opening of a special office over a public house near the War Office, to deal quickly with official communiqués. The man who was put in charge of it was George Smith, who over a long career with the Press Association achieved a very high reputation which spread far beyond the news agency itself and indeed beyond the world of newspapers. George Smith, who had been a schoolmaster before going into journalism, joined the P.A. in 1891. Three years later he was appointed Court reporter and in time was to be known as 'Royal Smith'. He was never a member of the staff, preferring to be paid 'linage'. He was also registrar of births and deaths for Finchley and Friern Barnet and, for a time at any rate, an agent for an insurance company. Because it would obviously be impossible for every newspaper to have its own reporter attached to the Royal Family, the practice grew up of a few news

The paternal touch

agency reporters—today there is just one—acting as representatives for the whole press. Whatever publicly involved the Royal Family involved the Court Correspondent of the Press Association. Smith was in Westminster Abbey for the Coronation of Edward VII when, for the first time, the Post Office made arrangements to distribute direct from the Abbey the descriptive messages which he and other reporters were writing as the ceremony proceeded. Soon after that, when Edward VII was ill, Smith was practically resident at Buckingham Palace with a royal telephone placed at his disposal. George Smith held the title of Court Correspondent for thirty-three years and the message which George V sent to Mrs. Smith when her husband died showed that the relationship between him and the Royal Family had matured into a more than formal one. There were certainly occasions when George Smith performed more than his formal duties. Philip Gibbs has told (in *The Journalist's London*) of one such instance:

'When the Peace of Vereeningen was signed, ending the war in South Africa, he [Smith] went down to Windsor to obtain what he believed to be the inevitable proclamation of King Edward to his people on this historical event. But it had not occurred to the King that such a message was necessary. So Smith was informed, somewhat icily, by Lord Knollys, the King's secretary. Smith pressed the point, to the annoyance of his lordship. The King was taking tea with a lady in Windsor Great Park and was likely to be back late.

' "I'll wait," said Smith, quietly but firmly. He waited a long time. To pass the hours he composed a message to the nation in royal phraseology with which he was familiar. King Edward returned only in time to dress hurriedly for dinner. Dinner was served when Lord Knollys came to see Smith again, advising him, and almost ordering him, to go home.

' "I've drafted out something," said Smith, in his quiet way. "Perhaps you would be good enough to submit it to His Majesty?"

'Lord Knollys stared at this audacious fellow almost with stupefaction, but reluctantly took the bit of paper on which Smith had written the draft of a Royal Proclamation. After an interval it came back. Below it was written "Edward, R.I."

'It was Smith of the P.A. who was the author of the King's message to his people.'

In fact, the King did make one or two small changes in Smith's draft, but the Proclamation, as released, was substantially the work of the P.A. man. It read: 'The King has received the welcome news of the cessation of hostilities in South Africa with infinite satisfaction, and trusts that peace may be speedily followed by the restoration of prosperity in his new dominions, and that the feelings necessarily engendered by war will give place to the earnest co-operation of all His Majesty's South African subjects in promoting the welfare of their common country.'

George Smith enjoyed the trust of the Royal Family for the simple reason that he never betrayed it.

The essential discretion of a Court reporter cannot be classed as suppression of news. But throughout its history the Press Association has been asked, sometimes by private individuals, often by solicitors, not to put out certain news stories, usually about cases in the police courts or law courts. Whether the appeal is accompanied by offers of money or of a contribution to the Newspaper Press Fund the answer has always been the same: No. To have succumbed to that kind of pressure would have meant the rapid tarnishing of the news agency's status not only in the eyes of the newspapers it was built to serve but also in those of the public at large. It takes a long time to achieve a reputation for integrity and a very short time to destroy it. There was no doubt that by the beginning of the present century the P.A. had 'arrived'. A small example of the appreciation of its importance by the political parties was to be found in 1908. It seems that the practice was growing of public dinners in London being held later and later. Consequently, after-dinner speeches were also reaching newspapers later than they would have liked. Edmund Robbins went into action. He explained to the Prime Minister's private secretary 'the real urgency' of the matter. Then it was put to Sir Henry Campbell-Bannerman. Both the Liberal Party and the Tory Opposition quickly mended their ways.

Just how serious a matter it could be from the P.A.'s point of view can be judged by the way they covered the Lord Mayor's Banquet at the Guildhall. This was the outstanding news event of the year in the speech-making line. Before the first world war it was the occasion when a number of Cabinet Ministers would speak. The P.A. reckoned to put out some 10,000 words and virtually the whole organisation was involved, not least Walter Cattermole, superintendent of messengers. To rush the reporters'

The paternal touch

copy to the telegraph office and the London newspapers about thirty messengers and perhaps five despatching clerks were needed, with Cattermole in supreme command of them. Before they left the P.A. he inspected the messengers to make sure that their boots, their buckles and buttons were all highly polished. Then they were marched in military formation to the Guildhall. At the Guildhall the police court was turned into a despatching room, with Cattermole seated high up in the magistrate's chair, smoking a huge cigar, a glass of whisky at his side. The reporters and clerks, too, could rely on getting bottles of whisky, wine and beer, and the messenger boys, as well as getting a shilling supper money, were certain to get plenty of food from the kitchens both to eat there and to take home.

The monetary value to the P.A. of such occasions as the Lord Mayor's Banquet was calculated in the less giddy and much less luxurious atmosphere of the Counting Room in the basement of 14 New Bridge Street. Here, for many years, reigned Henry Wright, a portly man with mutton-chop whiskers who was nicknamed 'Curry'. Wright, whose coat was powdered with snuff, was, according to a contemporary, an eccentric. On Sundays he was a very religious man who went to church morning and evening and took a Bible class in the afternoon; on weekdays he exercised a Billingsgate vocabulary. Nothing could deter Henry Wright from his duty of pricing up the 'specials' and 'locals' sent out by the P.A. the previous day and checking the Post Office accounts for telegrams. Even when a thunderstorm caused the Fleet River to overflow into the basement where he worked he merely tucked up his legs on his high stool and went on with his work. Alas, according to one of his colleagues, 'religious mania got him in the end and he died in Bedlam'.

Six / The perils of the law

One day in December 1886, the slightly melancholy, military-looking figure of Henry Whorlow could be seen getting out of a cab in Clapham. He went up the steps of 62 New Park Road, one of those dignified, upstanding, bourgeois residences which proclaimed the respectability of its owner. He had come to see Lady Aylmer, the recently divorced wife of Sir Arthur Percy Fitzgerald Aylmer, the 12th baronet. Whorlow came in his capacity as Secretary of the Press Association and his mission was an urgent and delicate one. It was to persuade Lady Aylmer to drop the libel actions she had started against fifty-five newspapers.

There was no doubt that the newspapers had libelled her and there was no doubt either that the report they had all published had been sent out by the Press Association. The report was of the hearing on 4th November 1886 of Lady Aylmer's petition for divorce. According to the evidence, Lady Aylmer, an American divorcee called Anna Reid, had married Sir Arthur, an Irish baronet, at Kensington Register Office in August 1884, the same year in which his first wife had died. (Curiously, all the reference books now give the date of his second marriage as 1885.) Now she had sued him for divorce, chiefly on the grounds of his misconduct with a flower girl. She was awarded a decree nisi with costs. In her evidence Lady Aylmer said she had known her husband for some months before marriage. The Press Association reporter, a man named Saunders, was not in court at the time and he copied a paragraph from the flimsy of another reporter. Unfortunately, he misread it. The report he wrote for the P.A. said that Lady Aylmer admitted in cross-examination that 'she had been intimate with the respondent [her husband] more than once before

The perils of the law

marriage'. The report went out to a large number of evening papers, most of which published it without alteration, although they put their own headlines on it.

The Press Association, in the shape of Edmund Robbins, the Manager, was not aware that it had sent out a libellous report until three weeks after it had been published. He heard about it from a Dublin newspaper which had been threatened with a libel action initiated by Lady Aylmer. Robbins wondered what he should do. Should he send out to the newspapers which had published the libel a correction and an apology? Or would the publication of an apology draw attention to something which had escaped notice for so long and thus aggravate the original libel? He decided to ask the advice of the Committee of Management which was due to meet a couple of days later. The Committee considered that a circular should be sent to all newspapers which had published the libel, advising them to publish an apology without delay.

All fifty-five papers did publish apologies, but writs for libel were issued against each of them and Lady Aylmer's solicitor, called Manning, refused to consider any suggestion of a compromise settlement out of court. The Press Association itself was not directly involved, for Lady Aylmer had been advised to sue the papers which had published the report and not the news agency which had supplied it to them. But Edmund Robbins and the Management Committee felt an obligation to try to mitigate the harm done by the reporter's 'indefensible blunder'. Until the writs were issued the P.A. had been unable to deal directly with Lady Aylmer because it was impossible to find out where she was living. But the writs gave her address as the one in Clapham Park. Edmund Robbins got in touch with the Chairman, Robert Leader, of the *Sheffield Independent,* and they agreed to try to bypass the obdurate solicitor, Manning, and make a direct appeal to Lady Aylmer herself. But Leader stressed that the operation would have to be carried out with great discretion and care as well as speed, for it was essential to its success that any deal should be clinched irrevocably before Manning heard about it. The Chairman felt strongly that an effort should be made to get Lady Aylmer's signature to any terms on the spot.

So off went Henry Whorlow to Clapham. What he did not know as he rang the bell of 62 New Park Road was that the house

105

Reporter Anonymous

belonged to Lady Aylmer's solicitor, Manning, and that she was merely lodging there. Luckily for him, the solicitor was not at home. Nor was Lady Aylmer, but Whorlow had a long talk with her mother, who was also staying there. He told her that the newspapers which were being sued were willing to give Lady Aylmer a total of £500 to settle the actions. She promised to talk to her daughter as soon as she came back.

The next morning Henry Whorlow, in his office at Wine Office Court, received a short note. It came from another solicitor called Wynne, of Chancery Lane, and stated that Lady Aylmer was with him and would see Whorlow if he would call. Whorlow went there and had a long discussion with Lady Aylmer and Wynne, who said he was acting not as a solicitor but as a friend. The outcome was an agreement to pay Lady Aylmer £500 in settlement and an additional fifty guineas to cover Manning's costs. Each of the newspapers concerned was called upon to meet its share of the settlement. The maximum contribution was £20, a cheap escape by any measurement.

On 23rd December the Chairman, Robert Leader, wrote a letter to Edmund Robbins which the Management Committee resolved should be entered in the minutes: 'I congratulate you and Mr. Whorlow on the tact you have displayed in very delicate circumstances. You are, I am sure, entitled to the warm thanks of all of us, though I know you will feel the relief equally as well as any of us.' The Manager read to the Committee a letter from Saunders, the erring reporter, expressing great regret. While waiting for the Committee to meet and consider how to deal with Saunders, Edmund Robbins had removed him from his duties in the Law Courts and placed him in a junior position in the office. At the annual meeting five months later the Chairman reported on the way the directors had dealt with Saunders.

'The first inclination,' said Leader, a man of austere but humane features, 'was to discharge him forthwith. He was, in point of fact, suspended for some weeks, until the whole thing could be investigated, and a motion was made at the Board that a man who could make a blunder of that kind was evidently unfit to be on the staff of the Association—[hear, hear]—and he ought to be discharged [hear, hear]. But considerations of mercy intervened. He had been in the service of the Association for a great number of years, and it was thought that the justice of the case

The perils of the law

would be met if he were removed entirely from reporting in the Law Courts, and given a subordinate position on the staff in the office at a considerably lower salary. [Cheers.] I do not know whether we made a mistake or not, but there is this to be said—that we took the more merciful course towards a man who had been in our service a great number of years, and who had a wife and large family. [Hear, hear.]'

From the point of view of the members of the Press Association and its subscribers the handling of the affair by Edmund Robbins and, particularly, Henry Whorlow had been an almost—but not quite—complete success. Not quite, because apart from the unfortunate Saunders who lost his job in the Divorce Court and had his salary cut from £3 5*s*. a week to £2 10*s*. a week, there was one other man who came out of it at a substantial loss. That man was E. Dwyer Gray, M.P. for a Dublin constituency and the proprietor of the *Freeman's Journal* and the *Dublin Evening Telegraph*.

From the very start of her discussion with Henry Whorlow, Lady Aylmer had insisted that, whatever else she might concede, under no circumstances would she settle out of court the action against the *Dublin Evening Telegraph*. She did not give any definite reason, but Whorlow discovered later that she considered Dwyer Gray had aggravated the original libel by the way he dealt with her complaints. Nothing Whorlow could say could make her change her mind and so he had to make the agreement for settling the actions against only fifty-four out of the fifty-five newspapers involved. The *Dublin Evening Telegraph* had to be left to face the music alone.

The action was heard in the Nisi Prius Court in Dublin before the Lord Chief Baron Palles. Lady Aylmer claimed £5000 damages. As Whorlow reported in a circular to members of the Provincial Newspaper Society, of which he was Secretary and therefore doubly concerned about the case, he, Edmund Robbins and Saunders, the reporter, all gave evidence for Gray. They explained how the offending report (which the *Evening Telegraph* had headed innocuously, 'Irish baronet in the Divorce Court—Elopement with a flower girl') had come to be sent out. They also told the court about the negotiations Whorlow had conducted with Lady Aylmer to get a settlement of the actions. According to Whorlow's version of the court case, Dwyer Gray proved that

Reporter Anonymous

Lady Aylmer had been wrong to accuse him of having aggravated the libel. In fact, he had seized the earliest opportunity to publish the following apology:

'Aylmer Divorce Suit. Out attention has been directed to a telegram published in our issue of the 4th inst. containing certain statements injurious to the petitioner, Lady Aylmer, who was represented as having in examination made admissions of a discreditable character. We are assured that there was no foundation whatever for these statements with regard to Lady Aylmer. The report was supplied to us in the ordinary way by the Press Association—a most respectable source of public information. It was published by us in perfect *bona fides*, and in the full belief that it was an accurate report of a proceeding in public court. The instant our attention has been called to the fact that the report was inaccurate and injurious to Lady Aylmer we take the earliest opportunity of offering her our full apology and an expression of regret that we should inadvertently have been led to publish statements calculated to cause her Ladyship pain and annoyance.'

Nevertheless, the jury awarded Lady Aylmer damages of £250 and costs. Dwyer Gray reckoned he had lost altogether between £500 and £600. Not surprisingly, he felt sore—not so much at the loss of money, he said, as at having been made a 'scapegoat'. At the P.A. annual meeting Gray put forward his complaint with much dignity and with a remarkable lack of rancour. He was a man of great personal courage and an impassioned defender of the poor and the oppressed in Ireland. Now he was pleading his own cause. He attracted a deal of sympathy. E. A. Mason, of the *Worcester Evening Post and Echo*, made a move, supported by Alexander Grigor Jeans, one of the two great pioneering names of the *Liverpool Daily Post*, to compensate Gray. Mason proposed that the Press Association should pay him £250. But Mason was persuaded that this would be a breach of the principles on which the P.A. was based and Gray said, with a courteous word of gratitude, that he was not looking for charity from his colleagues. It must be all or nothing. The Press Association either did or did not recognise what he considered its moral obligation to meet all his expenses, he said. The answer of the meeting, the compassionate but unambiguous answer, was that the P.A. did not and could not admit such an obligation.

The perils of the law

About three weeks after that annual meeting in May 1887 a Dublin solicitor, acting for Dwyer Gray, asked the Press Association for compensation. The P.A. denied liability and resolved to defend all the way the action that was then threatened. Even now the atmosphere in which the two sides squared up for battle was one without hostility. Both Gray and the P.A. instructed their solicitors to conduct the action in 'a perfectly friendly spirit'. There were many legal comings and goings at a high level to decide whether the case ought to be heard in England or Ireland. Eventually the Court of Appeal ruled that the Irish courts had jurisdiction to try the action. The machinery of the law started to move and a claim for £1000 damages was made on Gray's behalf. But before the action could be heard Dwyer Gray died suddenly. He was only forty-two. The P.A. still had to pay £270 in costs—after persuading its solicitor to cut his original account by £53. To cap a sad story, a matter of months after his severe reprimand and his demotion, Saunders, the reporter who had blundered, also died. There was little doubt, it was said, that his death had been hastened by the 'unfortunate business'.

The Aylmer case was finished but it had raised issues of continuing significance both to the Press Association and to all newspapers. William Lewis, of the *Bristol Mercury*, the chairman who had the job of reporting the unhappy ending to the story, defined the position of the P.A.

'We have felt all along Mr. Gray's position was one of great hardship,' he said, 'and his rebellion against it was only natural. But,' said Lewis firmly, 'we could not allow our sympathy to warp our judgement, and admit a contention contrary to the fundamental principle upon which all our business is conducted, and upon which alone it is possible for the Press Association to continue to exist. We act,' said Lewis, spelling out that basic principle, 'as agents to our customers, and are in fact in the same position to them as their own reporters. We use all the care in our power, but they must publish the news they receive from us on their own responsibility. Upon any other basis it would be impossible to carry on the Press Association.'

Answering questions, William Lewis elaborated. In the same way, he said, as no newspaper proprietor could make a reporter pay the damage arising from any error or lapse of judgement on his part, so the P.A. could not possibly take the legal responsibility of all their customers. To take that responsibility on behalf of 500 or 600 papers all over the country, he said, would require a reserve fund not of £9000 but of £900,000. The meeting seemed to agree that a record of just one court action for libel arising from news supplied by the P.A. in seventeen years of service did not suggest that the agency was run by wild men or staffed by irresponsibles. But to this day the Press Association is protected, in its conditions for the supply of news, against claims from subscribers for compensation for any unfortunate consequences which may follow publication of a P.A. message. In practice, this principle, at the Board's discretion, has been occasionally modified. Sometimes the P.A. has dealt directly with threats of action and so saved individual members from receiving claims.

Writs for libel and threats of libel actions are a chronic occupational hazard of journalism. But in the late nineteenth century the hazards were even more acute and abundant than they are today. As we saw earlier, James Lancelot Foster, of the *Yorkshire Gazette*, in 1880 spoke of 'plenty of wolves prowling about ready to devour anyone making a false step'. Provincial Newspaper Society circulars throughout the early 1880s contain numerous references to the frequency of libel actions, many of them frivolous. There were also observations about solicitors who spent many hours poring over newspapers at the British Museum to discover causes of action.

The Lady Aylmer case came at a time when newspapers were already discussing the possibility of amendments to the law of libel. Early in 1887 Henry Whorlow, as Secretary of the Provincial Newspaper Society, circularised every daily and weekly paper in the metropolitan area and in March that year a conference on libel law was held at the Salisbury Hotel. Twenty-five London papers, as well as the Newspaper Society, the Press Association, the Exchange Telegraph, the Central News and the National Press Agency, sent representatives. The ultimate outcome of this conference was a Bill to amend the law of libel, introduced in the House of Commons by Sir Algernon Borthwick, M.P., of the *Morning Post*. It became law in 1888. One section of it may well have been drawn up with the Lady Aylmer case in mind; certainly it was important to all news-agency operations. Quite simply, it made it possible, where the same person was bringing two or more actions for what was, in effect, the same libel, for a judge to order all the actions to be consolidated—to be tried together. This reform was put to the test in 1897 in another libel action arising out of a message circulated by the P.A. Writs were issued against sixteen newspapers and, in this instance, also against the Press Association itself. Legal arguments about the procedure to be adopted led to a decision by the Court of Appeal which confirmed the intention of the 1888 Act: all seventeen actions could be considered as one and tried together.

Another libel action which was brought against the P.A. in the nineteenth century made legal history because it raised and fixed the right of recording proceedings which take place in open court. In 1891 the P.A. had sent out a report of an *ex parte* application made to, and granted by, a Canterbury bench of magistrates for the issue of a summons for alleged perjury against a solicitor named Edmund Kimber. As it happened, there were no members of the public in court but the hearing was not *in camera*. The three justices had been called together by their clerk to hear the application; they sat in their customary room; they made no order to exclude the public and in fact the reporter, who was the P.A. correspondent, was present throughout. He took a note of the proceedings and sent in his report which the Press Association circulated. The solicitor, Kimber, sued the P.A. for libel on the grounds that this report of *ex parte* proceedings—those in which only one side is heard—was not covered by the privilege which extends to a fair, accurate and contemporaneous report of judicial proceedings. His action was heard in July 1892, and judgement was given for the P.A., with costs. Kimber appealed, but the Court of Appeal confirmed the judgement in favour of the P.A., again with costs. In giving his judgement, the Master of the Rolls, Lord Esher, said, 'Public policy requires that some hardship should be suffered by individuals rather than that judicial proceedings should be held in secret.' He said a court was an open court unless the justices exercised their discretion by ordering it to be closed to the public.

Kimber tried one more ploy. He told the P.A. that he would not take the case to the House of Lords if, in return, the Association waived his payment of costs awarded by the Court of Appeal. Edmund Robbins was outraged. 'A more impudent proposal,'

Reporter Anonymous

said the Manager in all his dignity, 'has never been made.' Kimber did not take his appeal to the House of Lords—and he did have to pay the costs.

In 1891 the Manager had faced serious trouble personally when he was cited for contempt of court. The Press Association had put out an incorrect statement to the effect that a pending lawsuit (the celebrated Tranby Croft baccarat case) had been settled out of court. The error was that of a P.A. journalist at the Law Courts. The Manager was ordered to name him, but Edmund Robbins refused to do so, taking upon himself the responsibility for having circulated the story. As soon as the error had been discovered another message was circulated correcting the first. This came out when Edmund Robbins was charged with contempt in the High Court. The promptness with which the P.A. had acted to correct its error so impressed the judge that he ordered Robbins merely to pay the costs of the contempt hearing.

The virtues of presenting a bold, unified front when under attack were proved once again in 1912. The Press Association had circulated 'a slight misreport' about a divorce case and gave the impression that a woman against whom a decree had been obtained had committed adultery not only with the co-respondent named in the case but with another man as well. Writs for libel were served on four daily newspapers and on the Press Association. The P.A. and three of the papers combined to fight the action. They stood together so firmly that when the time came for making a decision the woman's solicitors dropped the action.

In the words of the P.A. Chairman, 'Without departing from its rule of repudiating liability on account of any erroneous statement which it may unfortunately be misled into communicating to its members for publication by them,' the Management Committee decided that the Association should, 'as a matter of grace', pay all the costs from the moment the combination was formed. The fourth paper which had been sued fared less happily. Its proprietors, said the P.A. Chairman, 'are, perhaps, too much afraid of going to court in matters of this kind'. It cost them £25 more to settle than if they had joined in the combination to defend the action. Ultimately, this newspaper also bore its share of the costs paid by the Press Association on behalf of the other three papers. The newspaper in question was the *Yorkshire Post*. The P.A.

Samuel Storey, M.P. (now Lord Buckton), P.A. Chairman 1938–39, who served as Chairman of Reuters from February to October 1941

RIGHT: Sir Roderick Jones, Chairman of Reuters 1919–41

Neville Chamberlain at Heston airport on his return from Munich in 1938. Immediately on his right is P.A. reporter S. T. A. Rosindell

The editorial floor of the P.A. as it is today
Punched tape carrying news to Britain's provincial newspapers

The perils of the law

Chairman was John Phillips, himself the editor of the *Yorkshire Post*, one of its greatest and most loved figures and an editor, incidentally, who enjoyed the most harmonious relations with his proprietors, despite their reluctance to fight libel actions.

Seven / No holds barred

In establishing itself, the Press Association had to fight against competition from other agencies. It was often ruthless competition, although when it came to it, the P.A. knew a trick or two itself. This competition was at its height during the thirty-seven years of Edmund Robbins' reign as Manager. The chief competitor was the Central News, which was the P.A.'s rival almost from the start.

The Central News grew out of the Central Press, a news agency which, as we saw earlier,[1] was founded in 1863, five years before the formation of the Press Association, by Edward Spender and his brother-in-law, William Saunders, of the *Western Morning News*, Plymouth. William Saunders, a man of reputation and resource, lent his experience to the Press Association for a few months as a member of the original Management Committee. It was he who suggested that his own news-agency business might be in competition with that of the Press Association and he felt it proper to retire. His colleagues pressed him to stay and he agreed to serve for another year on the Consultative Board of the P.A. His help and advice in those preparatory days were most valuable, but his reward was a smack in the face. His final break with the P.A. came when he tried to do a deal with the news agency whereby he would buy the full general news service from the P.A. and he would use what he wanted of it in his own service to London and provincial papers. He also offered to supply the P.A. with its provincial news. Not surprisingly, the Management Committee turned down all his proposals after 'a very long and grave discussion'. The Press Association, he was told, was going to gather its

[1] See page 22.

No holds barred

own provincial news and it was going to sell its own service direct to London and provincial newspapers. It was obvious from then on that the P.A. and the Central News—which Saunders formed in 1871 to sell telegraphic news—were going to be fighting each other for business. That fact, however, scarcely seems to justify the comment of one member of the P.A. who accused Saunders, while on the Management Committee, of 'having sucked its brains'.

The battle between the Press Association and the Central News was on. It went on for the next seventy years and for the best part of the first fifty the fighting was hot and sometimes bitter. From the start there were those among the members of the Press Association who favoured tactics which would have meant a short, harsh and expensive war ending in the destruction of their opponents. In other words, they advocated cutting Press Association charges so savagely that no competitor would be able to stand the pace for long. But at the beginning such notions were rejected. John Jaffray, for instance, welcomed the prospect of competition as a stimulus.

'With respect to the general principle of cutting out competition at a loss to ourselves,' he said, 'I think no principle could be more vicious or undesirable. There is no doubt that the competition of other agencies does sometimes impede the transmission of our news, but it is not an unmixed evil. If we had no competition in this as in any other business, we might get rich and fat, and not attend to our business.'

The competition, especially that of the Central News, did keep the staff and management of the P.A. on their toes. (The story of how the P.A. man, McCallum, dished his rival over the Druce exhumation is a good example.[1]) Although their criticisms were often rejected as unjustified, members of the Press Association and subscribers to it often made unflattering comparisons with the services offered by competing agencies, saying they were either cheaper or better or faster—or all three at once.

When P.A. reports did sometimes arrive in newspaper offices later than Central News ones, the P.A. could not always be fairly blamed. During the 1880s there was a curious series of incidents at post offices in towns where P.A. and Central News reporters were competing. Although P.A. telegrams were handed in to the

[1] See Chapter 5, pp 98–100.

local post offices first, the Central News reports of the same events were somehow transmitted to London before them. The Press Association protested. The Post Office was compelled to agree that something did seem to have gone wrong but it refused to admit any possibility of corruption. Could it be then that in those places the Post Office clerks had such a high personal regard for Central News reporters they would give priority to their messages? Edmund Robbins thought it most unlikely. In one instance his investigation came very close to establishing bribery. The Telegraphs Department must have sent out a strong warning about dealing with press telegrams strictly in order of their receipt because the apparently preferential treatment of Central News messages ceased.

At about the same time, though, the Press Association learned of instances in the Midlands where newspapers had been asked by post-office telegraphists why they did not take Central News Parliamentary reports in place of the P.A. service. A few years later a postmaster was severely reprimanded for 'milking' messages from P.A. correspondents and a postmistress was dismissed for 'milking' a private telegram sent to Hawarden Castle, Gladstone's residence.[1]

In both cases the Central News benefited. It is only fair to add that the Post Office produced a letter addressed by John Lovell to a post-office clerk offering 5 per cent commission on any subscriptions he might obtain for P.A. news services. It is impossible to say now under what circumstances the offer was made, but by the time the letter was produced John Lovell had moved to his editorial chair and the letter was disowned by the Committee of Management and Edmund Robbins.

The time came when the Press Association deserted the principle enunciated by John Jaffray and had to join in a cut-price war with the Central News. In 1887 the Central News slashed its charge for special reporting—such as major political speeches— from fifteen shillings to ten shillings a column. The P.A. followed suit at a cost of £3000 a year. The Manager's views on Central

[1] The telegram was one of condolence from Queen Victoria to the widow of the Archbishop of Canterbury who had been staying at the Castle but had died while attending morning service at Hawarden Parish Church. The postmistress was dismissed at first, then her dismissal was cancelled but her 'post was declared vacant'.

News competition were unqualified. They are revealed in letters which he wrote to Charles Pardon, the P.A.'s sporting editor, in 1888. Pardon was travelling in the north on the P.A.'s behalf.

'The *Edinburgh Evening News* detailed order arrived this morning', wrote Robbins. 'During this session we have sent them our ordinary Parliamentary report at 15s. a week, supplemented at their own request with a special report of Scotch questions, and also having the report carried on to a later hour than the ordinary evening paper service. Do I understand from you that Mr. Wilson expects to receive at a cheaper rate than that charged by the P.A. the ordinary supply from the C.N.? We charge 15s. a week for an average of 1000 words a day and I can assure you there is scarcely a penny profit after paying reporting and transmission expenses . . . Your description of the C.N. Parliamentary is a very just one. It is always straining after effect, and is always crying "Wolf, wolf" when, as a matter of fact, the reportable scenes in the House of Commons are few and far between.'

And again:

'I . . . hope and believe that you will be enabled to get back the *Manchester Guardian* for law cases. It cannot be denied for one moment that the Press Association's staff in the Law Courts is greatly superior to that of the C.N., and a great paper like the *Manchester Guardian* ought not to put the £. s. d. question first when it is well served by its own Association. We have stood the test of time and no fault can be found with our work, yet papers rush off to any outsider who promises what he cannot perform.'

But a tentative suggestion put forward in 1889 at the annual meeting that the P.A. should get together with the Central News to cut out wasteful competition—such as both agencies sending out the same Court Circular, or weather reports or the text of the Queen's Speech—got nowhere. The idea that the P.A., a cooperative organisation representing a substantial part of the British press, should do a deal, amounting to a form of amalgamation, with an ordinary trading concern, appalled some members. Apart from that, as John Lovell said, competition was healthy. The war went on but the P.A. charge for special reporting went halfway back to what it had been—to 12s. 6d. a column.

Central News competition was not confined to home news. From the 1870s onwards it was sending its own correspondents

Reporter Anonymous

overseas and offering a service of world news. It was fighting Reuter for the British market and that meant, once more, it was also fighting the Press Association which relied upon Reuters for the foreign news it supplied to its own customers. For the most part, the P.A. were well satisfied with the Reuter service, but there were moments of friction and criticism of its shortcomings. In the nineteenth century Reuters was stodgy and conservative in its presentation of news. (So, for that matter, was the P.A.) In 1889 the Press Association told Reuters that some provincial newspapers were beginning to think that Reuters was a channel for official messages rather than a news agency. Later, the P.A. appealed for a 'flesh-and-blood' service. Reuters was naturally jealous of its high reputation for accuracy and did not want to jeopardise it. The Central News, on the other hand, while never matching the thoroughness or the extent of the Reuter operations, was more lively, colourful and, as it sometimes seemed, much faster. Its correspondents did not feel so diffident about using their imaginations when the facts were unexciting. An example of this tendency was severely castigated in the columns of *Judy, or the London Serio-Comic Journal* in October 1883. Under the heading 'Political Palaver', it said:

'Last week we were startled by the announcement in the newspapers that a plot to murder the new Governor-General of the Dominion of Canada had been discovered, and its execution prevented. Intense excitement, it was announced, on the authority of a press agency, had been caused in Quebec on "the alarming fact" becoming known.

'This startling intelligence was pretended to have been received in Quebec on the 22nd. On the 22nd, however, a Reuters telegram informed us that "so far as Quebec is concerned, no information is forthcoming with regard to the supposed plot, and there is not the slightest indication of the existence of any excitement".

'There now. Of course Reuter was right. It was a bit of bogus business. What is to be done with the concoctors of false news and those who, without the expense of verification, disseminate for pecuniary gain? . . . Were the bogus telegram agency forced to return the money received for the falsehood, and the newspapers reproducing it fined, more care might perhaps be taken in announcing one moment what has to be contradicted the next.'

No holds barred

Also in 1883 Reuters reported from St. Petersburg news of a disastrous fire in a provincial Russian circus. C.N., too, issued a message about it. In letters to some P.A. members Edmund Robbins alleged that the Central News had used the Reuter message as the basis for its own. C.N. issued writs for libel against him and the Press Association. While Robbins was giving evidence, the judge suggested a consultation between the parties. The result was a settlement, each party paying its costs.

The Central News made the running at the beginning of the Sino-Japanese war of 1894-5, when some P.A. subscribers complained that the Reuter service was inferior. The Press Association agreed to pay its share for an extension of the service. Reuters protested that the Central News was 'padding' and 'expanding' its reports far beyond the limits justified by the hard news from the seat of war, and was very pleased when, in 1895, *The Times* printed a critical article 'exposing' the C.N.'s embellishments of cables. Ten years later, during the Russo-Japanese war, it was alleged that the C.N. fell for reports supplied by an imaginative Italian journalist who, after reading the meagre cables from the Far East, produced much more readable reports from his own head. In October 1907 the Central News broke an embargo by announcing the forthcoming issue by the Foreign Office of the text of an Anglo-Russian treaty. The P.A. was indignant, but its indignation was somewhat appeased when Reuters beat the Foreign Office to the tape by cabling the full text of the treaty from St. Petersburg.

Whatever the truth of these particular incidents, there can be no doubt that Reuters—and the P.A.—profited from the competition of the Central News and other agencies. It was forced to innovate and spend money when, if left alone, it would probably have continued in the old ways, making the minimum outlay necessary to provide a service. It had to rejuvenate itself, it had to widen drastically its concept of what was news. But the Press Association did recognise that Reuters could not be expected to improve its coverage, including the sending of longer cables, for exactly the same return as before. P.A. members were getting, through the contract with Reuter, a foreign service for £300 a year. London papers had to pay Reuter direct £1500 a year for the same service. The provincial papers asked for more and more. They wanted news which was more humane, more colourful, more sensational. Reuters was anxious to provide it, but not at the same price.

So in 1890, by agreement with Reuters, the P.A. started a special supplementary foreign service, later called Foreign Special. Reuters recruited new men, men who knew what newspapers wanted, resourceful, enterprising men, to feed this new service. In competition they would match sensation for sensation, drama for drama. Where the normal foreign service might send a quarter of a column these men would provide the Foreign Special with a column. Wherever anything important was happening there they would be. That is what the P.A. promised its members. Reuters kept a separate account of money spent on the Foreign Special and the Press Association paid half of it. The two agencies consulted about foreign assignments which would involve particularly heavy expenditure, and where the P.A. thought it worth while it was not mean. It arranged with Reuters, for instance, to share the expense of getting long reports of such sensations as the Dreyfus affair in France and the Harry Thaw trial in the United States. Several times the two agencies sent H. A. Gwynne, later a celebrated editor of the *Morning Post*, as their joint correspondent. He was with Kitchener, then with the Turkish army in the war against the Greeks and chief of the Boer War correspondents. P.A. members received the Foreign Special for 20s. a column of 2000 words. Just how cheap that was can be gauged by a glance at the cost of cables in 1890. The press rate from Europe was cheap enough—twopence a word. It was only fivepence a word from North America. But from India it was 1s. 4d. a word; from South Africa 2s. 3d.; from Australia between 2s. 8d. and 3s. 4d.; from South America between 6s. and 8s. 10d.; from China it was 7s. 1d. a word and from other distant parts of the world it cost even more.

It was these rates, apart from any question of the cost of correspondents, which made it so difficult for Reuters to compete successfully with, among others, the Central News. Reuters was expected to cover, and did cover, the whole world. Central News was more selective, tending, quite understandably, to choose those places where its operations would be profitable. On this basis it could afford to set the pace and it could sometimes appear to be outstripping Reuters. And, despite all the demands for 'flesh and blood', newspapers still expected accuracy from Reuters.

No holds barred

The P.A. never considered turning to any agency other than Reuter for foreign news and, the inevitable and legitimate grumbles apart, its members knew they had every reason to be happy with their service from Reuters. Through it the readers of the provincial press learned of the Commune in Paris, the Carlists in Spain, expeditions against the Ashantis, against the natives of Sierra Leone, the Somalis, the Afridis, the Mohmands; of Arabi Pasha's revolt, the Mahdi, Kitchener's Sudan expedition, the victory at Omdurman and the French humiliation over Fashoda; of Rhodes and the Transvaal, of insurrection in Mexico, revolution in China, trouble in Venezuela, revolts in Mexico and the Balkans. They had incomparable coverage of war: the Franco-Prussian, the Sino-Japanese, the Spanish-American, the South African (Reuters put out a report of the relief of Mafeking three days before the War Office knew about it), the Russo-Japanese, of the Turco-Italian and the Balkan conflicts and the first world war itself. Some of these were reported in the ordinary Reuter service or in Foreign Special without extra charge to P.A. subscribers. When the Foreign Special Service was established it was thought that the cost of cabling might reach about £1200 a year. Twelve years later members learned that the cost of the cables alone in covering just one news story—Joseph Chamberlain's South African tour—was very much more than that. To cover the bigger and more expensive troubles, 'war special' services were arranged, the two agencies sharing the cost.

Through the agreement between the P.A. and Reuters the provincial papers became the peers of the London ones. In 1903 William Brimelow, of the *Bolton Evening News*, was to say of the report he had received through the P.A. of the Durbar at Delhi, 'I never felt prouder of our evening paper than when we had over a column of well-written descriptive matter of those wonderful scenes at Delhi which had occurred early on the same day.' But some of the metropolitan papers, in particular *The Times*, displayed their jealousy in a practical way. In an effort to discomfort and damage Reuters *The Times* gave its backing to another news agency which was launching out into the international sphere. This agency was called Dalziel's and for a few years during the nineties it had some success and certainly caused Reuters a deal of anxiety and heartburn. Most of its backing came from America and most of its news, too; it dredged the American continent for sensations in a way which Reuters could not emulate. It seemed for a while in the 1890s as though America was in a chronic state of violence and disaster, natural and man-made. Dalziel's made headway in selling its gaudy wares to the London papers and by 1892 had also persuaded a number of provincial newspapers to switch over from Reuters by offering to accept half the subscription to their service in the form of advertising space. But the superior quality of the special service offered by Reuters, its comprehensiveness and its dependability, triumphed in the end. There were times when a Reuter correspondent was the only British journalist in the right place at the right time, sometimes the only man officialdom would trust to send fair and accurate despatches. It was not long before the London papers, including *The Times* itself, began to buy the Reuter special service and by the end of the century the threat from Dalziel's was no more than an unwelcome memory. Dalziel made what may have been a desperate last effort in 1898 by cabling Test scores from Australia at expensive urgent rates. Reuters countered by doing the same thing.

It was over sporting news that the Press Association met—and indulged in—some of the most uninhibited and extravagant competition. The Central News was in on this fight, too, but the P.A.'s chief rival was the Exchange Telegraph Company. Extel, as it came to be known, had been founded in 1872. At the start it dealt in financial and commercial news, but it soon extended its interest to sport. Then, in 1882, it wanted to buy general news from the Press Association to supply to its subscribers in Liverpool and Glasgow. The P.A. had no objection to this in principle but the two agencies failed to agree on terms. Later on, Extel went into the general news field itself in rivalry with the P.A. But it was over sport that the two agencies fought the toughest battles and hurt each other badly.

The P.A. had drifted into sports reporting. When it started in business it was just not geared to deal with sport. Nor was there any demand for a comprehensive service of sports news. The great days of soccer as a mass-audience sport or as the excuse for the Pools were still to come. Cricket, however, was sufficiently organised and had a strong enough following for newspapers to want dependable news about it. A senior sub-editor on the staff of the P.A., Charles F. Pardon, offered to organise a service. Why

No holds barred

he was not asked to do so inside the Association is not known, but it was certainly by agreement that he left the Association in 1880 —with a presentation silver flask—to found the firm of Pardons, or the Cricket Reporting Agency as it was to be formally known. Pardons expanded to take in football and other sports and for a time covered all the P.A.'s sporting interests, including some racing (but not the results or the betting from the course). In 1883 Charles Pardon was made the P.A.'s sporting editor, but he still operated from outside the Association. It seems a curious arrangement, but it clearly worked well, and it was not until 1901 that the P.A. took over the last of the racing work done for it by Pardons and appointed as sporting editor a member of its own staff. The connection between the P.A. and Pardons still went on, however, and in its time Pardons gave newspapers the benefit of such fine writers as Charles Stewart Caine, Sydney Southerton and Hubert Preston, apart from Charles and Sydney Pardon.

The P.A.'s original racing service was operated by C. H. Ashley, but he and the Press Association parted company at the end of 1883 because he refused to give an undertaking not to extend his own list of direct newspaper subscribers. The P.A. then turned to the Hultons of Manchester, who had successfully founded the *Sporting Chronicle* as the genesis of what later became a powerful newspaper group. P.A.-Hulton relations were stormy at times, but an arrangement was maintained for many years. It became gradually less important as the P.A. extended its own 'outside' racing staff to cover meetings.

One consequence of the P.A. break with C. H. Ashley was that he became a powerful competitor for a time. Apart from his racing service, he sold comprehensive cricket services at reasonably cheap rates. Edmund Robbins saw Ashley not only as a dangerous enemy but one whose existence was injurious to newspapers. It could well be that Robbins saw all other agencies in this light and only the Press Association as wholly desirable and in the public interest. At any rate he expressed his feelings in somewhat florid terms to Charles Pardon, who had obviously been disappointed in a visit to Manchester on behalf of the P.A. (Robbins seems to have used his correspondence with Pardon to confide some of his anxieties and emotions about the Press Association.) In December 1888 he wrote:

'I was not altogether surprised at Mr. Parkinson informing

you that he intended to discontinue our Sporting. At the same time, you took up a very proper attitude in denouncing the manner in which newspapers had, after reaping advantage from the Press Association's success in preventing what threatened to be one of the greatest monopolies of the age, so far as newspaper work is concerned, thrown over the P.A. when their ends had been gained. By this time Ashley would have been charging at least £300 a year for his full evening paper Sporting Service, and it should not be forgotten that the Press Association was the only organisation which could grapple with his monopoly and which, having grappled with it, had completely beaten it down. This, however, is not enough, and the *Manchester Evening News* and the *Manchester Guardian* should remember that it is only by still supporting the Association that the monster can be slain. At present he is only scotched, not killed, and if other papers followed in the wake of those at Manchester, they would find in a few years that the Press Association could not possibly spend its money in keeping up an expensive staff, and thus the old grievance would be renewed with increased intensity.'

When the competition between the P.A. and the Extel was at its height, the men whose job it was to get the racing results back to their offices were as resourceful as any of their more publicised counterparts today. On one occasion when the last race at Brighton was to be a match between two famous horses the course was hidden from the spectators as mist swirled in from the sea. But the race was still on and it was the job of the reporters to get the winner's name back to their offices as soon as possible. The P.A. man, Tim Harrington, made his way through the mist to a gipsy encampment on the Downs. He had been there that same morning to hire a grey mare for his own pleasure. Now he asked the gypsy who owned it to lend it to him again. Harrington led the mare as near to the winning post as possible, mounted, and waited for the two racehorses to finish. He heard them thud by. Number 5 was hoisted as the winner. Harrington galloped away, following the outside of the rails, knowing he must eventually meet up with his colleague, Arthur Winn, as they had arranged. Winn, who had not known exactly what Harrington intended when he went off into the mist, was astonished to see him galloping out of it again and shouting 'Number 5 won'. Winn did the rest and the P.A. had the result out to its subscribers ahead of its rivals.

No holds barred

Up to about the end of the nineteenth century reporters sent the racing results and cricket scores back to their offices by telegram. The Post Office had travelling staffs of telegraphists at racecourses and country grounds to handle the traffic. Chance played a big part in deciding which agency's telegram was sent first. The telephone offered a much faster and more efficient means of collecting and disseminating news but the Press Association was slow to perceive its value. The Extel, on the other hand, began to use it about the turn of the century. The P.A. was soon under pressure, especially from evening paper subscribers, to follow suit, but it was not until July 1905, at a special general meeting of members, that the idea of a telephone service to supply sports results and brief 'snapshots' of general news was given the go-ahead.

The P.A. service was organised by Alan Greaves, who had been running a business in Sheffield, supplying news by telephone to newspapers and bookmakers. That Greaves was given a seven-year contract at £1000 a year—an astronomical figure for those days in P.A. terms—shows just how determined the directors were to make the telephone service work and make it work quickly. For his part, Greaves lost no time. Special telephone centres were opened in Birmingham, Bristol, Leeds, Liverpool, Manchester, Newcastle, Nottingham and Sheffield and one in London at 150 Fleet Street. Each was fully equipped with staff and telephones. The new service began, accompanied by much enthusiasm, on the first Saturday in September 1905—at the same time as the new football season. Within a very few weeks the Manager and the directors were already counting the cost and perhaps Edmund Robbins, who had been so antipathetic to the telephone, found it impossible to refrain from an 'I told you so'. In October Robbins was telling his board that the one way of keeping pace with Extel in the telephoning of racing results and betting was to 'capture' a trunk line from each racecourse. This meant booking a long series of consecutive calls and so holding open the line to London. The costs soared and the only means of making the service pay, said Robbins, was to extend it to bookmakers. So it was decided to seek the custom of 'the more respectable commission agents' and also of clubs. The P.A. was already doing more and spending more than it had intended and Extel was regretting its early generosity in offering to supply the P.A.

with tape machines. It withdrew the offer. At the same time it asked the P.A. to consider the possibility of working together instead of in competition. The P.A. was not interested. Not yet. If Extel would not supply a tape machine someone else would. The P.A. chose one supplied through the London office of Siemens, but new machines meant teething troubles and there were many complaints. They were never given the time to prove themselves.

By the beginning of 1906, competition with Extel had reached a bitter stage. Good intentions perished, precious principles were abandoned. The rate-cutting which had seemed so repugnant a few months earlier was now introduced, though not, one imagines, with any relish. The P.A. telephone service was reckoned to be heading for a disastrous loss of £7000 a year. The Central News, which was also distributing news by telephone in London, offered to come to some working arrangement with the P.A.; the offer was turned down.

But things could not go on as they were. There was one sure way of ending the competition and that was to get control of the Exchange Telegraph. In March 1906 the first moves were made. Edmund Robbins and Wilfred King, the managing director of Extel, held secret meetings away from their offices, usually at the Howard Hotel. Extel, however, had no wish to be taken over by the P.A. King, instead, proposed joint working. Again the Press Association refused and the war entered an even fiercer stage. By April the P.A. was renting its own telephone lines on racecourses and football and cricket grounds. Where two men had been enough before to cover a race meeting, eight or more were now needed. So deep was the crisis, so desperate the fight, that for a short time the P.A. even agreed to co-operate in race reporting with the Central News. But the only result of a war carried on for long like this must have been the destruction of either the Press Association or the Exchange Telegraph—or of both. Only the Postmaster General and the National Telephone Company stood to profit.

At last, reluctantly, the P.A. reached the conclusion that Extel had reached a long time before: they must work together to produce one service. There were more meetings, often with lawyers to hand, to draft an agreement. By July it was ready for signature. The two companies agreed to do together what they had been doing separately. (Extel was given the right to operate alone within

No holds barred

the county of London.) They were to share the costs and divide the revenue. There were obvious and immediate economies. Each company staffed and managed a number of provincial centres. In towns where each had had a telephone centre one was closed. The staffs were 'fused', which means that a lot of men were sacked. But that, after all, was the inescapable and desired consequence of setting up a Joint Service.

Edmund Robbins and Wilfred King were to be joint managers of the new service under a joint committee of two directors from each company. It was a formula which, unless there were perfect understanding and sympathy on both sides, was surely guaranteed to promote friction. And so it did. In case of disagreement, the marriage document had said, there was to be arbitration. And the triviality of the first disagreement submitted to an arbitrator indicates just how imperfect their union was. What was still lacking was the will to make it work. The first argument was about the circular to be sent to prospective subscribers for football results in the 1906-7 season. The P.A. said there ought to be one letter, signed by both parties. Extel said there should be two identical letters, each agency sending out its own. Incredibly, they found it impossible to resolve their differences. Let there be arbitration. But who? What sort of man should he be? A lawyer, said the P.A. A commercial man, said Extel. In the end they agreed it should be the general manager of the Great Eastern Railway. But long before he had started to adjudicate on this quarrel there were others for him to sort out. The material of them is insignificant. They were merely a symptom of the fractious atmosphere. Joint committee meetings rapidly degenerated into squabbles over the phrasing of minutes and what they meant. There was a much bigger row, which went all the way to the High Court, over the P.A.'s claim that it had the right to telephone 'snapshots' of Reuters news direct from London to newspaper subscribers. Extel said it was entitled to share the revenue because the Joint Service covered *all* telephone news. Not *Reuter* news, said the P.A. *All* telephone news, Extel insisted. First the K.C. appointed by the High Court as arbitrator and then the High Court itself backed the Extel view.

The P.A. was unhappy and indignant with the way things were going. It felt it was getting the worst of the bargain. Arbitration was all very well but not when it went against you—and it seemed

Reporter Anonymous

to be going against the Press Association most of the time. The P.A. had two outstanding men as its representatives on the joint committee, Charles Clifford of the *Sheffield Telegraph* and William Brimelow of the *Bolton Evening News*. Clifford was the son of Frederick Clifford, one of the founding fathers of the Press Association, and in 1908 he himself became chairman of the P.A. William Brimelow provided the continuing link between the *Bolton Evening News* and the P.A. which had first been forged by William Frederick Tillotson. Brimelow joined the *Bolton Evening News* as its first editor in 1871. When he died in 1913 it was said that for more than twenty years no legislation affecting newspapers had been introduced or passed without his being consulted. He was three times Chairman of the Press Association, an uncommon achievement in itself. In other words, the P.A. could not have been better represented on the Joint Committee but Clifford and Brimelow had a worrying and depressing time. So did Edmund Robbins, who told them that Extel was always scheming to become 'paramount' and 'trying to get the better of us'. (It seems more than likely that the managing director of Extel, Wilfred King, and his colleagues, felt just as suspicious of the P.A.)

All these disagreements had very material consequences.

Both parties retained leading counsel and legal costs were piling up as legal costs have a way of doing. Sadly, Edmund Robbins wrote to the P.A.'s solicitor that it was better to suffer any injustice than to go to law. But both the P.A. and Extel kept on going to law. In an effort to find a simpler and cheaper method of settling disputes they persuaded the Hon. Harry Lawson (afterwards the 1st Viscount Burnham) to act as the friendly adviser of both parties as and when requested—a role which leading provincial newspapermen had prudently declined. But there is not much point in asking for friendly advice if you are not prepared to take it: the legal actions went on. It was not until 1911, five years after the Joint Service started, that both sides can be said finally to have lost their taste for arbitrations and High Court actions. Neither party loved the other any better, they went on finding points of disagreement, but nothing which could justify yet another line-up of lawyers.

Through all this time of conflict the Joint Service itself had been operating with a fair amount of success. Although tempers might mount high, the parties were agreed on the way the service

Monitoring incoming and outgoing wire pictures
Telegraph mechanics at work in the back room

Battery of copy takers typing telephoned reports

Main editorial floor on the night of the 1966 General Election

No holds barred

should be run. In 1909 they agreed to put out a joint General Election results service. This, said Wilfred King, with heavy humour, might be called the 'PAX' service. By the outbreak of the world war, the Joint Service was in fact pretty well established and even Edmund Robbins had accepted the telephone—at least as a means of collecting and distributing news.

The telephone was also an integral part of the London News Service which the P.A. launched in 1909. Thousands of cards were distributed among pubs, cafés and cab shelters, saying, 'We want news. Phone the Press Association, Central 7440. Remuneration given. Open day and night.' The news came in all right, by phone and by 'runners' who were paid 2s. 6d. or more for news of fires and accidents; a good many half-crowns were paid out for false alarms. The London Service was started because it was no longer possible to ignore the competition from a small agency, the London News Agency, which was supplying to London papers and the London offices of provincial papers longer and more numerous reports of London events than the P.A. could give in its general news services.

The London Service had its own offices in Red Lion Court, another alleyway off Fleet Street. More messenger boys were recruited to ride smart red bicycles, ten of which were stolen in the first week. The London Service had its own reporters and sub-editors, but they were paid less than those of the General Service and their status was lower. If a General Service reporter was sent on a job more than 100 miles from London, for instance, he received a guinea a day expenses, plus 12s. 6d. for travelling back the next day, and he was allowed to charge first-class fare. A London Service reporter received only fifteen shillings a day, nothing for travelling back and third-class fare. Expenses had to be passed by the Deputy Manager, Edmund Robbins' son, Harry, and reporters swore that he knew every fare stage in London. Harry Robbins came to be known as 'Farthing Robbins'.

The gulf between the staff of the London Service and that of the General Service was certainly more than one of physical separation and it was meant to be. The new service was run on lines of strict economy. When a sub-editor wanted to check a quotation in a sermon he found there was not a Bible on the premises. But there was not one at New Bridge Street, either, where the 'library' consisted of no more than a dozen reference

I

Reporter Anonymous

books. In the end the sub borrowed a Bible from Cattermole, the superintendent of messengers. Edmund Robbins prophesied at the outset that the fight against the London News Agency would be long and costly. The new service received little support at first but gradually found its feet. The London News Agency realised it must lose the battle in the end and offered in the first year to sell out, but its price was considered too high. The proposal was repeated from time to time, with the same result. The smaller agency found life getting harder and harder and the P.A. bought what was left of it in 1919. (Had the P.A. bought an independent offshoot, L.N.A. Photos Ltd., as well, as it could have done in 1920, it would have anticipated by twenty-five years its own entry into the news-photo field—an idea first suggested by the Federation of Northern Newspaper Owners as early as 1912.)

As the Press Association moved towards its first half-century it was catering more and more for the morning and evening newspapers. With the vast improvement in communications, with the further rapid development of urban and industrial society and with free, compulsory education, this was inevitable. The weekly newspaper owners often complained, with justice, that the P.A. was neglecting their interests, but it was a fact of life that the news gathering and the services of a national news agency could no longer be geared economically to the weeklies. The amount of general news ordered by weekly papers gradually diminished. Newsrooms had outlived their purpose and they went out of business. But small news services to some clubs and exchanges did continue.

This was the period in which mass-circulation journalism was born. It was bound to come. Newspapers could not ignore the new reading public which would be measured not in thousands, even hundreds of thousands, but in millions. This did not mean they all had to try to be like Northcliffe's *Daily Mail* which, within four years of its birth, during the Boer War, had touched a million circulation. Nor did they have to emulate W. T. Stead, the crusading, campaigning, innovating editor of the *Pall Mall Gazette*, in all his fervour. But even among those who professed to despise the new journalism there were editors and proprietors very much alive to the need for change. No one, for example, would have accused the *Yorkshire Post* of debasing its standards or of pandering to the multitude, but its editor during these years of journa-

No holds barred

listic revolution, H. J. Palmer, was not afraid of innovation. The *Sheffield Daily Telegraph* said of him, 'He was for ever improving his paper, and believed in being up to date. He flung aside the worn-out garments of a jaded journalism and dressed up his columns in the fashion of the day, but always with this proviso, that they remained seemly.' Similarly, Charles Russell at the *Glasgow Herald* let light into his pages with paragraphs and cross-heads, relieving his readers of the burden of solid, unrelenting type. But there were other papers, the *Birmingham Post*, for instance, which, from the height of its dignity and political reputation, refused to desert tradition, perhaps for fear of being thought sensational.

There are many misconceptions about this period of British journalism. The sensationalism of those papers which set out to win a mass readership is often exaggerated. No less false is the notion that the only material contained in the 'respectable' papers was such as could be read in Sunday School. In so far as Northcliffe sought 'sensation' he was only reviving a concept of news which had characterised all newspapers up to the Victorian era. For their part the 'serious' newspapers still relished a juicy crime story as much as anyone.

George Crosbie, of the *Cork Examiner*, as Chairman of the Press Association in 1911, reviewed the past year's work—a record both in the profit made and also in output. 'This has been contributed to,' said Crosbie, who possessed a lively sense of humour, 'by having two General Elections within the year, and also by the remarkable and sensational trial of Dr. Crippen. It would give me great personal satisfaction, gentlemen, if I could attribute any of that success to the fact that I was your chairman, but I am afraid that, though I do not suffer from modesty, I can hardly claim that I contributed in any way to the very satisfactory state of things that now confronts us. We may not have any further elections during the present year, but, as we say in my country, "God is good", and it is quite possible that some further picturesque scoundrelry will help to swell the coffers of the Press Association.'

The function of the P.A. was to provide its members and subscribers—or the majority of them—with what they wanted. What they wanted was, in Northcliffe's phrase, 'anything out of the ordinary'. The reflection of this can be seen in the guidance to

Reporter Anonymous

Reuter correspondents about the kind of story which would deserve longer treatment in the Special Service: 'The wreck of an ocean liner or steamship; a calamitous railway accident; a fire or explosion involving serious loss of life; a destructive earthquake, cyclone or inundation; especially startling crimes and outrages; popular disturbances; the sudden or tragic demise of any illustrious or famous personage; an attempt upon the life of a monarch or statesman, or the discovery of a far-reaching plot.' From the viewpoint of a modern journalist the list states the obvious. But seen in the context of 1890 it represented an emphatic change of direction.

This new emphasis was reflected also in the kind of news items sought by the P.A. itself, in addition to its coverage of the kind of events which were entered in advance in the chief reporter's 'diary'. Queen Victoria's Diamond Jubilee[1] came into this category, but it also ranked as something out of the ordinary and received very special treatment. On that day the P.A. put up a 'record' by telegraphing 45,622 words and some morning newspaper telegrams were even sent at the day-rate which normally was simply not done.

The Press Association remained conservative, though stodgy indeed, in the form in which it presented much of its news. When the young Winston Churchill came one Sunday night in 1908 to the offices in New Bridge Street and handed over a brief and formal announcement of his engagement to Miss Clementine Hozier,

[1] The provincial press is a particularly valuable guide to the understanding of popular British feeling. For a taste of the superb arrogance of the nation at the time of the Jubilee take this quotation from a leading article in the *Southern Echo,* the Southampton evening paper: 'Politicians came as patriots from the Colonies to our parade of thanksgiving. They were at the centre of movement, the great throbbing heart of our civilisation. They had come home, descendants of the men and women who went out as humble emigrants, to cast happy eyes on the land of their fathers, to be honoured as part and parcel of the Empire. The dark-skinned men who were not united to us by race or religion were warmly welcomed. . . . They must have felt it no humiliation to be attached to such a vigorous, teeming people, whose sons traverse the world. Our American cousins must have been glad of their kinship, and looking forward to the time when the English-speaking race shall dominate the earth. Strangers and pilgrims from other lands must have caught some quicker insight into the greatness of the British people, the affection with which the Queen is regarded, the vitality which has compelled us to explore, to colonise, and to build up free States afar off.' No wonder the Europeans loved us!

No holds barred

with the request that it be sent to the daily newspapers for publication next morning, the P.A. sent it out exactly as received. No elaboration, no background material, no dressing-up of any kind. But it was under pressure to move with the times. In 1906 G. F. Gratwicke, of the *Exeter Daily Gazette*, described some of the long reports of political speeches as 'an intolerable nuisance'. 'The public demand now,' he said, 'is not for long speeches and I think the staff of the Press Association should have this point impressed upon them . . .' 'There never was a speech in this world,' he added, 'the pith of which could not be put into a column.' The 'ohs' which greeted his assertion suggest that some of his colleagues still believed in the verbatim reporting of leading statesmen but Gratwicke was speaking the language of the new journalists.

The statesmen themselves were slow to admit any change, particularly in the way they themselves communicated official news. Despite all that Edmund Robbins and his colleagues had done over the years to impress upon politicians that it was wrong to give *The Times* preferential treatment, the practice persisted, as Lord Northcliffe discovered.

In the early days of the Boer War, soon after the birth of the *Daily Mail* and while he was still Alfred Harmsworth, he called one evening at the P.A. offices. H. C. Robbins went down to see him. Robbins invited him into a private room, but Harmsworth had his carriage and pair waiting outside and he stayed in the front office. He had just been dining, said Harmsworth, with Lord Selborne (who was then Under-Secretary for the Colonies). Selborne had said he would like a small correction made in a communication which the Colonial Office had issued to the press earlier that evening.

'I told him,' said Harmsworth, 'that the best way was through the Press Association and as I was going down to the *Daily Mail* offices after dinner I would call at your office myself.' Harmsworth went on to tell Robbins he had complained to Lord Selborne about Government departments giving information exclusively to *The Times*. 'I said that all the papers should be on the same level in this respect and that what the Government should do is to issue all such information through the Press Association.'

Harry Robbins thanked Harmsworth who continued, 'I told Lord Selborne very frankly that if the practice continued I would

Reporter Anonymous

not support the Government in my papers. Why should *The Times*, Mr. Robbins, be favoured in this way?'

'I suppose,' said Robbins, 'because *The Times* is *The Times*.'

'That is what everybody tells me,' said Harmsworth who, a few years later, in 1908, was himself to become chief proprietor of *The Times*.

Eight / Struggles with the censor

On the 27th of July 1914, a week before the first world war began, Sir George Riddell, of the *News of the World*, representing the London newspapers, and H. C. Robbins, for the Press Association, went to the War Office. They sat at a small table with two top civil servants, Sir Graham Greene, from the Admiralty, and Sir Reginald Brade, of the War Office. Sir Graham found difficulty in getting to the point. At last he said, 'I have a very serious communication to make to you gentlemen.' Sir Reginald Brade kicked him under the table, warning him to be careful in what he said. Sir Graham went on, 'It is highly probable that in the next few days the country will be involved in a war with Germany; the Government are very anxious to make arrangements with the press so as to secure that no news shall leak out as to the movements of battleships and troops.'

As Sir George Riddell recalled later when telling the story, 'We knew things were in a critical state, but we had no idea they were so critical. . . . Mr. Robbins and I picked up off the table a dirty piece of paper, almost too dirty to write on, and wrote out the draft of the letter which was circulated to the press, in which the press were requested to make no references to the movements of battleships or troops.' The two civil servants approved the draft. Harry Robbins took it with him and the P.A. circulated it to the newspapers.

Very soon after the war had actually started Riddell went again to the War Office, this time accompanied by Edmund Robbins. (At the time of the previous meeting Robbins had been in Switzerland, where he invariably took his annual holiday, his only break from work.) They had a further talk with Sir Reginald Brade

Reporter Anonymous

about the press and secrecy. As they left the War Office, Robbins turned to Riddell and said, 'You know, old chap, I think we are in for a devil of a mess.'

What Edmund Robbins meant was that newspapers were going to have a hard time because of the war. He knew well enough how little excuse governments need to restrict the liberty of the press to publish the facts. He had had first-hand experience of it over many years. During the Boer War, for instance, the war correspondents faced such ruthless censorship that in July 1900 Baron Herbert de Reuter wrote to Robbins, 'The censor's action is nothing short of a scandal . . . the censor (undoubtedly acting under orders) suppresses everything which is not favourable . . . the way in which the British public are being continuously misled and the honesty of the correspondents frustrated is a disgrace to the authorities.' This affected the P.A. directly, of course, and by 1902 it had become so disgusted it wanted to make an appeal to the Minister of War. Reuter, curiously, advised caution, believing the only result of a protest would be even more destructive censorship.

But there was obviously plenty to protest about. The Chairman in 1902, Thomas Bullock of the *Staffordshire Sentinel,* expressed his views of the censorship with a splendidly controlled indignation. It was so drastic, said Bullock, 'that if anyone had told us three years ago that Englishmen would be subjected to such treatment we should have said it was impossible'. The censors did not even confine their interference to news of the war being sent back to England. Bullock gave as an example a telegram about Princess Radziwill, 'which had nothing to do with the war'. Even this 'was got through with the greatest difficulty'. Further, censorship went so far that telegrams from London to the correspondents in South Africa were stopped.

It was also during the South African war that Alfred Harmsworth and the *Daily Mail* had a head-on collision with officialdom. Harmsworth saw the war not only as an occasion for patriotic exhortation—which he ladled out in abundance—but also for lavish journalistic enterprise. He had his own team of correspondents, including Edgar Wallace, with the Army, but they were altogether too enterprising for the taste of the authorities. The *Mail* was accused in the Commons of having gathered 'secret information'. The House agreed that the newspaper had committed a breach of privilege. But it was left at that; the editor was not called to the Bar of the House. The War Office, however, had banned the *Daily Mail* from receiving any official news and statements. The military went so far as to call upon the news agencies, too, to withhold War Office releases from the *Mail*. The P.A., Extel and Central News made a joint protest to the War Office. For his part, Harmsworth put pressure on the Press Association. He had a contract for news supplies, he said; if necessary he would go to law to enforce its fulfilment. He also challenged the Secretary of State for War to say on a public platform that the *Daily Mail* had 'purloined public documents'.

Luckily, perhaps, for the P.A., caught between the guns of the Army and Alfred Harmsworth, the War Office relaxed its ban on the *Daily Mail* before the situation reached crisis-point. *The Times*, while sniffing loftily at newspapers with a lower concept of public duty than its own, rejected the assertion that the *Mail* had committed a serious breach of privilege. There were various kinds of official secrets, it said. 'In some cases they are really state secrets, but, in the majority of cases, they are official and nothing more. That is to say, their publication, however inconvenient to a Minister, does not involve injury to public interest.' As valid an observation nearly seventy years later as at the time it was made.

For years before the outbreak of the first world war the Government had made known their desire to control 'secret' information about the armed forces. They went as far, in 1907, as to draft a Parliamentary Bill to provide for such control in cases of emergency—one need scarcely add that it was to be the Government's responsibility to determine what amounted to an emergency. Edmund Robbins and Baron Herbert de Reuter joined a Newspaper Society committee to consider this Bill. The Government did not go any further with it, however. Instead, they set up the Admiralty, War Office, and Press Committee, which was charged with the duty of giving guidance to editors in times of crisis.[1]

[1] Later this Committee had the task of deciding whether matters brought to its notice by Service representatives should be considered 'secret', that is whether they should be disclosed to the newspapers, or referred to in any detail by them. This in turn led to the system of issuing confidential 'D' (Defence) notices to newspapers, asking them not to refer to certain matters, or to consult before doing so. This arrangement was a voluntary censorship. As we saw in 1967 when Chapman Pincher of the *Daily Express* was accused by the Prime Minister of having committed a breach

Reporter Anonymous

Edmund Robbins was much concerned with the setting-up of this Committee, he represented the news agencies on it and he became its secretary.[1] It was very much more than a merely titular responsibility and during the early part of the war at least it was a task full of frustration. It must have been a strain for Robbins, who was now in his late sixties and white-haired. (The previous year the Press Association had promised to reduce his burden.)

Whatever could be done to enlighten the authorities about the needs of the press Edmund Robbins did and the whole newspaper industry owed him much for his efforts. Even so, it was an uphill fight all the way and often one without any reward at all. The war had been going on for eight months before the authorities were persuaded that it would be safe to allow a journalist anywhere near the actual fighting. They then allowed a single war correspondent, representing the Press Association and Reuters, 'to tour the British lines' on the Western Front. Then another covered the attack on the Dardanelles from on board a British battleship.

For the first few months of the war the P.A. had to pick up crumbs of news about the war from wherever it could, from anywhere in fact except where it was being fought. Only in South Africa were correspondents allowed to accompany the forces—one was appointed to each of the four columns sent against the enemy. Otherwise, the P.A. and Reuters arranged for a regular service of telegrams from Paris, Vienna, Rome, Petrograd, Athens, Cape Town, from India and from Japan. They relied heavily on statements published in foreign newspapers. They also made a special arrangement to receive war news from *The Times*. Altogether it was an inadequate as well as a very expensive business. A description of the naval battle fought off the coast of Chile was telegraphed from Santiago at the rate of $1s.\ 4\frac{1}{2}d.$ a word. And whatever scraps of information the P.A. did manage to acquire had to pass through the crude sieve of the censorship. After eighteen months of war it was reckoned that more than £1000 worth of cables had been stopped by the censors. But the

of the 'D' notice system, it could only work when the newspapers themselves felt it was not being used by the authorities to restrict the freedom of the press unnecessarily.

[1] His son, H. C. Robbins, continued as Secretary until his own retirement in 1938. The news agencies' representative on the Committee nowadays is the editor of the P.A.

Struggles with the censor

chief cause of frustration was the refusal of the authorities to allow the press to do its job of reporting the war. The only firsthand stories to go out to the provincial press and the London papers through the P.A. were those written by 'able but anonymous officers', issued by the authorities themselves under the by-line 'Eye-witness'.

It took the Government and the military a long time to catch up with the new role and status of the press and news agencies in time of war. Their difficulties in relaxing the restrictions were explained to the 1916 annual meeting of the P.A. with surprising tolerance and charity by Meredith T. Whittaker, of the *Scarborough Evening News*.

'It must be remembered,' he said, 'that this is the first war in which Great Britain has been involved with a European power since the campaign with Russia which ended sixty years ago when comparatively few daily newspapers were published in this country. And,' Whittaker added, 'the distance between England and the Crimea was so great that there was no possible chance of the papers being able to publish information from Headquarters which might give either political, naval, or military secrets to the enemy.' Since the Crimean war, telegraphic communications had transformed news-gathering and dissemination. Newspaper readers now expected to hear what had happened on the day it happened. Those responsible for the conduct of the war had not grasped the consequences of these developments. They had no more appreciated the need for accurate, undoctored news than they had realised the whole nature of waging war had changed. Of course, there was need for censorship in the interests of military security. It was a necessity which newspapers and news agencies did not question. According to Meredith Whittaker, 'it occurred occasionally in the earlier part of the war that the enemy ascertained from articles published in the newspapers our positions at the Western Front, so that they were in a position to accurately fire upon them'. The press was obviously as anxious as the authorities that this should not happen but the needs of security were used as an excuse for a severity of censorship and restriction of movement which could not be justified.

In 1915 the *Southampton Pictorial* was prosecuted under the Defence of the Realm Act. Its offence was the publication of photographs calculated to furnish the enemy with useful information. The pictures were of a Red Cross fête at which wounded soldiers assisted. The court came to the conclusion that it was unlikely the picture would help the Germans to win the war, but the paper was fined for having committed a technical offence.

Slowly, the efforts of the various newspaper organisations, of the news agencies, and of particular individuals like Edmund Robbins (and Admiral Sir Douglas Brownrigg, the commonsensical chief naval censor), brought about modification in official policy.

By 1916, through its arrangements with Reuters, the P.A.—and hence the provincial press—had war correspondents at British headquarters in France and the Canal Zone, in the Balkans and in East Africa. There was also, by a very curious agreement, a correspondent with the British army in Mesopotamia. The military had decided they would allow only one correspondent to represent the whole British press. But the services of the man who was sent—Edmund Candler, who had accompanied the British Expedition to Tibet several years earlier—were to be shared by the Press Association, the London newspapers and the India Office.

This was not the first time the Indian Government had sought to make an arrangement with the press. In 1908 members of the P.A. heard with understandable misgivings of a deal which the Indian Government had done with the correspondent of a London paper in India, whereby in return for his supplying them with news they would give him preferential treatment with their news. The P.A. felt that if any individual journalist were to be given this privileged treatment it ought to be the Reuter man, as representing all the British papers. The Indian Government was persuaded to adopt 'a less questionable attitude' after the British Government had heard how strongly the P.A. objected. The arrangement with the Indian Government over Mesopotamia, however, lasted two years. It was ended when, belatedly one would have thought, the London papers felt 'it was more in accordance with the independence of British journalism that the Government connection should be removed'. The P.A. agreed and the India Office dropped out.

Although the war correspondents never attained the freedom of their counterparts in the second world war, the men appointed jointly by the Press Association and Reuters endured both heavy

Struggles with the censor

physical strain and very real danger. For much of the British press they were the sole links with the fighting. (The P.A. continued its arrangement with *The Times*, and also arranged to receive telegrams from the correspondents of the *Morning Post* and the *Daily Telegraph* in particular theatres of war.) Two of the most distinguished of the P.A./Reuter correspondents, Herbert Russell, with the British Army, and Lester Lawrence, with the French, broke down after the war was over; Lawrence was seriously ill for some time. Russell received a knighthood; Lawrence was honoured by the French Government.

What the war correspondents serving the Press Association during the 1914–18 war did was to soothe the atavistic suspicions of the military about journalists. By their unrelenting concern for accuracy they gradually invested reporting of the war with an integrity which had been dangerously absent in the early stages, again because where the facts were hidden, rumour and invention flourished. The P.A. sometimes felt, during the war, that it was penalised through 'playing the game'. It submitted to the Official Press Bureau any news which related directly or indirectly to the war. It felt that it had an obligation to be safe rather than sorry, so that no paper buying its news from the P.A. would run any risk. Individual papers were not always so scrupulous or cautious and the P.A. often had to wait and wait for the Press Bureau to 'pass' items of news which had already appeared in some papers. But it is certain that the reputation of the Press Association suffered no harm in the long run.

There was one occasion when the P.A. came close to very serious trouble when it put out a Reuter message without submitting it to the Press Bureau. The P.A. had assumed that, as usual, Reuters had done so—but it had not. The report said that an armistice had been signed. Seventeen minutes later the P.A. sent out another message telling newspapers to kill the story which had turned out to be false. The Director of Public Prosecutions told the P.A. it had committed an offence under the Defence of the Realm Act. The Attorney-General 'found it difficult to restrain from some drastic action in a case where such large public mischief had already ensued'. But because the P.A. had taken immediate steps to stop the report, and because the armistice was in fact signed eighty-four hours later, he let it drop.

The value for money offered by the P.A. in its War Special

Reporter Anonymous

service can only be described as astonishing. Morning papers paid six guineas a week for it. In return they received an average of 4600 words a day. Evening papers received about half the number of words for half the price. (The provincial evening papers, whose importance and success in many towns and cities had by now outstripped that of the morning papers, frequently complained of the preferential treatment accorded to the mornings. This could be explained by a need on the part of the P.A. to hold back certain news items so that the London mornings, with whom joint arrangements had been made, could have first publication of them. It was also the practice of the authorities, abiding by long tradition, to place an embargo 'For morning papers only' on some releases. But the evenings had reason to feel resentful.) During the five and a half years the War Special service existed it had a financial turnover of nearly a quarter of a million pounds. At the end the adverse balance was estimated at under £1500—'a truly remarkable illustration of the advantages of co-operative enterprise,' as Sir George Toulmin, of the *Lancashire Daily Post*, said. It was also a remarkable tribute to the way it was organised and administered.

Many of the P.A.'s normal services were hard hit during the war, services like Reuter's New York Prices, Lloyd's Mail and Shipping News, the London Stock Exchange, Racing, Cricket and Football. The Association paid subscribers to these services rebates which amounted, over the whole period of the war, to more than £50,000. Elsewhere, the P.A. was affected by the war like any other business. Men went off to the fighting and were more and more difficult to replace. Towards the end it was especially hard to get messengers, girls just as much as boys. The P.A. was also handicapped by the drain on the Post Office staff of skilled telegraphists; more than 10,000 out of a total of some 13,000 had been taken for service with the Army or Navy. The old, old complaints of delays in the transmission of telegrams were exacerbated and when, as was bound to happen, the receipt of important war news was held up the newspapers which suffered felt very sore. But now the Post Office had a genuine excuse and in 1917 the Management Committee of the Press Association recorded a rare and sympathetic tribute to the efforts of the Telegraphs Department to cope and for its willingness to do its best.

Early in 1916 a blizzard which hit Britain, especially in the

South and Midlands, affected the efficiency of the telegraphs for months afterwards and must have reminded Edmund Robbins of the storms which battered the country in the very first days of P.A. operations. The weather played a heavy hand again on the night of 16th December 1917, as the P.A. was receiving a most important and most expensive message from Jerusalem. The correspondent was Fergus Ferguson who had gone to the Holy Land from Salonica the previous April. For months there was not a word of copy from him. He wanted to send despatches with 'interesting details as to the general conditions of the life of our gallant troops in the hot weather'—but the Censorship had other views. But with Allenby's dramatic advance at the beginning of November, which ended within a few weeks with the arrival of his forces at Jerusalem, Ferguson's long wait began to pay off. During those few weeks he sent many first-class despatches which reached a peak with his descriptive account of the capture of Jerusalem and Allenby's formal entry into the Holy City. That despatch made nearly two columns. Sent at the express rate of a shilling a word, the cabling alone cost nearly £150. How sad, then, that this message should arrive on a night when a great gale was raging and seriously interfering with telegraphic traffic, especially to the north and west. Despite this, the Post Office got the message through to most towns 'in fair time'.

In 1917 Edmund Robbins, who had been with the Press Association from the first day of operations and who had composed its first message for transmission over the State telegraph system, retired. He was now seventy, he had been with the P.A. for forty-seven and a half years, he had been Manager for thirty-seven of them, he had been working for nearly sixty years, and he wanted a rest. The strain of carrying the P.A. through the war had taxed even his resilience. Though his son, Harry Robbins, had borne a much larger share of the administration, the Manager had scarcely enjoyed that relief he had been promised. Everyone realised this and knew that it was right for him to retire while he still had his health, but there was the sadness at his going which went far beyond the ritual expressions of regret.

Edmund Robbins, after all, was the physical embodiment of the Press Association. He, more than any other individual, had a right to say that whatever the Press Association had become it was largely of his making. And in many ways his own character and personality epitomised or reflected that of the organisation he had served so capably. His virtues were not florid or glamorous ones; they did not strongly impress at first encounter; in his quiet, conscientious, moderate way, he ran the risk of being underestimated. But time brought proper recognition of his qualities. His temperate, courteous manner certainly did not mean weakness, as successive Postmaster Generals and senior civil servants were to discover. He was firm to the point of being stubborn in defence of the P.A.'s interest. He had evolved in his own mind a very clear concept of the rights and responsibilities of the press and the principles by which journalists should be guided. Like the P.A. itself he was unflashy to the point of stuffiness but he and the organisation he piloted were still there and the more widely esteemed when more gaudy and flighty competitors had gone down or were in decline. As he grew older, it is true, he grew more conservative in his ways. He responded less quickly to new ideas and as a result the Press Association itself occasionally had to follow where it should have led. As is almost inevitable with any man who enjoys virtually unqualified power for so long, he played the despot in his own house. But, as we have seen, he never lost his humanity.

As annual meeting followed annual meeting, as directors rotated and new chairmen took their seats at the head of the Management Committee year after year, Robbins must have felt an increasing loneliness. Not only did he outlive all the founder-members of the P.A.—the last of them, Frederick Spark, of the *Leeds Express*, died in 1919—but he saw them succeeded by their sons and even by grandsons. While Edmund Robbins was still sitting there, in his accustomed place, his face still youthful despite his white hair and fluffy white moustache, with his memories of the origins of the P.A. still fresh, he had to listen to younger men talking of them as though they belonged to some misty, unimaginable past.

Of those with whom he had worked at the beginning of the P.A., only one, Henry Whorlow, who had become Secretary when Robbins became Manager, survived him. John Lovell, his predecessor as Manager and the man who had given him his job at the P.A., had died young, in 1890, at the age of fifty-four. By the time of Robbins' retirement, the last of the original quartet who had acted as midwives to the P.A.—John Edward Taylor, Frederick Clifford, John Jaffray and George Harper—had been

Struggles with the censor

dead for more than ten years and none of them had taken any active part in P.A. affairs for much longer than that. Indeed, Clifford had been succeeded by his son Charles, who had become Chairman of the P.A. himself in 1908, and in 1915, as Colonel Clifford, was 'in the thick of it' on the Western Front. Others, too, who had been big names in journalism and in the growth of the Press Association from its earliest days had gone. Those who now looked to Edmund Robbins with something like veneration knew little or nothing of them, except perhaps where their family's newspaper connections had survived, like Henderson of Belfast; Crosbie of Cork; Scott of Rochdale; Toulmin of Preston; Glover of Leamington Spa; Jeans of Liverpool; Tillotson of Bolton; Lewis of Bath; Duncan of Cardiff; and Hawkins of Bristol.

Despite the existence of these, to Robbins, familiar names, the atmosphere of P.A. meetings and the character of the membership had changed considerably over the long years of his service. Slowly, perhaps almost imperceptibly from year to year, the old 'family' feeling of the P.A. was dying. There were fewer and fewer of those 'private' jokes which could be appreciated only by the audience composed of men well known to each other. The number of personal proprietorships was rapidly dwindling. More and more newspapers were owned by companies and the men representing them at P.A. meetings were executives of those companies. In the conduct of business the genial intimacy of the past was gradually giving way to a friendly professionalism. The Press Association reflected in its membership the changing nature of newspaper ownership.

Until Harmsworth showed the way to mass circulations with his new journalism and his *Daily Mail*, the big newspapers had been owned, almost exclusively, by men interested in journalism and public affairs. They used their papers as platforms from which to participate in political life. The most successful papers prospered but not in a way to excite the kind of man whose primary interest was the making of money. Harmsworth demonstrated that newspapers could be commercial propositions. The impact of this discovery upon the provincial press was small at first, but as early as 1904 William Brimelow, of the *Bolton Evening News*, voiced his awareness of the changes to come. 'I am not quite sure,' he said, 'we shall know in the future that we are dealing with newspaper men, as distinct from those who engage in newspaper enterprise from the point of view of commercial speculation.'

John Lovell said on one occasion that the Press Association 'had had to struggle severely against the dead weight of indifference that arose from the absence of any feeling of proprietorship in the Association'. Lovell was arguing in favour of paying a small dividend as a way of creating a sense of proprietorship in the minds of members. Lovell was speaking in 1885, and it was in that year, for the first time, that a dividend was paid. (The original Articles of Association did not give the power to pay a dividend; a special resolution was passed in 1885 to permit it.) There have been only four times in the history of the P.A. when a dividend has been paid; the last time was in 1890. It was a subject which provoked lively argument at many annual meetings, but the view generally held was that the aim of the P.A. should be to supply news to its members as cheaply as possible and not to make profits or pay dividends. When it did make a profit, despite the most precise calculations of cost, the money should be ploughed back.

The Press Association was created by provincial newspapermen and developed by them. But from 1903 onwards some London newspapers which have separate printing establishments in the provinces have been P.A. shareholders. The P.A. had always maintained the principle that separate newspapers, although published by the same proprietor or otherwise closely linked, must pay separate subscriptions for P.A. news. In 1900 Harmsworth began to print his *Daily Mail* in Manchester as well as London and it was a triumph for the P.A. when he agreed to pay for the news services in both places. Despite this, the Committee of Management hesitated long before creating the precedent of issuing twelve shares to the *Daily Mail* to qualify its Manchester edition as a member of the Press Association. Other London newspapers have since taken shares in the same way. The privilege of receiving news at members' rates applied only to the provincial editions.

On his retirement in 1917, Edmund Robbins received a knighthood to mark his achievements. When he died in December 1922, at the age of seventy-five, a bronze memorial tablet was erected to him in St. Bride's Parish Church, Fleet Street. On it was an epitaph which briefly, simply, characterised his qualities:

'An upright Man, an able Journalist, and a great Organiser.'

Nine / Private wires for all

In its first fifty years the Press Association reported the doings of a world transformed by scientific invention, by social legislation and by war. Yet at the end of that half-century the means by which the P.A. itself was sending out the news had changed scarcely at all.

When the Great War ended, the Post Office telegram, delivered by messenger, was still the principal way of distributing news-agency 'copy'. It still took about an hour for any but the briefest messages from the P.A. to reach a provincial newspaper office. If the wires were particularly busy, or the weather was bad, it could take even longer. Although the performance of the State telegraph system had certainly improved upon the inefficiencies and disasters of its early days, it never reached a standard to satisfy the press. Throughout his career Edmund Robbins was embattled with the Post Office. Unbelievable though it may seem now, it took him more than twenty years to get the Post Office to make a minuscule concession over the time at which it would accept messages for transmission at the cheaper, night rate. The P.A. sent all telegrams for morning papers at the night rate which began at 6 p.m. Of course, the sub-editors were writing the copy for those messages throughout the afternoon. But the Central Telegraph Office would not accept them before 6 p.m. Anything handed in before six o'clock, said the Post Office, must be paid for at the day rate which would push up the cost by one-third. So the messages piled up in the P.A. offices and then, on the dot of six o'clock, they were unloaded at the C.T.O. The result was a traffic jam which meant frustration in morning paper offices waiting for the telegrams to arrive.

Reporter Anonymous

The P.A. wanted the Post Office to accept the telegrams before six o'clock so that they could be copied ready for transmission. There were 'insuperable difficulties', said the Post Office, the chief of which, it seems, was that the hour between five and six was the tea hour at the Telegraph Office. It was not until 1908 that the then P.M.G., Sydney Buxton, agreed to an experiment first suggested by the P.A. early in the 1890s. Copy for the morning papers was handed in from five o'clock onwards and the Telegraph Office prepared it for despatch at six. Delivery of the telegrams to provincial newspaper offices was speeded up by between twenty minutes and half an hour. The Post Office agreed to make the concession part of the normal service.

One other example of the official mind at work. It was the practice of the P.A.—and of other news agencies—to send out reports in sections. Thus, if covering the story of an election at Dundee, a first telegram would be followed by a second perhaps an hour later, supplementing the initial message. This second telegram would be prefaced 'Add Dundee'. These two words, like the rest of the telegram, were paid for at the cheaper, press rate. But suddenly, in 1908, the Telegraphs Department said that because the word 'Add' was not a piece of news it must be paid for separately, as a private message. The local post office at South Shields had tried the same game a few years earlier. George B. Hodgson, editor of the *Shields Daily Gazette*, fought a battle lasting some three months, arguing with officials in person and by letter. The Post Office view was that if a reporter used the word 'continued' that would be passed at press rate but if he used 'add' it must be paid for as a private telegram.

From the nineties onwards a focus of dispute, sometimes impassioned, especially on the part of Edmund Robbins, was the leasing of private wires to individual newspapers. These private wires gave newspapers a direct link between their London and head offices in the provinces for, at first, twelve hours a day and, later, for twenty-four hours a day. Only the bigger, more prosperous papers could afford this luxury, which gave them a great advantage over smaller competitors. This was especially so with evening papers. An evening with a private wire from London might have an important item of metropolitan news in the paper and being shouted in the streets before its rival had even heard of it. True, P.A. services could not be sent over these private wires

Private wires for all

because the P.A. would not allow it; the P.A. took its stand on the principle that it existed to provide 'absolute equality of service'. But even without being able to send P.A. news—Central News did not place the same restriction on its reports—the paper with a private wire still had a real edge over its rivals.[1]

Edmund Robbins took the view that all should have private wires or none should. He said that not only should individual papers be allowed to lease private wires but so should groups of papers acting together and so should news agencies. If the P.A. could lease private wires they would be able to cut out most of the work done by the Post Office and eliminate delays. The Post Office would not agree. When is a private wire not a private wire? When more than one newspaper—or a news agency—uses it, said the Post Office. Once again officialdom remained impervious to the protests, the somewhat overpitched protests, of Edmund Robbins. The Post Office policy, he said, would see the destruction of smaller papers.

It was nearly thirty years before the P.A. set up the private wire system that Edmund Robbins had asked for in the nineties. That it took so long, however, was not wholly the fault of the Post Office. A distinct impression emerges from the records that Edmund Robbins was not wholehearted in his enthusiasm for private wires. There was more than a suspicion of the negative about his attitude. If the Post Office had given in to pressure and had withdrawn the private wires from individual newspapers Robbins, one feels, might have been content. He probably felt that so long as everyone received the same treatment, with none able to purchase privilege, it was better to leave the job of transmitting the news over the telegraphs to the Post Office. Certainly it was cheaper than leasing private wires, but this was to ignore the mounting demands for faster news services.

Not all the members of the P.A., however, were concerned to the point of doing anything very active to remedy the situation. But there was a vigorous pressure group of evening newspapers in the early years of the century and they did much to bring about a change in the official attitude. These newspapers did not have private wires but they wanted five or six papers to be able to combine to receive their news over the same 'joint' wire. They were

[1] Later the P.A. also allowed some of its material to go through London offices, but not its main news services.

Reporter Anonymous

led by George Hodgson, of South Shields. Hodgson was a small man, with an easy, pleasant manner, but an enthusiast who campaigned relentlessly for what he believed in. He was a native of Bishop Auckland, Co. Durham, and it was in the north-east that he made his reputation as a journalist, working on the *Northern Echo* and the *North Eastern Gazette* at Middlesbrough before joining his paper at South Shields. He did not believe in letting sleeping officials—or fellow-newspapermen—lie; he nudged them and prodded them until they got up and did something.

With Sydney Buxton at the Post Office, the press felt they had 'a thoroughly sympathetic' Minister and a positive change in the relations between the Department and the press can be observed from that time on. There were still disagreements, of course, but Buxton played an active part himself in trying to understand and meet the needs of the newspapers. He even arranged for newspapers and the agencies to send complaints of delays and other inefficiencies to his private house. He set up a Departmental Committee to look into the whole question of transmitting news at press rates and Edmund Robbins, as well as many members of the Press Association, gave evidence to it. The Committee recommended a change in Post Office policy. They saw no reason why newspapers should not have joint wires or why news agencies should not operate a system of private wires, if they found the staff to man the wires. It seemed a considerable concession—and so it was—but the cost of it was too much for the P.A. It was not just the difficulty of finding and paying for the staffing of the wires but also the cost of renting the wires themselves—£7 a mile for underground wires and £5 a mile for overhead wires, always vulnerable to the weather. 'Exceedingly stiff' terms, thought the P.A. The smaller evening papers thought so, too. Much as they wanted to get on even terms with the bigger papers, there was a limit to how much they were ready to pay for the pleasure. The Press Association continued to think and talk about the possibilities of a private wire system but nothing came of it. They also examined the potentialities of new high-speed telegraph instruments but nothing was done about them, either, until after the first world war.

Some imaginations were excited by the ultimate possibilities of wireless. Among them was, once more, that of George Hodgson. Through him a demonstration was arranged in 1912, at Whitley

Private wires for all

Bay—in his own part of the world. He persuaded Edmund Robbins and the P.A. Chairman for that year, John Phillips, of the *Yorkshire Post*, to journey to that beautiful but bleak part of the north-east coast of England. They were not much impressed. As Phillips reported in his dry, sceptical way, 'We saw—so far as complete non-experts in electricity could see anything—a large number of words rapped out by the apparatus, and printed by photography upon a long and narrow slip of sensitised paper. The message, it was said, came from Denmark, and apparently with little interruption. But we discovered that what was transmitted was a continual repetition of one short word and we agreed that this was not such a test of the capabilities of the system as in itself to suggest an early application to newspaper work.'

George Hodgson continued to look forward to the time when P.A. news would be transmitted to the provincial newspapers by wireless but that did not come about, either in the immediate future or later. Before the first world war, indeed, the principal interest of the P.A. and other news agencies—Central News and Extel—was in protesting against the Marconi Company's practice of issuing a press service of wireless news, chiefly of shipping items. Jointly and repeatedly the news agencies protested and won the day. The Post Office said that Marconi's should not distribute news although it was not considered they had damaged the news agencies by doing so.

The most potent impetus to change in the ways of transmitting news came from a Post Office plan to increase the charges for press telegrams. At last, the 'cuckoo-cry' of the Post Office—as newspapermen regarded it—that the press were enjoying a cheap, preferential rate for news telegrams at the expense of the nation, had been heeded. After nearly fifty years at the same price could the press fairly protest? Whether justifiably or not, they certainly did protest. The proposed increases were sharp ones and this was 1915, a time when many newspapers were having a tough time. Several papers died during the year. Edmund Robbins said later that if the rates had been increased as the Post Office proposed, seven out of ten of all provincial daily papers would have died. But after Robbins had talked or written to nearly every member of the Government, the Postmaster General accepted compromise proposals drawn up by a press committee. These new rates did mean increased charges but they were far below those

Reporter Anonymous

initially suggested by the Post Office.[1] They were to come into operation at the end of the war or on 1st January 1917, whichever might be the earlier. The Post Office, for its part, promised to improve the service by installing extra plant at provincial post offices. But in the end it failed to get the extra revenue it had hoped for and, perhaps, deserved. As the war dragged on, the press made strong pleas to delay the operation of the new rates. The Press Association was very much in the front line of this campaign which was so successful it achieved three successive postponements. It was not until January 1920 that the higher charges finally took effect.

By that time the P.A. had decided it must organise a new and more efficient means of sending its news services to its subscribers. If a push from behind was necessary to get the directors to decide to modernise, the thought of paying those higher charges for press telegrams provided it. Before the war the P.A. had turned down the idea of running a private wire system because it was too expensive. Now it was a choice of paying more and carrying on in the old, unsatisfactory way or of paying more for a new, better system. Another incentive to make the change was the development in the actual machinery for transmitting messages.

Even in the early days of telegraphy it had been possible to transmit messages at a very high speed—at up to 400 words a minute—by means of the Wheatstone machine. This machine printed the message in Morse code symbols on a tape at the receiving end. But the regular use of this system would have been wholly uneconomic because a small army of clerks (as the original telegraph operators were called) would have been needed at both ends of the wire. At first, therefore, the usual system employed was point-to-point working with the Morse key and sounder. The messages were transmitted letter by letter with, of course, recognised contractions to speed up the process. The receiving clerk still had to write out the message as he read it off his sounder. All this was rather slow and laborious and, during the nineteenth century and

---

[1] The Post Office had said the basic rate should go up from 1s. to 2s. 6d. for a reduced number of words and the duplicate rate should rise from 2d. to 8d. The compromise plan kept the 1s. rate but the wordage was cut from 75 to 60 by day and from 100 to 80 by night. The duplicate rate went up to 3d. The press had good reason to be pleased with itself —and with the Postmaster General.

Private wires for all

later, the ingenuity of inventors and engineers was devoted to constructing and developing transmitters and receivers which would produce the messages mechanically and in clear English at the receiving end. There were many inventors and many failures.

In the news agency field, the Exchange Telegraph led the way. Early on, it had developed the sturdy and reliable tape machine which produced messages in clear English on a continuous paper tape—a convenience to clients, such as stockbrokers, who wanted to glance quickly at the news. It was not suitable, though, for sending long news services. Extel also led in the later development of teleprinters—called column printers or page printers in the early days—which would print the messages at a faster speed. Some systems still delivered the product on tape, usually gummed, to be pasted up into pages. The later and more complete system printed successive lines on paper rolls to be torn off as 'pages' whenever the receiver wished. Central News also used such machines in the later years of the nineteenth century. Both P.A. and Reuters rented Extel printers for the distribution of some of their news in London.

The system which the P.A. was to use after the war, however, was the one invented and developed by F. G. Creed, who, for many years before the war, had been experimenting in Glasgow (and was indebted to the *Glasgow Herald* which gave him the freedom of the paper's private wire for his most important experiments). In 1920 the P.A. installed the plant necessary to operate an experimental Creed transmission service over private wires to the morning and evening newspapers in the West of England and South Wales. This called for the opening of the first provincial telegraph centre at Bristol.

The experiments were successful. The speed of transmitting P.A. news was revolutionised.[1] A Swansea paper, the *Cambria*

[1] This was achieved by a sequence of operations. The news message, prepared by the editorial staff, was 'punched' in Morse code at the Press Association in London in the form of a perforated slip. This slip, which was in fact a tape, was fed through a transmitter and produced an identical punched tape at the provincial telegraph centres. The centre staff then made a similar retransmission over circuits to which two or more subscribing newspapers were connected and in each newspaper office the punched tape was produced for the first time. This in turn was passed through another machine which printed the message in clear—at the beginning on gummed tape but within a few years in page form. In theory,

Reporter Anonymous

Daily Leader, told how the Creed had transmitted the text of a Lloyd George speech at Llandudno. The great man started speaking at a quarter to three in the afternoon. By the time the *Daily Leader* went to press at half past four it was carrying four and a half columns of the speech. As the P.A. Manager said, 'That would have been absolutely impossible over the public wires; we should not have dreamt of attempting such a thing.'

Another Welsh newspaperman, however—from the *South Wales Argus*, Newport—could not see the need for these new-fangled methods.

'If all the newspapers are getting their news at the same time,' he said, 'the only people who are going to get the advantage of the new scheme are the public, and the newspapers will be going to a very large expense in order to satisfy the public. My opinion is that the public are not anxious or waiting on our doorsteps ready to grasp the news that comes more quickly over the Creed than over the ordinary telegraphic service.'

Such reactionary views did not prevail. The P.A. went ahead with the Creed system, rapidly extending it until practically all morning and evening newspapers in the British Isles were connected to it. The P.A. leased from the Post Office all the telegraph circuits needed for the system and opened additional telegraph centres at Birmingham, Manchester, Leeds and Glasgow. In London the P.A. set up a fully fledged telegraph department and its first chief, John (Jock) Newlands, was to play a most significant part in these years of experiment and advance. Newlands had retired from being controller of the Post Office's Intelligence Department. He went to the P.A. in 1919.

The introduction of the private wire system began the transformation of the relationship between the Press Association and the Post Office. As the morning and evening newspapers changed over to the new system, the P.A.'s use of press telegrams declined until it was confined to minor news supplies to weekly newspapers. The chronic disputes about delays virtually ceased. Gone were the hold-ups at the Central Telegraph Office in London. No longer did provincial papers have cause to fret about deliveries of telegrams from the local post office. Complaints to the Post Office

this system (carrying tape produced by more than one puncher, of course) was capable of transmitting 140 words a minute; in practice, the average was about 90.

Private wires for all

were far fewer and were mostly about failures in circuits and the time taken to repair them or supply alternative facilities.

The new system also removed the inequalities which had worried Edmund Robbins for so long. Now every daily paper was a private wire paper. With the Creed system, which was to remain in operation until 1948, the Press Association advanced mechanically into a new phase of its history. Behind was a brave, in some ways romantic, era, but it was more than time to move on.

Ten / New men for a new world

When Walter Runciman proposed the toast of the Press Association at its jubilee dinner at the Savoy in 1920, he described the P.A. as 'one of the most important of British institutions'. He was not merely being polite to his hosts. The days of bitter and anxious strife were over. Other news agencies still competed with it but the P.A. had established its predominance. In 1919 it had taken over what was left of the London News Agency. The Central News was still in the fight and it, too, had leased some private wires to link it with the provinces, but the scale of its operations could not compare with those of the P.A.

In his book *The Decline and Fall of Lloyd George* the late Lord Beaverbrook gave a dramatic illustration of the way in which the P.A. was accepted as *the* instrument for giving important news to the nation. Beaverbrook told how he went to see Bonar Law on the evening before the fateful meeting in October 1922 of Conservative M.P.s at the Carlton Club. At stake was the life of Lloyd George's Coalition Government. Would Bonar Law go to the Carlton Club meeting and call for an end to the Coalition? For a quarter of an hour Beaverbrook put to Bonar Law the arguments for going to the meeting. Then he waited for an answer.

'He calmly refilled his pipe and said quite simply: "I am going to the meeting." It was a dramatic moment. I was going hot and cold on account of my temperature. But it seemed to me I then went hotter and colder. I asked if I might make a statement to the Press Association that he would be at the Carlton Club. He concurred. I fled. Not a moment did I waste in reaching a telephone. I called through to the Editor of the Press Association, gave him

New men for a new world

my name, and told him I was authorised to publish the statement: "Bonar Law will go to the Party meeting at the Carlton Club."

'Then I returned home and to bed with two hot-water bottles and one of rum with a bowl of sugar. One last word of warning on the telephone to the *Daily Express* to make the most and the best of the great news. And then a night of sleep.

'It was eight o'clock in the morning when I was called imperatively to speak with Bonar Law on the telephone. When I got on he told me he had not slept all night; that he feared so much for the future of the Conservative Party; that he believed so greatly in the need for that instrument; that he worried so much lest it be destroyed; that he would like to have another talk with me at once.

'I replied, "Have you seen the morning newspapers?" which was a conclusive answer to his suggestion for more talk. The front page of almost every newspaper displayed the statement that Bonar Law was going to the Carlton Club.

'Every political writer in Fleet Street knew that the announcement foreshadowed the fall of Lloyd George's Government that very day. And so it was.'

So the value and the status of the Press Association as Britain's premier news agency were now beyond question. But, as seems to happen at some stage in the life of any established institution, the P.A. was suffering from more than a touch of arthritis. Its virtues —its unrelenting insistence upon accuracy and impartiality— were real enough. But in its style of presenting the news—and the kind of news it chose to present—it seemed to be possessed of the notion that to be trusted and respected it must be dull and stodgy. The world had been maimed and shattered, the people's faith in their leaders had been soured, the most successful newspapers peddled sensation and set out, primarily, to entertain. But the P.A., in some respects, conducted itself as though it was still servicing a pre-war world in which newspaper readers were presumed to have the leisure and the inclination to absorb column after solid column of verbatim political reports. This attitude was epitomised in the reply given to a member who dared to ask why the P.A. did not report, as the C.N. did, some of the more interesting interjections in Parliament. Because, came the lofty reply, we report the Parliamentary proceedings that matter and interjections are usually unimportant and sometimes irrelevant.

Reporter Anonymous

There were times, of course, when the P.A.'s capacity to provide at high speed a reliable verbatim account was much valued both by newspapers and, at one remove, by newspaper readers. But this was in the reporting not only of politics but of crime. Teams of P.A. reporters, highly proficient shorthand-writers, achieved a standard of performance which few, if any, newspapers could match. Most papers did not try. There was the Kidwelly poisoning trial at Carmarthen Assizes in November 1920, for instance. According to contemporary accounts, this aroused the 'greatest public interest since the Crippen poisoning drama'. Some of the P.A. subscribers said they wanted every word the agency could get. The P.A. did not let them down. On the day on which the celebrated and histrionic Marshall Hall opened for the defence, the Press Association created a record by putting out a report of 14,339 words.

In covering a sensational murder trial, the P.A. performed a valuable but unimaginative service. The facts and evidence were such that they needed no dressing-up to make them interesting. But even if they had they would not have got it, because the P.A. did not believe in 'dressing-up' the news. 'Brightness and anything savouring of elaboration were taboo', according to Andrew Gray, who joined the P.A. as a reporter in 1907 and later was to become news editor. Richard Eccleston, one of the P.A.'s outstanding reporters between the wars, found this tradition intolerable. When he joined the reporting staff in 1919, there was a set form for introducing a report. A report of a speech, for example, would always begin, 'Mr. Baldwin, speaking at Birmingham tonight, said . . .' To Eccleston 'this was more than flesh and blood could stand'. So he began introducing the highlights and some descriptive matter, 'but I couldn't count the number of letters I received from the General Manager explaining that was not the way they reported on the P.A.'

The General Manager to whom Eccleston refers was H. C. Robbins, who succeeded his father in 1917. He was known to the staff as 'H.C.R.' and as he peered at them through his thick lenses he attracted some of the awe they had felt for his father. Harry Robbins joined the P.A. as a junior sub-editor in 1894. He started off on what was called the 'victim turn', which meant coming on duty at midnight and working through until 8.30 in the morning. He had ten years on the editorial staff before moving over to the managerial side. There was some muttered criticism inside the office when he was promoted, over the heads of more experienced men, to be Deputy Manager. P. A. Shaw, who later succeeded Henry Whorlow as Secretary, was imprudent enough to write a letter to the *Westminster Gazette* protesting, without mentioning names, about the unfair practice in some firms of giving an important executive appointment to a man whose chief qualification was that he happened to be the son of one of the heads of the business. A contemporary has said that this letter did not amuse either Edmund Robbins or his son Harry, and that neither of them ever really forgot it. There were moments of friction between Shaw and Harry Robbins and when the latter became the senior executive of the P.A. there were occasions when he had to remind the Secretary of their relative responsibilities. But it would be wrong to exaggerate the extent of any animus between them. After all, Percy Shaw remained Secretary until 1940 and for nearly the whole of that time he and Harry Robbins were working closely together. That would have been impossible if their working relationship had not been firmly based in mutual respect.

It must also be said that whatever justification there may have been for the initial criticism of Robbins' appointment as Deputy Manager (does a young man ever leap-frog to a top position without resentment somewhere?), he quickly established his ability to hold the job. This was particularly so during the war when from the very start he carried much of the burden of organising the special war services and of adapting the P.A. to radically changed conditions.

When Harry Robbins succeeded his father as Manager it meant much more than a perpetuation of the family name. Having worked at the P.A. for more than twenty years and having been his father's deputy, it was not surprising that Harry Robbins shared many of Edmund Robbins' views about what the Press Association was, what it stood for, and how it should conduct itself. In that sense he must be seen as exercising a conservative influence, but it was not a harmful one. It might fairly be seen as a moderating influence, tempering the forces of change.

Those forces were strong ones. After the war there were powerful personalities in the boardroom who were determined to give the P.A. a modern look. Among them was Colonel Sir Joseph Reed, of the *Newcastle Daily Chronicle*, who was sometimes im-

Reporter Anonymous

patient of the niceties of protocol in his resolve to get things done and to get them done quickly. Another important figure, though a less aggressive personality, was Arthur Pickering, of the *North Eastern Daily Gazette*, Middlesbrough. Chairman of the Association for two crucial years in the mid-1920s was Sir Charles Hyde, of the *Birmingham Post*, a man who expressed eloquent contempt for the mass-circulation press and for the newspaper kings from London, but who put his energies and his distinctive talents behind the reshaping of the P.A. for a new world. Towards the end of the decade Sir James Owen, of the *Exeter Express and Echo*, took a leading part. These men had one thing in common—a persistent vision of how the Press Association must change and grow; they also had the drive to see it fulfilled.

It was Colonel Reed, a tough, square-faced industrialist, and Sir George Toulmin, with ancestral and long personal experience of the P.A., who pushed the Association into a new headquarters. For some years there had been talk of the need to find somewhere more adequate than the New Bridge Street offices. But whatever premises were examined were found to be unsuitable in some way or other. It began to look as though the only answer would be to put up a new building on the New Bridge Street site. That would have cost £100,000 and there would have been the problem of where to live while it was being built. Reed and Toulmin tired of the inconclusive discussion and delay. Colonel Reed found that the leasehold of Byron House in Fleet Street, with a frontage running from Bride Avenue to Salisbury Court, could be bought for £20,000 and he and Sir George Toulmin, the then Chairman, bought it. Then they went to their colleagues on the Management Committee and said to them, 'You can have it at the same price. But if you don't like it we'll keep it ourselves.' The P.A. directors decided to like it. Those with a taste for history and symbolism will note that the Press Association was planting itself alongside St. Bride's Church just as Wynkyn de Worde did when he brought Caxton's press to Fleet Street in 1500. (The first stone church was built on the site of St. Bride's in the sixth century; the church is often called the 'Printers' Cathedral'.)

Byron House was decorated in various places with tiles inscribed 'crede Byron'. Presumably, it had been built for a Byron enthusiast. No one could have called it a beautiful building, with its fussy façade, its bits of mock Gothic and its clusters of chimneys. Nor was it an easy job to adapt it for use by the P.A. Beginning in 1921, it was well over a year before all the departments from New Bridge Street and the London Service from Red Lion Court—known to its inmates as the 'Black Hole of Calcutta' —were in their new quarters. It was also a costly business and it turned out later that the construction of the building had not been first-class and expensive repair work was needed. Nevertheless, Colonel Reed was justified, when presiding over the 1922 annual meeting, in patting himself on the back, without affecting any false modesty, as he said, on the good stroke of business he and Toulmin had done.

In 1922 the P.A. bought the freehold of Byron House for £75,000 and also the leasehold and freehold of an adjoining building in Salisbury Court. By 1923 the P.A., which had worked for its first fifty years in rented offices, was the owner of over £100,000 of real estate (with a mortgage of £55,000 which was paid off in 1925).

The man who had the task of adapting Byron House to the P.A.'s needs was George Hodgson, the man from South Shields, who had campaigned so vigorously for a private wire system. Reed said of Hodgson that 'if he had not become a successful journalist he would have made a first-class architect'. But Hodgson's work in getting Byron House in shape was only a small part of his total contribution to the successful expansion of the Press Association. When Harry Robbins became Manager in 1917 Hodgson was appointed Assistant Manager. Two years later he and Robbins became Joint General Managers. On the face of it this looks like an uncomfortable arrangement, with abundant opportunities for misunderstandings. In practice, however, the partnership between the short, thin Robbins and the big, stout Hodgson worked out extremely well. Robbins obviously maintained his seniority but Hodgson took on certain responsibilities which formerly would have been the Manager's. Above all, he carried through—with Jock Newlands looking after the technical side—the creation of the private wire system which had been his dream. Even after the initial decision had been taken, the establishment of the system took years of hard, often frustrating, work.

At the end there were 3000 miles of wire, radiating from Byron House, linking the P.A. with practically every morning and evening paper in Britain. Robbins paid ungrudging praise to Hodgson for this achievement, never seeking to take any part of the credit to himself. There is no doubt, either, that Hodgson, with his successful experience as an evening paper editor, brought a valuable stimulus to changes on the editorial side of the P.A. He was an innovator and an enthusiast, two qualities precious to the P.A. at that time.

During this period the directors played a much more active role than they had during the reign of Edmund Robbins. This was probably no reflection upon Harry Robbins but a response to the much more urgent and complex demands in the post-war years. An indication of this was the decision taken in 1921 to enlarge the Committee of Management—from five to seven. The directors felt that if one or two of them were ill or found it impossible to attend meetings, the Committee, under the original constitution, could be dangerously small to take important decisions. The P.A. was a growing business and its affairs needed more care at boardroom level. An effect of the change was that, although the procedure of electing a new director every year remained as before, each director would now serve on the Committee for seven years instead of five before transferring to the Consultative Board—the panel of elder statesmen—for a further five years. Thus bigger Committee meetings were assured, the continuity of control was extended, and the principle of the regular infusion of 'new blood' was confirmed.

With the strong men in the boardroom providing the drive, with George Hodgson injecting journalistic flair and enterprise and Harry Robbins keeping the Association steady with his indispensable administrative ability, the Press Association began to throb with a revived vigour. On the editorial side, it not only continued to turn out the routine coverage which its members took for granted but it also achieved some spectacular journalistic successes.

In news-agency work, success usually means sending out a piece of news before your rivals, getting a 'beat', to use the jargon. To achieve this may call for every bit as much exercise of resource and ingenuity as getting an exclusive story. To an outsider, one agency beating another by a matter of minutes in the transmission of an item of news may seem of negligible importance. But in newspaper offices minutes may mean the catching or losing of an edition and, when the news is big enough, this in turn may make

New men for a new world

a significant difference to sales, particularly of an evening paper.[1]

The result of the division in Dail Eireann over the Irish Treaty in January 1922 was such a story. The man who was there to cover the story for the P.A. was Richard Eccleston, whose reporting of the Irish situation was to win him much praise from both inside and outside the Press Association. He was in Dublin in competition with something like four hundred journalists from all over the world, special writers from the London papers, top reporters from the American news agencies as well as his rivals from the British ones.

It was Eccleston's formidable task to try to beat everyone else with the news of whether the Dail would accept or reject the treaty which Michael Collins had signed in London. Acceptance of the treaty would make Ireland a Free State and end, at last, the terrible, bitter conflict between Great Britain and the Irish Republicans. Many of the reporters with whom Eccleston was competing had been throwing their money around to effect, buying up what seemed to be the best channels of communication. The private wires to London from the three Dublin daily papers, for example, were barred to Eccleston. The P.A.'s own private wire system was not extended to the Dublin papers until 1923. If he were to rely upon using the telephone or the telegraph to London in the ordinary way he was bound to trail behind his rivals in putting the news across. His solution was to use the British Government's private line between Dublin Castle and the Irish Office in London. Basil Clarke, who was at the Castle, acting for the Irish Office as liaison officer with the press, took some persuading to allow the use of a Government channel for a newspaper message. Eccleston eventually won him over—and Clarke in turn persuaded his superiors—by stressing the Government's own anxiety to hear the news as quickly as possible. Then Eccleston arranged the other links in the chain. There was to be a colleague inside the Chamber waiting to hear the result of the division. He would rush it to Eccleston himself who had made sure of being able to use a telephone inside the Dail. Eccleston would

---

[1] The Economist Intelligence Unit report on the national newspaper industry, published in 1967, questioned the validity of certain journalistic assumptions such as that exclusivity or late news influence sales. In the absence of any convincing evidence to the contrary, however, a journalist must continue to believe in their significance.

Reporter Anonymous

pass on the news to another colleague at Dublin Castle. From there it would be flashed to the Irish Office in London where another P.A. man would be holding a phone open to the P.A. in Fleet Street.

It was late in the evening when Michael Collins demanded an end to the talking. The House was made ready for the division. Eccleston left the chamber and made his way to the telephone. He had no trouble in getting his colleague in Dublin Castle. Now it was a matter of waiting for the news. As arranged, he talked on the phone of anything but the debate. Gossip, reminiscences, sport, it did not matter what so long as they kept talking. No one could say how long the division would take. The minutes went by with Eccleston straining for the sound of footsteps. The Irish girl on the exchange interrupted the conversation. 'Haven't you finished on this line?' she wanted to know.

'Ah, now,' said Eccleston, 'just give me time to talk about all me troubles.'

'Sure,' said the girl, 'you men are worse than any women, you just can't stop talking.' But she let them talk on.

More minutes limped by. At last, Eccleston heard his colleague leaping down the stairs from the chamber two at a time. He gasped out the result to Eccleston. At that moment the Irish telephonist butted in again.

'You'll have to finish with this line,' she said.

'One second,' Eccleston begged. She agreed.

'Treaty accepted,' he said. Inside three minutes of the announcement in the Dail, the result of the division was being flashed to the world by P.A. and Reuter. Eccleston had got his scoop over the world's press.

In May 1923 a random check was made to see just how fast the P.A. service had become since the introduction of the private wire system. A news item which had been sent to the P.A. in London from a town 300 miles away was back in a newspaper office in that town as a P.A. message eight minutes later. Before the P.A. had its private wires, that news item could have taken three hours to make the same journey.

Racing results were being received in newspaper offices within two minutes of the winning horse passing the post. (The Joint Service continued to use the telephone and the tape for sports results even after the P.A. set up the Creed network; there was little to

New men for a new world

choose between the three methods from the point of view of speed.) This can be appreciated as all the more remarkable when one realises how the men at the racecourses had to collect the results. This was done by the ingenious but hazardous means of 'tick-tacking'.

One man took up a position, perhaps on the roof of the grandstand, where he could see the winning-post and the board showing the numbers of the runners. A colleague stationed himself beside a telephone with a telescope trained on the first man. This phone might be in a building or it might have to be a field telephone out in the open. The observer at the course would 'ticktack' news of the race, using an elaborate system of signalling by arm movements to pass on information about the runners, incidents during the race itself, the numbers of the first three horses and the starting prices. The man with the telescope had to read these signals and transmit the news by phone to the nearest Joint Service centre from which it could be flashed throughout the country. The uncertainties of this system in bad weather are obvious. There were also places—Goodwood, for example—where the telephone was two miles from the observer and an intermediate man was needed to receive and pass on his signals. Yet, most of the time, the system worked extremely well.

What it was really like for the men doing this job was recalled more than forty years later by Ebenezer Eden. Eden was a telephonist with the P.A. then and he often went to racecourses with two colleagues, Len Coldwell and Arthur Winn. At Windsor, he had to carry the wooden box containing a field telephone to a meadow which backed on to the course. There he had to find a tree-stump to which terminals and telephone wires were attached and hook up the instrument. Coldwell would then adjust a telescope 'of considerable length' on a portable tripod and they were ready for work. Their 'pitch' at Windsor was on the banks of a stream and it always seemed to rain. The level of the stream rose and Coldwell and Eden often had to operate standing on chairs borrowed from a nearby cottage. At the end of the afternoon they had a train journey home in soaking wet clothes. The racing journalists of today, courted and cosseted by the authorities, may care to count their blessings.

Early in 1926 Harry Humphries, a well-known member of the P.A. racing staff, was given a contract to produce a daily forecast

Reporter Anonymous

of Probable Runners and Jockeys. Apart from the service of actual results and starting prices, the Probables became the P.A.'s most celebrated racing service.

Important as this innovation in the sports service was, the year 1926 was notable for a development of much wider significance. In March George Hodgson died after a brief illness. It seems likely that the P.A. directors had been looking to Hodgson to improve and brighten up the editorial department and, indeed, he and Harry Robbins did have some plans in hand at the time of his death. When he died the Management Committee quickly held a special meeting, at which attendance was confined to directors—even Robbins was excluded. The meeting decided that the only way now of getting the radical changes they wanted was to appoint a new executive—an editor-in-chief. This meant taking away from the General Manager the ultimate control of the editorial department which had been his responsibility from the first day of operations in 1870. True, he still had to be consulted about matters affecting staff or involving new expenditure and he also remained the senior executive, of course; but Harry Robbins could not have been expected to see it as anything but a blow to his own status and authority. There is no doubt, however, that the decision was the right one and was to complete the process of change to fit the P.A. for its future role.

The man chosen as the first Editor-in-Chief was A. L. Cranfield. He came to the P.A. in November 1926, and resigned in December the following year. Yet in that short time his impact was powerful, distinctive and enduring. Arthur Cranfield was only thirty-four when he became the Press Association's first Editor-in-Chief but behind him was a solid and successful career first in provincial journalism in Warwick, Sheffield and Birmingham, and then in London; in the four years immediately before joining the P.A. he was chief sub-editor of the *Evening News*.

Cranfield—'Cran' to Fleet Street—was unencumbered by P.A. tradition. The way he reshaped the news agency's editorial services was little short of revolutionary. Generally speaking, the staff themselves were infected by his energy and enthusiasm, although there were those who resented his bustling intrusion into their settled lives. He recruited new men, young men, men who were attuned by outlook and temperament to the demands of modern journalism. He brought to London men who had worked

New men for a new world

on provincial papers and who knew what was wanted at the other end of the private wire. The old, heavily stylised P.A. reporting was abandoned. Now the order to reporters was to put the most important and most arresting facts at the top of their stories so that newspapers nearing the time for going to press could be sure of running at least the guts of the story either in news columns or as a 'fudge' (stop press). Reporters were encouraged to elaborate the bald facts, where appropriate, with descriptive material. So were P.A. correspondents who, more and more, were to be professional journalists. Cranfield insisted that P.A. reports should give much fuller background than before, relevant previous history, comparable occurrences, brief biographical sketches of newsworthy figures. This necessitated a newspaper library worthy of the name, with cuttings regularly and systematically filed and an adequate supply of reference books.

There were other advances in P.A. reports which lightened the burden of sub-editors working against the clock in individual newspaper offices. The main facts of an important story were sent ahead of the full report. The private wire system was cleared to take these brief messages—'snaps' and 'rushes', as they were called. Carefully written summaries of stories which could be used either as introductions to the full reports or as complete stories in themselves—these were called 'intros'—were sent out. Summaries of White Papers, Blue Books, and similar weighty documents from Government departments and elsewhere, were prepared in advance of publication and often circulated with a note of the time at which they were released for publication.

Not all of this was new, for even in the days of press telegrams efforts had been made to expedite important messages and publications were summarised. But the difference now was that all these things—and more—could be done to much greater effect by a bigger staff with better equipment and facilities, and they could cover a wider field.

Cranfield had the advantage of coming in as a new man, with unprecedented powers, with the directors wholly behind him as he made his radical breaks with the past. The principles upon which he directed editorial operations were the ones which had always inspired the P.A.: speed, accuracy, impartiality. But he interpreted them in a wholly contemporary way. He took what was best in the new journalism, its humanity, its sense of curiosity, its enterprise, and applied it to news-agency work. He eschewed its worst qualities, its tendency to mistake a stunt for a genuine news story, its distortion of values, its pursuit of sensation for sensation's sake, and, far from debasing the reputation of the Press Association, he lifted it to a new peak.

The newspaper industry regarded the P.A. with enhanced respect and admiration. The reporters and sub-editors felt a fresh pride in their work and the P.A. attracted to its ranks some bright and outstanding young journalistic talents. Many of them moved on to take up big jobs in newspapers and, later, in radio and television. This must be seen as inevitable for, although the P.A., like any other sensible management, was ready to pay a little more than the average to hold on to men whose services it specially valued, it could not hope to compete with the big London papers if it came to a question of the highest bidder getting the man. Between the wars, as now, there were journalists who were attracted by the glamour of by-lines, or recognition, attracted by a more subjective form of journalism, a more positive projection of their personalities. These men left the P.A. sooner or later, their years in the news agency an acceptable credit-card wherever they might go. There were also the men who stayed with the P.A., who responded to the peculiar appeal of news-agency work, who were conscious of their role as servants to the whole British press, who found lasting satisfaction in knowing that, while they would rarely be credited by newspapers for their work, their reports occupied column after column, page after page, of newspapers all over the country, every day. They knew, too, they were contributing, by their care, to the collective authority of the P.A., an authority expressed in the attitude of all newspapermen: 'If it's from the P.A., it's safe.'

Under pressure from the National Union of Journalists, the P.A., along with the other news agencies, agreed to a minimum wage for journalists. This went up after the first world war by quick steps until it reached eight guineas a week in July 1920. It stayed there until after the second war. (The cost-of-living actually fell during the 1930s: none of us needs reminding of the human misery and waste which made that possible.) In his attitude to money, as in other things, Cranfield showed little respect for the P.A. tradition. If getting the news meant spending more money, then Cranfield spent it. To make up for getting lower

New men for a new world

wages than some Fleet Street men, P.A. reporters were encouraged (not directly by their Editor-in-Chief, of course) to put in their expenses 'thick and heavy'.

Cranfield's actions brought quick results. In May 1927, only six months after he had arrived, the Consultative Board recorded its opinion that there had been 'a very considerable improvement in the news services'. The General Manager, however, could not be expected to react with unqualified enthusiasm. The old, well-recognised boundaries of responsibilities had either been changed or eroded by the entry of the Editor-in-Chief. An indication of the different order of things was to be found in the decision to call on the Editor-in-Chief and the chief of the Telegraph Department to present separate monthly reports to Board meetings and, if required, to attend while their reports were discussed. (A few years later, it was laid down that the Editor-in-Chief should be present throughout all normal Board discussions.) In March 1927, and again in February the following year, the Management Committee had to define the responsibilities of the General Manager and the other executives, particularly the Editor-in-Chief. Percy Shaw, the Secretary, was reminded, not for the first time, that he was responsible to the General Manager and was not to promulgate independent policies of his own.

It was obviously an awkward, embarrassing, edgy period in the life of the P.A. administration; but it was a necessary one. The P.A. directors were naturally sorry when Cranfield left them after such a short stay.[1] But he had done all that could have been wished from a new broom and they were confirmed in their opinion, as Sir Charles Hyde said, that they had come to 'a wise decision' when they had appointed an Editor-in-Chief.

---

[1] Arthur Cranfield went from the P.A. to be assistant editor of the *Evening News*. In the 1930s he spent five years as assistant editor of the *Daily Mail* and then three as editor. For the first three years of the war he was managing editor of the *Evening Standard*, and from 1941 until his death in 1957 he was editor of the *Star*.

Eleven / A losing battle

History books are full of stories of men who could not see the future that was staring at them. The records of the Press Association can add another example or two. At the annual meeting in May 1923 Sir Robert Baird, of the *Irish Daily Telegraph*, Belfast, brought cheering news to his colleagues. He had recently paid a visit to the United States. 'From my experience there,' he said, 'you will be gratified to know that broadcasting is on the wane. People are getting so tired of it that it reminds one of the almost forgotten skating-rink craze. I was in one of the largest hotels in Chicago one evening when the broadcasting instruments were working after supper, and there was not a soul listening in.'

But few indeed shared Sir Robert's views. The corporate opinion of the P.A. in the early 1920s towards broadcasting was that it was 'a wonderful scientific invention' which might turn out to be 'a new and terrible rival' if it were not properly controlled and confined in its activities. Right up to the outbreak of the 1939 war, the efforts of the newspapers and news agencies were devoted to trying to hold back the final emancipation of broadcasting in Britain. They retreated, step by reluctant step, until they were forced to acknowledge the accomplished fact. Their fears were understandable enough. Others might talk with philosophic vision of the potential blessings which lay in store for mankind with the transcendence by wireless of physical barriers. John (later Lord) Reith, managing director at thirty-five of the British Broadcasting Company, could write[1] in evangelical terms of the power of the microphone. 'By it,' he said, 'the voice of a single man may command a nation, and through its agency the ideals of universal

[1] *Quarterly Review*, October 1924.

brotherhood be broadcast over the whole world. If culture, embracing religion, and in its broadest and noblest sense, be the paramount need of the world today, the master-microphone is at hand, and the service of broadcasting is at the service of culture.' But journalists and newspaper proprietors saw their own interests threatened and they reacted with qualified enthusiasm.

The Newspaper Proprietors Association (representing the national newspapers), the Newspaper Society (the provincial press) and the British news agencies (P.A., Reuter, Extel and Central News) acted together. The attitude of the newspapers can be simply summarised. The B.B.C., they said, should not broadcast paid advertising. It should pay for the publication of its programmes in newspapers. It should broadcast news only at the time when least harm would be done to newspaper sales, namely, after 7 p.m. each day. The news agencies' approach was a little more complicated. They were naturally in favour of measures to safeguard the interests of their principal customers, the press; on the other hand, they wanted to be the suppliers, if possible the sole suppliers, of the news to be broadcast.

The aim of both newspapers and news agencies was to effect an arrangement whereby the B.B.C. would have free play to develop 'on its own legitimate lines and not encroach on what we regard as the legitimate interests of the press'. In trying to define these territorial limits and in trying to apply them to the detail of day-to-day news coverage, the press came up with proposals which are fascinating in the nicety of their distinctions between what was legitimate and what was illegitimate. A quotation from Colonel Egbert Lewis, of the *Bath Herald*, P.A. Chairman in 1924, gives the full flavour.

'Broadly,' he said, 'the principle adopted has been that the Company [the B.B.C.] can broadcast ceremonies and speeches by microphone . . . The event will be announced and thereafter the microphone will reproduce the speeches, utterances, and other sounds, such as music, the ringing of bells etc., without the interposition of the broadcaster to comment on or link up the various speeches or sounds. With reference to Studio Narratives, as they are called, the Company will be able to invite well-known people to their studio to talk of an evening on matters of topical interest, but not to describe actual events which have just taken place, a dissertation on which would anticipate the press. For example . . .

Reporter Anonymous

Mademoiselle Lenglen on arriving in England might broadcast at 2L.O. her impressions of a lawn tennis meeting on the Riviera a few days before, but it would not be open to the Broadcasting Company to arrange for her to talk of her impressions of the play which had taken place at Wimbledon the same afternoon, as the latter would in the view of the press be competing with the newspapers.'

John Reith recognised that time was on his side. There was a great deal to be done apart from the broadcasting of news. It would have been stupid to have provoked a head-on collision with the powerful press interests—and neither Reith nor his colleagues were stupid men. He also had to recognise that, during the early years at any rate, he could not look for support in official places against the press. The Government and the Post Office were prepared to encourage the B.B.C. but not at the expense of alienating the press; broadcasting must advance by gradual, negotiated steps.

Reith played his hand with increasing confidence and with great skill. Occasionally he dug his heels in, but for the most part he showed himself a master tactician, pushing forward here and there, sounding out the defences, but withdrawing wherever he found firm resistance. He conceded with grace all the early conditions upon which the press insisted. The B.B.C. did not wish to take paid advertising and, in any event, the Government of the day would not have allowed it. It would not broadcast news before 7 p.m. and the news would be supplied jointly by the British news agencies. The only substantial point on which he refused to compromise was in his rejection of the proposal that the B.B.C. should pay for the publication of programmes in newspapers. That demand collapsed when a London paper broke away and announced that it would print them as editorial matter. The others had no choice but to follow the lead.

The first B.B.C. news bulletin was broadcast at 7 p.m. on 23 December 1922. It was prefaced with an acknowledgement to the news agencies. For the next four years, each bulletin was to be preceded by the prescribed form of words: 'Here is the news, copyright by Reuter, Press Association, Exchange Telegraph and Central News'. Curiously—because one might have expected the P.A. to do the job—these bulletins were compiled for the B.B.C. by Reuters, on behalf of the four agencies. The B.B.C. paid the

A losing battle

agencies royalties on a sliding scale, according to the number of wireless receiving licences. The agencies arranged between themselves the basis on which this money should be shared but none of them was satisfied with what it got.

Reith began to find irksome the restrictions upon what the B.B.C. could broadcast and what it could not. In 1925, still in tones of sweet reasonableness, he put forward proposals for covering four big sporting events in a way previously forbidden. He wanted to broadcast a running commentary on the first half of the England and Scotland Rugby international; 'coded narratives' of the Boat Race and the F.A. Cup Final,[1] and a broadcast from Epsom on Derby Day, which would not only give impressions of the traditional local colour but also an 'actual microphone record of the noises of the race'.

The press saw the danger signals bright and clear. They turned down all four proposals. Not surprisingly, in view of their opposition and because the whole question of broadcasting was going to be reviewed before the end of 1926, the Postmaster General procrastinated. The first major breakthrough in news broadcasting came by accident. Although the P.A., with the agreement of the unions, carried on without trouble during the General Strike and although most newspapers outside London managed to publish in one crude form or another, the restrictions on the B.B.C. had to be waived. While the Strike lasted, five news bulletins were broadcast every day.

By the end of 1926, the number of wireless licences in Britain was more than a million. No one now needed binoculars to see into the future. The British Broadcasting Company ceased to exist and the British Broadcasting Corporation was created by Royal Charter. In January 1927 the new Corporation was given permission to broadcast earlier news bulletins, running commentaries and eyewitness accounts. The concessions which Reith, still proceeding with circumspection, managed to extract from the press were admittedly very limited ones. The B.B.C. still had to take its news bulletins exclusively from the four British news agencies, for instance, and although the announcer need now say only 'Copyright Reserved' before each bulletin, the old, longer formula still had to

---

[1] The 'code' meant a plan of the course or pitch to which the commentator could refer to indicate where the boats had reached or where the ball was being played: e.g. 'Square Four'.

be used once a week. Nevertheless, from that time forward the B.B.C. could feel the wind on its back. It was in April 1927 that the then Chairman of the Press Association, Sir Charles Hyde, described that year's broadcast of the Boat Race as 'one of the most thrilling half-hours' he had ever spent. 'Not until then,' said Hyde, 'did I realise how wonderful the wireless is and how more wonderful it may become . . . Broadcasting has come to stay, and the newspapers must realise the fact.'

The B.B.C. had created the nucleus of its own news section after the General Strike. By 1930, it had grown big enough and sufficiently self-assured to produce its own bulletins at Savoy Hill, although, even more curiously than before, Reuters continued to prepare the Parliamentary report for broadcasting.

In the early hours of a Sunday morning in October 1930 the airship R101 crashed in flames at Beauvais and, although it was a breach of his agreements with the press, Reith ordered the news to be broadcast. Protestations by the newspapers and news agencies about the expansion of B.B.C. activities were received in official quarters with less and less sympathy. Yet if the whole history of broadcasting between the wars is seen from the narrow view of the press, the men who negotiated on behalf of the newspaper industry, frequently including Harry Robbins for the P.A., could congratulate themselves on having held back the inevitable for so long.

Of course, the ultimate freedom of the B.B.C. in news coverage was inevitable. Just before the second world war, after a number of revisions and renewals of its original contract with the British news agencies, the Corporation had decided it would drop joint negotiations and agree with each agency separately about what news supplies it wanted and how much it would pay for them. Nevertheless, in 1939 it consented reluctantly to make another joint contract. By now, television had begun, and this argument was accompanied by an assurance that the B.B.C. would not transmit on the screen a reproduction of a teleprinter message[1] or make a visual presentation of news which resembled that of a newspaper. That joint contract was the last of its kind. The Central News was soon to drop out of the running and the war itself

[1] B.B.C. Television has tried in recent years to heighten the dramatic impact of the football results by showing them being spelled out on the teleprinter.

A losing battle

was to destroy all the old conventions and restrictions.

As war became more and more likely, plans were laid for a service of B.B.C. news bulletins, twenty-four hours a day, with no limitations on the times at which they would be put out. There were some protests that this would damage the press. The B.B.C. would not budge, although in the event it did show its sympathy for evening papers to the extent of abandoning the 4 p.m. bulletin which it had introduced. It was the end of the long and skilfully fought battle for freedom. The principles and the liberties for which Reith had fought were ones familiar and sympathetic to journalists but, not unnaturally, what they perceived as their immediate self-interest had blunted their response.

Compared with the struggle that went on inside the newspaper industry itself between the two world wars the conflict between the press and the B.B.C. was conducted throughout with gentility and humanity. A sketch of these bloody hostilities must be hung as a background to the story of the Press Association.

It was a war for circulation and for ownership. With their development as a medium for display advertising, newspapers became potentially desirable commercial properties on a scale that not even Northcliffe had approached. What mattered to the advertisers was how many people would see what they had to sell and come and buy it. Almost their only measurement of a newspaper's value to them was the number of readers it could offer. In those terms, a circulation of one million which, when Northcliffe's *Daily Mail* had first touched it during the Boer War, had seemed so astonishing, was now no more than a starting point in the race.

A new generation of journalists was already applying the lessons taught by Stead and Northcliffe to the titillation of the public appetite. Many of them were men of unquestionably outstanding talent and they displayed an inventiveness, an ingenuity and a resourcefulness in producing papers which sold in ever increasing numbers. But the sales of these popular papers did not go up fast enough to satisfy their proprietors. They decided that what journalists could not achieve by skill must be bought. All manner of bounty was practised to seduce new readers. Bigger and better free insurance; competitions involving the minimum of skill but prizes worth as much as £5000; free gifts in profligate variety: rarely indeed has the great British public been so extravagantly courted. And all the newspapers wanted in return was a promise to fork out a penny a day for ten weeks. This was the war fought out in the papers themselves and on the doorsteps by armies of canvassers by the *Daily Herald* and *Daily Express* and, at a slightly diminished level of fantasy, by the *Daily Mail* and *News Chronicle*.

But ownership of a mass-circulation national newspaper was not the only goal that beckoned. It seemed to the commercial men that there were rich deposits of gold in the provinces, too, just waiting to be mined. When Northcliffe died in 1922, the newspaper combines—the 'chains' which linked many newspapers to one proprietor—were still in the early and relatively unambitious stages of development. That situation changed rapidly and turbulently.

After Northcliffe's death, his brother, the first Lord Rothermere, acquired his controlling interest in the *Daily Mail*, the London *Evening News* and the *Weekly Dispatch*—he did not get *The Times*—and added them to his already substantial newspaper interests in London and Glasgow. Then Rothermere bought Sir Edward Hulton's papers and so had in his control three national morning newspapers, three national Sundays, two London evenings, four provincial dailies and three provincial Sundays. For a while, but only a short while, Rothermere was top dog of the newspaper world—and a very big dog at that. He was soon to be dethroned by the Berry Brothers—later Lord Camrose and Lord Kemsley—who ranged far and wide in the search for properties to add to their empire. But it was not only Lord Rothermere and the Berrys who were marauding in the cities and towns of Britain. The bald statistics of newspapers controlled by five big chains in 1929—the peak year between the wars for the concentration of ownership—will show how vigorously and successfully they had campaigned. At the end of that year the Berrys controlled twenty-five daily and Sunday papers; Rothermere, fourteen dailies and Sundays (with a fat interest in another three); the Westminster Press thirteen daily and Sunday papers; the Iveresk Paper Company had nine and another brother of Lord Northcliffe, Sir Leicester Harmsworth—who was not really in the same league, either in the size of his possessions or the way he went about his business—controlled four dailies. (These figures do not include the ownership of periodicals, in which the Berrys in particular, had vast interests, but which are irrelevant to this story.) These

The 1965 Derby with P.A. man Dai Davies first on the spot for the winning jockey's story

Sports picture of the year 1956 by John Horton of the P.A. which won an Encyclopaedia Britannica *award*

Winston Churchill, then Prime Minister, speaking as guest of honour at the P.A. annual luncheon, 1952. Beside him, Laurence Scott of The Guardian

Duke of Edinburgh leaving the Press Association after touring the offices

A losing battle

five chains controlled between them no less than 44 per cent of all Britain's morning, evening and Sunday newspapers. They had 40 per cent of all provincial morning papers and 43 per cent of the evenings. Eight years earlier, the percentage of all newspapers in chain ownership had been only 15 and it was even lower in the provinces: 12 per cent of morning papers and less than 8 per cent of evenings.

The bloodiest battles were fought out between Rothermere and the Berrys in cities where they had rival papers and each was determined to destroy the other. In 1928 Lord Rothermere declared his grandiose ambition of building a chain of provincial evening papers—each to be called *Evening World* and each with its own Northcliffe House. The Berrys determined to meet the challenge. They engaged him in a war which knew no rules, no quarter. The principal battlefields were Bristol, Derby and Newcastle. There was no victor and the injuries sustained by both sides were severe. Both squandered huge sums of money in the hope of forcing a conclusion. It has been said, for instance, that the Newcastle battle cost Rothermere over £1,000,000. In the end he agreed to quit Newcastle and the Berrys withdrew from Bristol and Derby. The only new paper Rothermere could show for four years of war was the *Bristol Evening World* (although it is true he had bought up other existing papers as part of his projected provincial chain).

The war between the chains was not fought in isolation, of course. Others were grievously hurt by it. Between 1921 and 1930 no fewer than ten provincial mornings and seven evenings disappeared from view. From 1930 to 1939 another six mornings and five evenings were lost. In 1935 the Press Association estimated the annual loss to itself, as a result of the death over the preceding seven years of newspapers which had been subscribing to it, at £29,000. It is all too easy, however, for a journalist to erupt into florid indignation against the men of money. The fact is that the commercial exploitation of the provinces by the expanding chains was not the only and probably not even the major cause of the death of so many newspapers.

Without doubt, the chains operated with single-minded purpose. Independent papers which impeded the growth of the chains had to face a rigorous struggle for survival. To compete they, too, had to spend money on improvements and on promotion. But some could not afford to and some did not try. Economically, these were hard years for independent provincial papers, particularly morning papers. For many of their proprietors, the production of a newspaper had never been a profitable enterprise; they had kept their papers going for other reasons. After the 1914–18 war they faced a formidable combination of circumstances. The national newspapers, backed by superior organisation and lavish promotion, plundered their local markets more and more successfully. The nationals opened offices in Manchester and, later, Scotland. They published separate editions, slanted to appeal to a region and even to particular segments of that region. Not before time, as some would say, journalists and printers received substantial rises in pay. In the years immediately after the war the price of newsprint, too, soared. Later, there was the financial crisis and the Depression, from which newspapers suffered like everyone else. As a consequence, all but the strongest provincial papers were highly vulnerable to attack by invaders who did not count the cost. The death-roll makes melancholy reading, but the 1948 Royal Commission on the Press came to the conclusion that only in extremely few cases could the cause of death be attributed directly to the operation of the chains. It must also be recognised that many of the papers which were bought up by the chains—their former proprietors often getting a handsome price for a shaky property—were kept alive when they might otherwise have died sooner or later from malnutrition.

There were still men running newspapers in the provinces, however, who represented the kind of sturdy independence, the incorrigible, sometimes eccentric, individuality which contemned metropolitan values and whose papers reflected their pride in local achievements and an intimate involvement in local affairs. Such a man, above all, was Sir Charles Hyde, the sole proprietor of the *Birmingham Post* and its stable-companion, the *Birmingham Mail*, an evening. H. R. G. Wates, the *Post*'s historian, has described Hyde's reactions to the news that Rothermere intended to make Birmingham one of the places where he would start an *Evening World*.

'Charles Hyde welcomed the prospect of a fight on his own ground. A lively poster campaign was waged around a city centre site acquired by the invaders for building offices for the proposed *Birmingham Evening World*. It came to Charles Hyde's

A losing battle

ears that Lord Rothermere had been advised that the established Birmingham papers were merely an old family property and would fall into his hands like a ripe plum. "Tell Lord Rothermere," he replied, "that, far from being a decayed old family property, the papers are owned by a young bachelor who will fight him till his blood's white if he comes to Birmingham." '

There was a spirited reaction at Bristol, too, where Rothermere and the Berrys clashed head-on. Before the fight began, Bristol enjoyed two independent morning papers, each of them with an evening paper attached. When the Berrys and Rothermere finally reached their agreement to a cease-fire, both the independent evenings had gone and only one of the mornings survived. It looked as though Rothermere's *Evening World* had captured the city but a group of local people refused to submit. They started their own paper, the *Bristol Evening Post*, and for three years Lord Rothermere had another fight on his hands. It was an expensive one for both sides but the Bristolians endured—helped, it may be said, by Sir Charles Hyde, who sent them a printing press. So well did the *Evening Post* fight that in the end Rothermere had to come to terms.

The struggle between the established provincial papers, especially the mornings, and the chains and the mass-circulation dailies, must also be seen in editorial terms. The invaders offered readers all the aids of style and presentation which the new journalism had evolved. Lively writing, typography and layout easy on the eyes, the emphasis always on entertainment rather than instruction or edification. Their selection of content, the intellectual level at which news was communicated and interpreted, and the angle from which it was approached, called for the minimum of effort by the reader. Some, like Charles Hyde again, deplored this playing down to the mass audience. Another was Sir Ernest Benn, Chairman of Benn Brothers, an individualist of the old school if ever there was one. The *Newspaper World*—a Benn periodical—published in 1935, the Silver Jubilee of George V, a retrospect of the press over the previous twenty-five years. In it Sir Ernest wrote:

'When King George ascended the throne we had completed twenty years of compulsory education. Forty million fools could read and write and a great industry was just arising to supply the new reader demand. At the beginning of the century we had everything that we possess today, but in smaller quantities, better organised and, more important, better classified.

'There was the *Police Budget*, with its pictures of women in nightshirts being murdered on the front page, of which there were sold a few thousand copies to those who cared about that sort of thing. The rather elaborate wood-cuts which depicted these events got rather nearer to the actual thing than the faked photographs which now serve the same sordid purpose. There was *Sketchy Bits* to supply the eternal need for the spicy and the disreputable, and there was the old *Standard* for those who wanted to study the news of the day. Three separate and well-defined departments satisfying three definite and different demands. The mammoth popular daily has killed all three and performs the functions of them all in a far less satisfactory manner.'

A more temperate and perhaps more qualified analysis was written in the same issue of *Newspaper World* by H. A. Gwynne, the distinguished editor of the *Morning Post*, whom we met earlier as a great war correspondent operating on behalf of Reuters and the Press Association.

'Looking back', wrote Gwynne, 'to the files of pre-war newspapers, we cannot be surprised that modernism in journalism came in with such a rush and with such persistent force. Then we journalists seemed to have taken up the attitude that we alone knew what was good for our readers to absorb. "Take it or leave it" was really our motto, though we boasted that our only aim was to give the public pure, unadulterated and unbiased news. There were no indications that one particular "story" was more important or interesting than another. Speeches, parliamentary debates, learned disquisitions on foreign politics by distinguished but dull foreign correspondents, were all served up on the same page with no sort of guide being given to the reader of their real importance....

'In revolt against this state of affairs came the desire for "human interest" stories. It was time that something lighter and brighter should take the place of the stodginess of the early twentieth century. No longer were people content with reading a political speech. They began to be interested in the fact that the speaker wore an orchid in his frock coat and indulged in a hearty meal before or after his speech.

'The only doubt in my mind', Gwynne ended, 'is not whether

A losing battle

the change should or should not have come but whether it has not swung the pendulum too far.'

One man who had no doubt at all and who never diluted his own journalistic standards was C. P. Scott, editor of the *Manchester Guardian* for fifty-seven years from 1872 to 1929. Yet Scott's *Guardian*, whose circulation was counted in thousands, achieved the kind of political influence and international reputation which eluded the proprietors of papers selling to millions, Northcliffe, Rothermere, Beaverbrook. It was to Scott—and it still is—that journalists looked for standards to which they could aspire and for a criterion of journalistic integrity. But, again, it would be the easiest thing in the world to place C. P. Scott on a pedestal and to sneer at all lesser mortals who applied their talents and their skills to the attainment of less exalted journalistic aims. Scott deserves his place in newspaper history. His *Manchester Guardian* deserved the singular respect which its educated and influential readers accorded it. Scott was right to insist that the news in the *Guardian* should be untainted by partisan bias. He was bound to imbue his beloved leading articles with the qualities of lucidity, moderation and liberal fair-mindedness, for it would have been alien to him to do otherwise. He was abundantly right to allow the brilliant journalists he gathered about him their freedom to indulge and exhibit their idiosyncratic talents. All this is to confirm that C. P. Scott was a great editor who created a great newspaper. What we must beware is the assertion of a false antithesis. Scott must not be misrepresented as the epitome of the Old School, uncompromisingly attached to some infallible and unchanging body of journalistic dogma. C. P. Scott accepted the need for change. He recognised the duty of a newspaper to make itself appealing to the eye as well as the mind. He did not confuse a sense of responsibility with a posture of unbending hauteur. What he found repulsive in the frenetic chase for circulation was the wilful distortion of values, the implicit denigration of the readers' intelligence, the pollution of news, the corrosive daily dose of triviality and sensation.

It is possible to pay C. P. Scott the highest reverence, however, without deluding oneself that the paper he was producing could ever have been bought, let alone read, by any but a minority. There was need to make newspapers for the millions. To do so meant adopting other ways than his. Perhaps only now are we learning, however, that it is not necessary to pervert our own tastes and talents.

Scott and his successors at the *Guardian* were greatly helped by the existence of the *Manchester Evening News* as a successful companion paper. The *Evening News*, under the extremely able editorship of William Haley,[1] propped up the *Guardian*. This was a common situation in the provincial press. The evening papers had little to fear from the national morning papers. They enjoyed an intimate relationship with their local readerships and their appeal was different from that of a morning paper. Until television established its dominance the reading of the evening paper, paragraph by paragraph, the titbits often being shared between husband and wife, was a firm and affectionate habit.

Generally speaking, those evenings which survived after the newspaper 'war' thrived. If it had not been for the prosperity of the evenings, even more provincial morning papers would have closed down. The 1948 Royal Commission learned from the evidence given to it that in 1937 'out of twenty-two provincial morning papers examined, as many as seven, including four quality papers, were losing in that year and were being maintained out of the profits either of a chain or, in the case of the quality papers, of a more profitable evening companion'.

It is here that we have to come to a sober assessment of the role of the newspaper chains. In their formation, the motives of the men at the top may have been much less than idealistic and their methods unpalatable, but it must be seen that they brought a transfusion of money and services, editorial and managerial, to many failing papers. They were able to achieve what are called 'economies of size'. From London they were able to provide certain common services to papers scattered all over the country. By and large, once established, they allowed a considerable autonomy to editors in the day-to-day running of their local papers and the evil of authoritarian control from London, imposing a uniform appearance and voice upon all dependent papers, did not manifest itself upon anything like the scale which had been properly feared. Local papers, though belonging to chains, con-

---

[1] Later Sir William Haley (he was knighted in 1946) became director general of the B.B.C.; then editor of *The Times* and, after the Thomson merger, its chairman; and, from the 1st January 1968, editor-in-chief of *Encyclopaedia Britannica*.

A losing battle

tinued to look like local papers and to serve their local communities.

They did not serve them in the same way, however. They suffered some inevitable loss of identity. Rarely did the distinctive personality of an editor appointed by a chain manage to assert itself. It is obvious that a proprietor or editor independent of outside financial interest or managerial control must be less circumscribed. The passionate, dedicated involvement in public affairs, the readiness to sponsor unpopular crusades, to offend local sensibilities: these were the qualities which had characterised so many outstanding provincial journalists of the late nineteenth century. Although there were to be a few notable exceptions, the chain-controlled papers were not generally conspicuous for those qualities. It would be naive to suppose that they would be.

Twelve / Squaring the circle

On the 8th of October 1936 Henry Martin, who had succeeded Cranfield as Editor-in-Chief of the P.A., issued a private and confidential instruction to his staff. It was headed 'Mrs. Ernest Simpson', and it said:

'The Press Association's attitude regarding mention of Mrs. Ernest Simpson may be governed by the following conditions:

'(1) Do not mention if she goes to Buckingham Palace privately or if the King visits her. If it is desired that her presence at the Palace be known the Court Circular will notify.

'(2) Do not mention if there is any real doubt about the taste of doing so. In any event, do not mention unnecessarily.

'(3) On the other hand, if she is at a public function with the King and both Press and public are in a position to note her, her presence may be indicated. For instance, if she went with the King to open a public building or accompanied him to the theatre, there is no reason for suppressing the information even though it may have been obtained in advance of the Court Circular.

'(4) It would have been in perfect order last week to have announced that she got out of the train on her return with the King from Balmoral.'

The position of the P.A. during the constitutional crisis arising out of Edward VIII's association with Mrs. Simpson was an extremely tricky one. It was difficult enough for an individual editor or proprietor to decide whether or not to give wider currency to the rumours and gossip which had been circulating for months in newspapers in the United States and the Dominions. But the P.A. was the servant of the whole British press and it was no part of its responsibility to act as the censor of news. In fact,

Squaring the circle

the Press Association—in common with the whole British press—conducted itself with a restraint which only the most assiduous of apologists would be able to distinguish from censorship. It can be justified in retrospect by the argument that it was self-imposed and that it was maintained only so long as the crisis did not become public property. Clearly, all those concerned with newspapers and news agencies saw it as their common duty not to precipitate that crisis.[1]

In the event it was the P.A. which was instrumental in bringing the crisis out into the open. When it did so it was because the Editor-in-Chief believed, quite rightly, that the Bishop of Bradford had projected the issue into the public arena. It would be tedious to dwell long upon the detail of an episode which has been so exhaustively mined but it is worth a momentary inspection to show once again the part that chance can play in the shaping of history. It was at a diocesan conference that the Bishop, Dr. Blunt, spoke those sensational words which were interpreted, understandably, as a direct reference to the King's private life.

A reporter on the Bradford *Telegraph and Argus*, Ronald Harker, heard the Bishop's speech. When he came back to his office he told his colleague, C. H. Leach, who was the Press Association's correspondent in Bradford, 'There's something good for the P.A. here. The Bishop has criticised the King.' On checking that his own paper was going to 'splash' the story, Leach decided he should send it to the P.A. although, as he has recalled,[2] he had a strong feeling that the P.A. would not use it.

The P.A. not only decided to use it but also called for both a complete verbatim of the speech and a carefully prepared summary of it. Furthermore, on the report it sent out, appended to the text of the speech was a long quotation from the leading article in the *Yorkshire Post* which had taken its cue—or so it thought—from the Bishop and referred soberly but portentously to the rumours. It is this leader which is often credited with particular significance

---

[1] One may doubt whether the press would view its responsibility in the same way today. The technique of disseminating juicy rumours while pretending to repudiate them as scandalous and offensive is now familiar. The way the story of Princess Margaret's friendship with Peter Townsend was made public in this country is a relevant example.

[2] Leach described the incident in the *Inky Way Annual*, Book Two.

in the story of the pressures and events leading up to the Abdication. It was a fine leading article, dignified and moderate in tone but ultimately censorious and apprehensive. It was not, however, the only one of its kind which appeared in the provincial press the next day. Arthur Mann, the editor of the *Yorkshire Post*, had decided to go ahead with it only after consulting on the telephone with the editors of the *Birmingham Post* and *Manchester Guardian*, both of whom also decided to comment. The leader in the Birmingham paper, at any rate, was no less outspoken than that in the *Yorkshire Post*. Many other papers decided to comment, among them the *Leeds Mercury*, the *Yorkshire Observer*, the *Northern Echo* and the *Nottingham Journal*. The quotation from the *Yorkshire Post* was the first to be sent out by the P.A., and this is almost certainly the reason why it has been credited with such historic importance, but the P.A. did send out quotations from other provincial papers during the course of the evening.

When the London papers learned of Mann's intention to comment in the *Yorkshire Post* and they read the quotation as it came over from the P.A., they also had to decide whether to publish leading articles and elaborate upon the Bishop's words by explaining the content of the rumours. They all held back, publishing only a report of the Bishop's speech. They waited another twenty-four hours before pitching in with their individual contributions to the crisis.

Just as the P.A. was the instrument by which the crisis was brought into the public view, so it wrote the postscript to the story. The reporter was once again Richard Eccleston who had distinguished himself many years before in Ireland. Eccleston had been sent to Portsmouth whence, it was believed, Edward would leave his country. Other reporters had tried to trail the royal car but lost it. Eccleston was staying at an hotel only a few yards from the main dock gate. It was after one o'clock in the morning when he strolled along to see if he could find out anything from the guard. While he was talking to him and being assured that Edward was not inside, he was caught in the glare of headlights from a car making for the docks. It pulled up within a few feet of Eccleston, who was astonished to see that the ex-King was in it. Eccleston rushed a story over to the P.A. Very soon afterwards, the other reporters were receiving phone calls from their papers which sent them hurrying down to the docks. By the time they got there, Edward had already sailed for France.

Through Reuters, the P.A. coverage of the Abdication crisis went out to the world's press and from the world came many messages of congratulation, including a most generous one from the great American agency, the Associated Press. Although, as in all P.A. operations, it had been a fine team effort, with the Lobby Correspondent, E. P. Stacpoole, playing a most significant part, it was a period of strenuous responsibility for the Editor-in-Chief, Henry Martin.

Martin was with the Press Association for twenty-six years and there is no doubt that during that time he contributed in a very positive way to the enhancement of the P.A.'s reputation. Cranfield was the pioneer who tore into his task of reorganising and modernising the Editorial Department and who administered the necessary shock treatment to the conservatives inside and outside Byron House. It is not enough to say, however, that Martin carried on where Cranfield left off. He impressed his own stamp on the P.A., elaborating the system created by Cranfield, introducing new ideas of his own, forging a first-class news-gathering organisation.

Henry Martin was thirty-eight when he became Editor-in-Chief. He had more than twenty years in journalism behind him, most of them in Fleet Street, and eleven of them with the old London News Agency. He had been its news editor during the first world war and he later held the same job with the *Daily Sketch* and the *Evening Standard*. As might have been expected, Martin had a highly developed news sense and this was of the greatest value to him at the P.A., where the work of the Editor-in-Chief is much more that of a news editor, selecting the stories to be covered and how they should be covered, than of an editor in the newspaper sense. But Martin did have to exercise the editorial responsibility in matters of taste and judgement and it was very much as an editor, conscious of the high standing of the P.A., that he made himself known throughout Whitehall, impressing on Government departments that *the* outlet for news was the Press Association. He also carried the flag in every part of the provinces so that newspapers knew the calibre of the man and the organisation serving them.

Henry Martin had an aggressive pride in the P.A. and he

warmly admired the qualities of the provincial press, of which he called himself 'an apostle'. Throughout his career, he was in tune with contemporary developments in news gathering and handling. The important changes in the provincial press, particularly the evening papers, which made them brighter, more readable, more informative, broader in outlook, owed a lot to the material sent them by the P.A.—and that meant they owed a lot to Henry Martin.

Martin was a man of strong personality and highly individual tastes. He was an antiquarian, he found great pleasure in music and literature and he had a pronounced interest in philosophy and religion. There was a strong flavour of the moralist in his utterances about journalism and though, as we have seen, he was a modernist in journalistic techniques, he was outspoken in his condemnation of the popular press. This brought him into collision with Arthur Christiansen, the editor of the *Daily Express*, at the time of the Royal Commission. He put his views into more permanent form when he published *The Place of Religion in the Post-War Press*.

The emphasis in the P.A. upon absolute impartiality in the reporting of news and the duty to serve newspapers, generally speaking, with the kind of news *they* want, must obviously make it very difficult for an Editor-in-Chief to express his own personality and interests through the material sent out. Yet Henry Martin did manage to do so to a certain extent. He felt that many newspapers held to a too narrow concept of what was news. He wanted to see them sharing his taste for the arts and for matters religious, and so, from time to time, he included such material in the P.A. services. There was a time during the 1930s when, for several months, Martin's mind was deeply engaged by the Oxford Movement. A consequence was an excessive attention by the P.A. to the Movement's activities. These occasional strayings from the beaten path were not universally appreciated but they could be viewed as a harmless by-product of Martin's redoubtable enthusiasm and as such easily countenanced by the directors of the Press Association. For they had no doubt of the value of the man. After only two years in office, they decided, in the words of the then Chairman, 'to grapple him to our souls with hooks of steel'—to continue his engagement on a long-term contract. At the end of his career, Henry Martin described, in his idiosyn-

Squaring the circle

cratic way, the difficulties of his job. 'The Press Association is an extraordinary child to father,' he said. 'You have got to square the circle; you have got to reconcile paradoxes; you have to blow north, south, east and west at the same time.'

With his staff Martin had the reputation of being a martinet. He drove himself hard and measured his achievement by the highest standards. He expected nothing less from those who worked for him. It was said that 'satisfied' was a word missing from his vocabulary. He believed in discipline and authority and was arbitrary in the exercise of his power. On one occasion this led to a strike.

The trouble arose out of the failure of one of the P.A. reporting team at the Law Courts to provide for the Joint Law Service a daily account of an action lasting several days about a claim under a motor insurance policy. The effect of his not reporting the case was that there was nothing in the London or provincial press about it. There were suggestions made that reporting of the action was being suppressed. Complaints reached Henry Martin. He sent for the reporter and demanded an explanation. The reporter said that the case had not seemed to him to deserve daily coverage but that he had intended to write an adequate account of it for general circulation when the judgement was delivered. Meanwhile, he had written a daily column or so only for papers with a particular local interest in the case and for a specialised London journal. This was not an uncommon way of dealing with certain cases and the reporter said he had the approval of his chief at the Law Courts in this instance.

Martin was not satisfied. He asked for the man's resignation. When the reporter refused to resign, Martin gave him notice. The Law Courts branch of the National Union of Journalists called a meeting which decided that its chairman and the general secretary of the N.U.J. should see the Editor-in-Chief. Henry Martin made clear in a telephone conversation that he had no intention of seeing them. He told the general secretary of the union the P.A. had the right to dismiss any member of the staff for incompetence. He had referred the whole matter to the Board who were meeting the following week. If the union wanted to make any representations on behalf of the reporter, said Martin, they should be sent in writing to the Board. The next development was a decision by the Law Courts branch to strike unless the P.A.

received a deputation. For one day, there was no reporter in the Law Courts. The P.A. Board held a special meeting and said they would not see a deputation until the men went back to work. The reporters did go back the next day. The Board received a deputation, the dismissal was at first suspended and then at their next monthly meeting the Board 'accepted the recommendation of the Editor-in-Chief that the notice be withdrawn'. The reporter had written a letter to Martin expressing his regret for an error of judgement.

There is little doubt that Henry Martin acted as he did because he felt that the reporter had let the P.A. down and had jeopardised its reputation. There was no higher crime in his book. In his defence of the honour of the P.A.—and of any member of its staff who had been unjustly attacked—he was inflexible and formidable, showing no regard for rank or status, as Neville Chamberlain, for one, discovered.

In April 1939 the P.A. Court Correspondent, Louis Wulff, was one of a large party of journalists invited on board the aircraft-carrier *Ark Royal* for an evening's entertainment to publicise the Royal Naval Film Corporation. They sat in an improvised cinema in a hangar along with officers and men. Among the party was Lieutenant-Commander Lord Louis Mountbatten and Lord Stanhope, the First Lord of the Admiralty, who was to do the appropriate piece of speech-making. Not an over-stimulating engagement for a journalist at any time and Lord Stanhope was not the most intoxicating of speakers. At the end of a dull, unprepared speech the First Lord said, without changing his flat tone of voice, 'Unfortunately there are others who are not with us tonight, because, shortly before I left the Admiralty, it became necessary to give orders to man the anti-aircraft guns of the Fleet.'

A statement of this kind, at a time when the nerves of Europe were stretched taut, was bound to be interpreted in the most dramatic way. What had looked like being a comatose evening for Wulff and the other journalists suddenly became one of high excitement. Louis Wulff asked immediately to be taken to the ship's telephone. While he was asking where it was, Mountbatten came to where the reporters were sitting at the back of the hangar and said, 'The First Lord has asked me to say that he has no objection whatever to his remarks being published.' Wulff put his report over the phone to the P.A. The Night News Editor called

Squaring the circle

him back and wanted to know whether he was sure of his facts and if Lord Stanhope knew he was being reported. Wulff assured him that the quotation was accurate and the First Lord had given his permission for it to be published. It was not until after they had all watched a George Formby film that Wulff was able to speak to Stanhope himself, who said he stood by his words and explained that he had wanted to show the Navy was always ready. Wulff made a note of what Stanhope said, read it back to him, and received his permission to publish it. While he was telephoning this additional copy to the P.A., he was told that a 'D' notice had been issued from Downing Street on the instructions of the Prime Minister, Neville Chamberlain, asking newspapers not to publish the quotation from Stanhope's speech on grounds of national security. Some papers had already done so in early editions; some continued to carry the report. Henry Martin pointed out to the Admiralty that the report of the First Lord's speech had already been sent all over the world by Reuters and it was impossible to recall it or cancel it.

In the House of Commons the next day Chamberlain was called upon to explain why the 'D' notice had been issued. He said, 'It was because I thought the words as reported would give a wrong impression and I thought it was desirable to make that request to the press.' Henry Martin felt that the honour of the P.A. was being impugned. He sent out a long, detailed account by Louis Wulff himself of what had happened on board *Ark Royal*. *The Times* was one of the papers which carried it. The Prime Minister was forced to make amends. When he had used the phrase 'as reported', Chamberlain explained to the Commons he had meant as reported to him at a Foreign Office dinner. 'I did not mean as reported by the reporter. It was the last thing that would occur to me to challenge the accuracy of the report. I know how extremely competent these gentlemen are who report these things. . . .' A distasteful piece of double-talk, but Henry Martin had won his point.

But it was as an organiser of news services that Henry Martin excelled above all else and no higher praise could be given to the editor of a news agency. In the end all the talents, all the enterprise and innovations, all the expensive and complicated equipment, must contribute to the transmission of accurate news at the highest possible speed; if they do not, they all have failed. A

Reporter Anonymous

conspicuous example of Martin's excellence came in the coverage in 1936 of the illness and death of King George V. 'Never,' said that year's Chairman, 'did the Press Association service rise to a higher level. . . .' The tribute was deserved. The P.A. scored at virtually every stage of the story. When it was over, Henry Martin bathed in the acclaim of the world's news agencies and of many newspapers. But he was honest enough and level-headed enough to say, in his confidential report, that the P.A.'s success had been a matter of chance—not because of any lack of preparation, not because of any shortcomings on the part of his reporters, but because the conditions under which they were working meant 'it was going to be a sheer gamble which of the agencies was first with the death'.

'It is with profound relief rather than with a sense of elation that I am recording our achievement', he wrote. 'For four nights and three days we had striven to this end, planning meticulously at each point, both outside and inside the office, so as to guard as far as possible against a failure of the human element, yet uncomfortably conscious that it was the technical, the telephonic side, that was menacing our chances of success, to say nothing of the stern competition.'

The news of the King's illness and the realisation of its seriousness—both of which came from the P.A.—happened at the end of a heavy but successful week for Martin's staff. His memorandum conveys the flavour of hectic, relentless news-agency activity.

'We had scooped the operation on Mr. Rudyard Kipling, and were on tension pending the fatal outcome; we had made the story of the discovery of Ellsworth[1] and his companion entirely our own on the Thursday and Friday; we had had a scoop with the Lancashire fire tragedy, when a mother and eight children lost their lives; we had emerged first of the agencies with the Shrivenham railway disaster; we had beaten opposition in the London evenings with columns of the Nottingham exhumation inquest; we were first with the suicide of Cynthia Stockley; we had reported successfully the inquest on the Westerham air-liner crash; and suddenly after the almost casual statement of the King's cold we realised that there was a much more trying time in

[1] Ellsworth, the American polar explorer who was missing for eight weeks on a flight across the Antarctic.

The board and officers of the P.A. 1967–8, L–R: *Jack Lush, Telecommunications Manager; John Williamson, Editor; Ernest Harvey, Secretary and Assistant General Manager; George Cromarty Bloom, General Manager since 1962; William Barnetson, Chairman; Angus Burnett-Stuart; Leslie Stallard; Kenneth A. Searle; Ernest Hoare; William Morrell; Gordon Linacre*

The headquarters of the Press Association (with flags flying)

Comings and goings at No. 10

R. A. Butler, as Chancellor, arriving for a Cabinet meeting in 1955. P.A. picture by Robert Turner which won an honourable mention in the Encyclopaedia Britannica award

The Queen leaves after dining with Sir Winston Churchill on the eve of his retirement as Prime Minister in 1955. P.A. picture by L. H. Abbott

Squaring the circle

front of us, in which cool heads and endurance were essential.'

There were two main problems in covering the King's illness and death: how to get the news and how to get it back to the P.A. There were no worries on the first account, for the P.A. Court Correspondent, Louis Wulff, was on the spot at Sandringham and if there was any news going he would get it. It was Wulff who had spoken by telephone on the Friday night to Lord Dawson of Penn who had been called to attend the King at Sandringham. From Dawson, Wulff learned the real significance of the 'bronchial catarrh with signs of cardiac weakness'—there was no chance of recovery and the King had three days at most to live. Louis Wulff set out by road through the night to Sandringham. Dick Eccleston followed next morning and on the Sunday afternoon, a third reporter, Louis Nickolls, who later became Exchange Telegraph Court Correspondent, went there, too. The weekend was largely a time of waiting. At Byron House in London the Creed was kept open continuously—'a drastic step', as Martin called it —so that if important news came not a second should be lost in getting it to newspapers. The papers, in turn, stood by. At Sandringham the world's press took possession of the local inn, The Feathers, some sixty of them from the news agencies and major newspapers. Reporters had no hope of a private telephone conversation with their offices. There was only one phone at the inn and whatever they put over could be heard by their colleagues. The length of calls was limited; often the connection was broken before the journalist had finished dictating his copy. Some motored to King's Lynn to telephone.

Faced with heavy foreign competition and the most precarious of links, the three British agencies, the P.A., Exchange Telegraph and Central News, made a pact of mutual assistance, whereby each would pass to the others whatever information it received. The Post Office, which had previously refused to lease private lines, now offered them to the agencies. Each of the agencies booked one line for £80 a month. That was on Monday afternoon, but by nightfall there were still four miles of wire to be laid and the Post Office made it clear the circuits could not be completed until Tuesday. As the P.A. had already warned several papers who had asked for guidance, the King's death was expected before morning. But all the Post Office had managed to do was to run more public lines into The Feathers.

Reporter Anonymous

When the news came at half past nine that Monday evening that the King was dying the atmosphere among the journalists became frenzied. Newspapers and agencies rushed to put in continuous calls both to and from their London offices. The P.A. had already booked a line from 10.30 p.m. until 10 a.m. the following morning. Luck was on its side. Dick Eccleston held on to an uninterrupted line throughout the critical period. Others were not so fortunate. Because of the pressure on the local post office many calls did not mature at all. But the news of the King's death, with which the P.A. led the world, was not given to London over the line held by Eccleston. It came in another call to Henry Martin. This is his record of what happened:

'At 12.4 a.m. I received a certain call. It was a link arranged in advance but upon which I had not relied in case it failed, as was quite likely. The line was very bad; a voice spoke from the far away. Yet the caller could hear my urgent questions. The replies revealed entirely unofficially that the King had died "at a few minutes to midnight". I took the decision to use it, and informed newspapers that it was unofficial. . . . The message was passed to the Exchange over the Joint Service line, which I had had transferred to our editorial table and kept continuously open. The Exchange refused to act upon it. The Central News accepted it, and timed their message a minute later than ours. There was quite that interval. . . .

'This unofficial statement placed newspapers for a moment in a dilemma. The *News Chronicle* acted on it without question, issuing an edition with the lead prepared. . . . The *Daily Express* editor phoned to ask me if he could rely on the news. I told him that he could. He went into action and the *Daily Express* special number was the first to reach the West End on sale. Similar assurances were given to the *Daily Herald* and the *Daily Telegraph*. Meanwhile I had followed up on Creed and D.P. [Direct Printer] with messages that although there was as yet no official confirmation we had every reason to believe that the King was dead, and two minutes later said definitely that he was dead and that the news was correct. By that time Mr. Wulff, our Court Reporter, had telephoned independent confirmation, still unofficially. At 12.15 a.m. we flashed the official confirmation, with the gist of the communiqué a minute later. We also supplied the Exchange, whose line broke down at midnight, and the Central News . . .'

Squaring the circle

Fortune did favour the Press Association but it was the organisation of the whole operation which brought ultimate success. Among the letters of congratulation which Martin received was one from Frank King, chief of the London bureau of the Associated Press of America, which read, 'Our staff man, Charles Nutter, who was at Sandringham, volunteered the opinion that the Press Association coverage of the King's illness and death was the "smoothest, most efficient thing of its kind he had ever seen in his newspaper experience in several countries".'

Arthur Christiansen, the editor of the *Daily Express,* wrote: 'There are times when one thanks God for the Press Association. . . . To you personally special thanks for just that piece of guidance when I telephoned at midnight. I am deeply grateful.'

There was one complaint. The *Scarborough Evening News* wrote an indignant letter of protest because the P.A. had phoned F. C. Whittaker, the proprietor, at midnight on the Friday with the first bulletin. 'They said,' Martin recorded, 'that if that was how we interpreted their instructions to phone urgent news, when no evening paper could print it at that hour, they would come off our emergency list! Mr. Robbins is more patient and long-suffering than I am, so I left him to answer.'

Of Louis Wulff, Martin wrote: 'I understand he made a tremendous impression upon the American journalists, who saw him drive through the gates of Sandringham House in a Daimler and be received with every mark of respect by those on duty, when the rest of the Pressmen were, so to speak, unrecognised. . . .'

The reputation of a news agency is built not upon isolated achievements, outstanding though they may be, but upon consistent competence and reliability and upon the cumulative effect of 'beats' and 'scoops' secured day after day, week after week, year after year. Of necessity, so many journalistic successes of this kind are things of the moment, ephemeral triumphs of which the readers of newspapers may be totally unaware, which are the currency of Fleet Street shop-talk for a few hours and which may linger only in the memory of the individual reporter who performed them. But they are the bricks with which a great news agency like the Press Association has been built.

As Norval Graham, of the Wolverhampton *Express and Star,* said as Chairman in 1935, reviewing the previous year, 'the Editor-in-Chief's records show a remarkable list of first-class "scoops". Unlike, however, the big London newspapers, who lose no opportunity of advertising their achievements day by day, the P.A. has no chance of blowing its own trumpet, and indeed has no wish to. Its reward is that a "scoop" is everybody's property. Provincial subscribers probably never pause to think how often the Press Association during its twenty-four-hour vigil snatches a first-class story from under the nose of a single newspaper which fondly imagines that it is going to have it exclusively. Where big news is, there the P.A. is invariably to be found.'

It would be impossible here to name all those who, between the wars, as part of the editorial team of the Press Association—and that must always include the hundreds of correspondents throughout the country—contributed to its advance. It is no doubt invidious to mention any but some were so outstanding the risk must be taken. Whatever Henry Martin achieved, for instance, was possible because of the able editorial executives who worked under his command: his deputy, Andrew Gray, one of the kindest as well as most conscientious of men; George Wettlauffer, the night editor; Frank Turner, who succeeded Wettlauffer and eventually became deputy editor, having spent most of his working life on the night turn, remaining astonishingly spry and tolerant throughout.

Of all the specialists, the man who probably enjoyed the widest respect and affection among his colleagues was Edmond Painter Stacpoole. Stacpoole—or Staccie as he was known—did not become Lobby Correspondent until 1936, by which time he had already been a P.A. reporter for twelve years. But he quickly established himself in the Lobby and he stayed there for the next thirty years. If ever a man lived for his job, it was he. The Lobby man is one of the privileged inner circle of political journalists. It is a relentless job, demanding, not least, deep reserves of physical and mental stamina. The Lobby Correspondent must be the confidant of politicians but he must also keep himself free of any personal or party political associations which might inhibit his ability to report political news without fear and without partiality. This is true enough even of those journalists who are the Lobby correspondents of newspapers with distinctly partisan political views. It is imperative for the man who serves the Press Association and hence the whole British press, and it is a role which Stacpoole filled until 1966 with distinction and without reproach. A gentle, modest man, he thrived in the assertive,

Squaring the circle

exhibitionist political world, the eyewitness, often a very eloquent one, of most of the historic episodes of our time. Yet, as he himself has said, it was the small incidents which stuck in his mind 'like little tabs to recall big events'. He has remembered the night Neville Chamberlain announced he would fly to Munich to meet Hitler. Stacpoole sprinted along Downing Street to a telephone box in Whitehall to pass on the news. A crowd surged round the box and pulled the door open to hear the story he was dictating to the P.A. He was hemmed in and had to be rescued by a policeman.

Then there was Frank King, the Diplomatic Correspondent, who enjoyed at the Foreign Office the same kind of trust accorded to Stacpoole in the Lobby. There was C. J. Robbins, younger brother of the General Manager, who became chief of the P.A. Parliamentary reporting staff—the largest Gallery team in the House—but who might well have remembered most vividly a macabre incident earlier in his career with the P.A. when he was sent to Watford to cover the police-court hearing of a trunk murder case. When he arrived the small press box was full. With police permission, Robbins had to use the trunk in which a body had lain for these summer weeks to write on. 'The stench,' he has said, 'was appalling.' The P.A.'s crime reporter for twenty-five years from 1930 was Bill Finch, whose dubious privilege it was to witness executions. 'This enabled me,' he said once, with chilling objectivity, 'to watch the reactions of murderers from the start of their crime to their end on the scaffold.'

News-agency reporters, like any others, benefit from competition. Between the wars, the stimulus of rivalry for P.A. reporters slowly dwindled. The London News Agency had been absorbed after the end of the 1914–18 war. Central News held out for long after that, still game, still frisky, but its end became more and more sure. The Central News had tried to underpin its news side by operating as an advertising agency as well, handling mainly financial and company meeting business. In the giddy 1920s this had paid off very well but in the hungover 1930s the income from this source declined. The C.N. also operated a subsidiary called the Column Printing Company which, over a teleprinter system, distributed news to clubs and betting and sports results to private subscribers. Although this business was very much smaller than Extel's in the same field, it was profitable—but not a strong enough buttress for the C.N.'s shaky finances.

Reporter Anonymous

By 1931 the agency had deteriorated far enough as to be in the market. There was some play with the idea that the other two agencies should buy it but it did not become a serious project. Then again, in 1937, it became known that the American-held majority interest in the Central News was up for sale and there were rumours of several possible buyers, including an American agency. The P.A. and Extel saw the threat of an invasion. Extel was primarily interested in the Column Printing Company and the P.A. in the general news and Parliamentary side. Hindsight suggests it would probably have been simpler if each agency had taken at once the portions it wanted. The P.A., however, pressed for joint action. Representatives of the two agencies sat in continuous conference for more than nine hours before deciding to act together. They did the deal with the Central News in half an hour. They put up equal sums to buy majority holdings in the C.N. and in the printing company. To cut down the rate at which the agency was losing money, the new joint owners put an end to its news activities overseas. The outbreak of war made its situation even more gloomy and general home news activities were stopped at the end of 1940. All that then remained of the C.N.'s once brave editorial operations were its Parliamentary service and the supply of a morning and evening London Letter.

This exercise in joint ownership by the Press Association and the Exchange Telegraph illustrated how well their relationship had developed from those stormy days of the Joint Service before the first world war. There were still differences between them in their interpretations of the agreements under which they operated and, from time to time, about proposed action, but never again did they lead on to the follies of litigation. In place of tempestuous Joint Committee Meetings, matters were settled quietly by discussion and correspondence between the P.A. General Manager on the one side and Sir Wilfred King (he was knighted in 1935) and his manager, Charles Wills, on the other. Because so much of the work done by H. C. Robbins was, by its nature, unspectacular, there is danger of underestimating just what he did do for the Press Association. Not the least of his contributions was the forging of this friendly working relationship with the Extel from which both sides profited. At the editorial level, too, where the two agencies were still fully competitive, Henry Martin established amicable relations with his opposite number.

Squaring the circle

By 1929 there was talk of extending this 'healthy cooperation' and in 1931 the two agencies combined their separate Law Courts staffs and set up the Joint Law Service. Each partner employed about half of the staff and there was a fifty-fifty pooling of all expenses and revenue.

That same year brought a legal action of concern to the whole British press. The context of the particular action was horse-racing, but its implications were much wider. The doping of racehorses was becoming a problem and the Jockey Club decided to take sterner measures to try to stamp out the practice. The stewards decided that a horse named Don Pat had been doped. Although there was no evidence that the trainer, a man called Chapman, had been in any way a party to it, they held him responsible for what, presumably, had been done while the horse was in his charge. They 'warned him off'—which meant that he lost his licence as a trainer. (It was restored a couple of years later.)

Notice of the decision was published in the *Racing Calendar*, the official journal. The P.A. circulated it and newspapers published it exactly as they had with hundreds of other disciplinary decisions in the past. But so far as Chapman was concerned, a brief notice that a horse has been doped and the trainer warned off is calculated to convey the impression that the trainer has some share, at least, of the guilt. He issued writs for libel against the Jockey Club, the *Racing Calendar* and various newspapers. A consolidated test action was fought. The jury found for Chapman with heavy damages. Although, on appeal, a new trial was ordered, it was plain that so far as the newspapers were concerned, they were likely to lose. A comprehensive settlement was negotiated by which Chapman received a substantial sum of money.

The P.A. and the press in general were left with a serious problem. Disciplinary decisions of the Jockey Club were certainly of interest to the large section of the public which followed racing. Furthermore, there were other governing bodies, the Football Association for example, which had wide and autocratic powers for control of their constituents and which also, from time to time, issued disciplinary decisions. Were these to be published at risk of a libel action?

The Jockey Club did amend the wording of future announcements about doping to avoid any damaging innuendo but this was not enough in itself to soothe the anxieties of the news agencies

Reporter Anonymous

and newspapers. After all, they were not present when such cases were investigated and they could not know how many legal pitfalls might be concealed in what seemed to be a straightforward decision.

At first, the P.A. decided to continue circulating all such notices. A few months later, they decided against. Finally, after another month, they resumed circulation, having warned all newspapers that publication was their own responsibility. The vast majority of papers took the risk.[1]

For all the enthusiasm which had accompanied the impulsive acquisition of Byron House soon after the first world war, it was not long before its inadequacy became apparent and before much more ambitious proposals were being aired to 'put up an edifice worthy to be the home not only of the P.A., the official representatives of the provincial press in London, but of Reuters Agency with its imperial and international importance and its world connections and ramifications'. The idea was first broached in 1928, only seven years after the P.A. had taken over Byron House. It must have gained some impetus, not only from the steady growth of the P.A. organisation, but also from the discovery, reported in 1931, of cracks in the fabric of Byron House. The foundations had to be strengthened at heavy cost.

In 1934 Sir Edwin Lutyens and H. Rogers Houchin were commissioned to design the new building which was to be built on the site of Byron House and of adjoining properties which the P.A. bought. There was now room for a most impressive building to run back from Fleet Street almost to St. Bride's Avenue. It was reckoned it would cost about £140,000 and that it could be put up in twelve months. In fact, it cost a great deal more than that; it cost with freeholds just under £450,000. It also took much longer than expected to build. The P.A. had to find a temporary home while the new one was being built. It rented the old *Daily Express*

---

[1] This uneasy state of affairs continued until, in 1952, a change in the law of libel extended qualified privilege to the publication of decisions by bodies which, although not courts of law, exercised quasi-judicial functions, either with the consent of their constituents or under statute (as, for example, some Marketing Boards).

Squaring the circle

offices in St. Bride Street and fitted them up at considerable expense. They were to be the headquarters of the P.A. for three and a half inconvenient and uncomfortable years.

The project ran into two big snags over the design. The original intention was a building of at least ten storeys and one hundred feet high. Sir Edwin Lutyens had been confident this would be allowed but the London County Council insisted on a maximum of eighty feet. This meant a complete revision of the plans to reduce the building to nine storeys. Then the Dean of St. Paul's asked for some modification of the upper storeys so that they would not interfere with the view of the Cathedral from Fleet Street; it was said to be 'one of the finest obtainable'. Reluctantly sympathetic, the P.A. agreed to set back the upper floors.

At last, in July 1939, 85 Fleet Street, as the new building was to be called, was near enough finished for the P.A. and Reuters to move in. (Reuters leased more than a half of the working space for themselves and their 'allies'—Commonwealth and foreign newspapers and news agencies with which Reuters had close relations. The P.A. occupied most of the remainder.)

It was the end of a phase in the P.A. history in more ways than one. There was now a new man in the General Manager's chair and, for the first time in nearly sixty years, he was not a Robbins. Although there were still two members of the family working for the P.A.—one as chief of the Association's London service, the other as chief of the Parliamentary reporting staff—the retirement of H. C. Robbins in 1938 meant the end of an era of paternalism. The P.A. was now the employer of many hundreds of men and women but so long as there was a Robbins at the head of it something of the old 'family' atmosphere had remained. With the coming of Edward Davies to take over from Harry Robbins, the administration of the P.A. became, necessarily, much less personal. Davies was certainly a most courteous and fair-minded man in his dealings with the staff, but he had come from outside, he did not share Robbins' sense of continuity and tradition, and the organisation he was to manage was much too complex and demanding to allow him to play the role of father to the staff. The days when the P.A. had still been intimate enough for Edmund Robbins to know everyone by name and to see that a man with a new addition to his family got a little extra in his pay packet were far away in the past.

Reporter Anonymous

Harry Robbins had a great deal to be proud of as he went into retirement. He had spent nearly forty-four years with the P.A.—twenty-one of them as its senior executive—and he had every right to claim a large share of the credit for the safe and successful way in which it had grown. He had laboured honestly and well, a likeable man with a pleasing lack of pretence. At the annual meeting of 1938, at which a presentation was made to him, he spoke of his retirement with a characteristic candour.

'I want to enjoy,' he said, 'what Charles Kingsley once described as the "Blessed, blessed feeling of having nothing to do". After half a century in journalism I feel that I can well enjoy and can deserve a perfect rest—I don't mind being frank and saying absolute laziness . . . You know, Charles Lamb, the day he left the service of the East India Company, wrote, "I have come home today for ever." I think it was a most beautiful phrase. Well, I am going home today for ever. I do not want to do another stroke of work as long as I live if I can avoid it.'

There were other indications of the passing of the old era. At the end of 1939 a man who had put in even more years at the P.A. than Robbins followed him into retirement. That was Percy Shaw, who had been Secretary since 1911 and, despite the occasional brush with the General Manager, had worked alongside him during some of the most important years of P.A. history.[1] It seems likely that Shaw would have liked to have spread himself beyond the responsibilities—heavy enough for most men—of Secretary. He was a man of strong opinions and felt bound to make them known publicly from time to time by writing letters to newspapers for publication.

There was one other change which, though only one of nomenclature, was reflective of the evolution of the P.A. In 1936 the term 'Committee of Management' was dropped. In its place came the more familiar 'Board of Directors'. In turn the Consultative Board became the Consultative Committee. The Board of Directors performed the same functions as the old Management Committee but there had been occasions, especially during the negotiations leading to the building of 85 Fleet Street, when the Committee of Management had felt themselves at a disadvantage because 'although there is no actual difference . . . a communica-

[1] At the time of writing, Harry Robbins was living at Eastbourne, aged ninety-five. Percy Shaw died in 1962 at the age of ninety-one.

Squaring the circle

tion from a Committee of Management does not appear to an outsider to have the same authority as a communication from a Board of Directors'.

Whatever the hostilities between independent papers and the 'chains' elsewhere, inside the P.A. their representatives met and worked together harmoniously in pursuit of common interests. It was recognised, in 1926, when William Will was made a director of the P.A., that a precedent was being established. Will represented the *Daily Dispatch*, Manchester, one of the many papers in the Allied chain. His election was proposed by one of the most tenacious of independents, Walter Scott, of the *Rochdale Observer*. 'We are not called upon today to discuss the question as to whether it is in the best interests of journalism that there should be this concentration and combination of a number of journals,' said Scott. 'Until that question is settled, there is no reason why we should not—in fact, there is every desirability that we should—avail ourselves of the best brains to be had in these combinations.' William Will became Chairman of the P.A. in 1931.

During the 1930s the P.A. enjoyed the services on the Board of a number of outstanding figures of provincial journalism. They included John Scott of the *Manchester Guardian*. His election to the Board in 1931 restored the link between the P.A. and the *Guardian*. During the long years of C.P. Scott's editorship, the *Manchester Guardian*, while buying the P.A.'s news supplies, had played no part in running the organisation which John Edward Taylor had sired; C. P. Scott never bothered to attend a single annual meeting. In 1939 William Haley, of the *Manchester Evening News*, the *Guardian*'s companion paper, became a P.A. director. Haley combined editorial ability with the managerial mind in an unusual and valuable way.

Among those who succeeded to the Chairmanship of the P.A. in the pre-war years were Alex McLean Ewing, of the *Glasgow Herald*, whose shrewd approach and long experience of P.A. affairs were to prove so opportune when he again became Chairman in 1941. John Scott occupied the chair in 1936–7 and was succeeded by that great editor of the *Yorkshire Post*, Arthur Mann. As Allan Jeans of the *Liverpool Post* said when Mann was first elected a director, 'it will do the managerial element . . . no harm to have let loose upon them an undiluted editor.' In the last

203

Reporter Anonymous

year of peace the Chairman was Samuel Storey, who had newspaper interests in Portsmouth and Sunderland and was a Conservative M.P. (He became Deputy Speaker of the Commons in October 1965, and was created a life peer, as Lord Buckton, in the 1966 Dissolution Honours.) As we shall see in the next chapter, Storey was to be deeply concerned in one of the most dramatic episodes in which the Press Association was ever involved.

Thirteen / A mysterious resignation

On the 5th of February 1941 the Press Association and Reuters put out an identical message announcing the resignation of Sir Roderick Jones, the Chairman and Managing Director of Reuters. It was a bald announcement. The reaction in Fleet Street, in the provincial press and among the Reuters staff was one of shock. Sir Roderick's resignation was, to all but a handful, sudden, wholly unexpected and inexplicable. No explanation was given at the time. No adequate explanation has been given since. In his autobiography,[1] published in 1951, Sir Roderick Jones said that the silence had been maintained at his own insistence. He cast out a few hints as to the reasons for his going. They did little to clear up the mystery, although they left a vague impression that Jones had been the victim of a gross injustice. The continuing silence has been unfair to the other men who were involved in the events which led to his retirement. It has not been fair, either, to Sir Roderick Jones, for, despite the impression he tried to convey in his book, the lack of information has fostered the suspicion that he had been guilty, in some way, of dishonourable conduct. That is not the truth of the matter. To understand what really happened we must first have a look at the career and personality of Sir Roderick Jones and also at the relationship between the P.A. and Reuters.

Roderick Jones had an impressive record of achievement. He had been born in England but in his youth went to live in South Africa. It was there, still in his teens, that he began his career with Reuters, distinguishing himself first as a correspondent and, later, from the age of twenty-seven, as the man in charge of all Reuters'

[1] *A Life in Reuters.*

activities and interests in that country. He was only thirty-seven when the 2nd Baron, Herbert de Reuter, died and Jones came back to England to succeed him as head of the agency. He took over the direction of Reuters at a time when it was weak and failing. The war had cut off its European contracts—for the exchange of news services—which had richly nourished it in the past. The foreign investments of the Reuter Bank were frozen. The British Government and the British press shared anxieties for its survival. Roderick Jones was the leading figure in the rescue operation. He gave it back strength, financial stability and brought it the praise and gratitude of Government and people for its wartime service. But in doing so he jeopardised its reputation for independence and editorial integrity. His actions in the first world war are very relevant to his resignation during the second.

For financial reasons and for genuinely patriotic ones, Jones—and Mark Napier, the Reuter Chairman and Jones's partner—decided that the agency must do all it could to aid the Allied cause. That there was need for a reputable British agency to feed the world with news of the war from the British and Allied point of view there was no doubt. What was in question was whether this could be done without incurring the suspicion that Reuter news was tainted by Government control or influence. Jones always believed that it was possible and that he succeeded. He made an arrangement with the British Government whereby Allied communiqués and officially inspired news were transmitted as a service separate and distinct from the normal Reuter service. This special service had a different name; it was called 'Agency Reuter' or 'Agence Reuter' instead of plain 'Reuter'. The Government paid £120,000 a year for its transmission. The nation was well served and well pleased. If there remained some who felt uneasy about this patriotic association of a great world news agency with the British Government, there was also, to be placed in the balance, the abundant admiration for the outstanding despatches by Reuters war correspondents issued by the P.A. in the War Special Service.

What caused much more profound misgiving than the separate transmission of official news was Roderick Jones's own position. In 1917, while continuing as Managing Director of Reuters, Jones accepted the Government's invitation to join the Department of Information—whose head, having given up a Reuter directorship,

A mysterious resignation

was John Buchan—to take charge of cable and wireless propaganda. He spent his mornings at Reuters, the rest of the day at the Department. He received a knighthood in 1918 and soon afterwards agreed to become Director of Propaganda in the newly formed Ministry of Information under Lord Beaverbrook. This was a full-time appointment but Jones refused to take any pay for doing the job and nor would he agree to resign from Reuters. As might have been expected, there were criticisms, including one by a Select Committee on National Expenditure, of the propriety of a top executive of a Government department—even if honorary —retaining his position as head of a commercial organisation which was receiving money from the Government for services rendered. Many felt that Jones could have done one job or the other but not both. There was also, of course, added anxiety over the role of Reuters as a news agency wholly free of Government interference. Jones's dual role was queried at the 1918 annual meeting of the Press Association. The Manager, Harry Robbins, defended it. Jones himself always maintained that the critics were misinformed and short-sighted and that he managed to serve his country and to run an independent agency without any conflict of interests or compromise of principles.

Ill-health forced Jones to resign from the Ministry in September 1918. Not long afterwards the Ministry itself ceased to exist and March the following year saw the last of the 'Agence Reuter' services. With Jones back at Reuters and with an end to Government financing, the heat died out of the controversy. In 1919, with the death of Mark Napier, Roderick Jones became principal proprietor and Chairman and Managing Director of Reuters. He pursued its interests with great energy and skill, and the international soil, in those early post-war years, was fertile. Reuter and Havas, the French news agency, dominated the European news scene and, to a large extent, the world one as well. With the acquiescence of the then General Manager of the Associated Press of America, Melville E. Stone, the British and French agencies carved up Europe, rigidly restricting the German agency, Wolff, and the Austrian one, Korrespondenz-Bureau, to operations inside their own countries. Havas and Reuter defined their respective spheres of interest and signed joint treaties with other European agencies. The forging of the 'National Agencies' Alliance' gave the British and French a dominating role.

Reporter Anonymous

Substantially cushioned against competition, it was a role which, for a while, brought prosperity and permitted them to expand successfully in other continents. But it was too good and too cosy to last. Apart from economic troubles in Britain and the rapidly mounting costs of world news-gathering, the Reuter-Havas supremacy was coming under challenge, most significantly by the Associated Press under a new chief, Kent Cooper. Cooper was a questing, ambitious man, temperamentally incapable of docile acceptance of the status quo. He was impelled idealistically by a belief in the virtues of competition and by a suspicion, shared by other agencies outside Europe, that both the Havas and the Reuter agencies were tainted and that their continuing dominance was inimical to the interests of free and objective news-gathering and dissemination. This is not the place to detail the battles Cooper, with the biggest home newspaper press in the world behind him, fought during his crusade. It is enough to observe here that the barriers to the free exchange of news and the free activity of the world's news agencies were gradually broken down and the more he succeeded the harder life became for Reuters.

Understandably, like any man or nation which sees its privileges threatened, Sir Roderick Jones strove over the years to resist the intrusions of Kent Cooper, the American who did not understand the rules of the European news agency game. But Jones was too wise a man not to prepare against the evil day. From time to time he had aired the idea that Reuters should be owned one day by the British press. In his book he erects this into an ideal that inspired his actions above all other considerations. When the second Baron de Reuter had died in 1916, said Jones, the future of Reuters had been in great danger, if not of dying, then of falling into undesirable hands. He and Napier had saved it then by finding the money—British money—to buy up the entire Reuter shareholding and to form a new private company to run the agency. He felt strongly, as he wrote many years later, 'that the future of so important a national and international organisation should not be dependent upon the life of one man, myself, and be open at my death to the danger that threatened it during the last war'. He saw ownership of Reuters by the British press as a means of ensuring its financial stability and its continuing freedom from injurious political or commercial influence.

Roderick Jones was a patriotic man and one with a grandiloquent concept of his public duty. Undoubtedly he saw the passing of Reuters from his own hands into those of the whole British press as a fulfilment of that duty. But Sir Roderick was also a very good businessman with a clear perception of his own interest. It is therefore possible to suggest that his wish to see the British press buy his interest in Reuters was given some urgency by his recognition that harder times lay ahead. He wanted to sell out at a good price while the going was good.

From the beginning of P.A. operations until 1925, the relations between the Press Association and Reuters had been fruitful and on the whole harmonious. They had worked closely together and each had strengthened the other. But they had been separate bodies, bound only by a recognition of mutual interest. In 1925, while retaining separate identities, their relationship underwent a radical change.

In that year Sir Roderick Jones offered for sale a half-share in Reuters. He offered it to the Newspaper Proprietors' Association, as representing the London press, and to the Press Association, representing the provincial press, the idea being that each should buy $25\frac{1}{2}$ per cent of Reuters. He also offered them an option to take up part of the remaining shares. Jones himself described in his book the fascinating comings and goings which followed. The result was that, after four months of negotiations and conferences, the London papers were unable to agree among themselves and the N.P.A. decided to stay out of Reuters. The provincial papers regretted this, for the P.A. shared the view that Reuters ought to be the concern of the whole British press. But the P.A. went ahead anyway, and bought a controlling interest of 53 per cent in Reuters for £160,000.

'Our primary object,' as Arthur Pickering of Middlesbrough, the Chairman at the time, said, 'has been to safeguard from the possibility of contamination and from exploitation the sources of foreign news.' It was a worthy, even noble, motive and the provincial newspapermen had every reason to be proud of themselves. They left open to the London papers the chance of buying part of the remaining Reuter shareholding, either as a body or as individual papers. Had the London papers taken up this option they would have bought only a minority share in Reuters. But as they had made clear during the initial negotiations that they wanted the upper hand and saw the provincial press playing a subordinate role—a concept Jones rejected—the provincials would have been more than charitable if they had offered to forsake the advantage they had bought for themselves. However, the London papers did not come in. At the end of 1930 the Press Association bought all the rest of the Reuter shares—with the exception of one thousand shares which Sir Roderick continued to hold until his retirement. The price this time was £157,500. So, in all, the P.A. had paid Jones £317,500.

The Press Association—the provincial press—now owned Reuters. After the first deal the P.A. appointed four of the seven Reuter directors. After 1930 every P.A. director was also a Reuter director. John Buchan, who had returned to Reuters after the war, continued as Deputy Chairman until, as Lord Tweedsmuir, he retired to become Governor General of Canada. Jones continued as Chairman and Managing Director, in the first place for ten years until the end of 1935. He received £6500 a year and a 10 per cent commission on all profits over £13,000. (The average net profit for the six years before the P.A. bought its interests had been between £25,000 and £26,000.) Jones was given a contract for a further five years until the end of 1940, during which period he received £8500 a year.

The ownership had changed hands but the executive control, and, to a large extent, the policy-making, stayed where they had been before, in the hands of Sir Roderick Jones. He was a man of high administrative calibre and the P.A. directors, for many years, were happy to leave him with a free hand. He knew the business, they did not. The traditional P.A. system, whereby directors served a term of years on the Board, passing through the Chair and then retiring, worked well enough in the home news agency. Limiting a man's membership of the Board to seven years did not seriously weaken its quality because any man elected as a director was already familiar with many of the problems of the P.A. Reuters was a very different matter. The jungle of the world news-agency business was unknown territory to the provincial news-papermen and seven years on the Reuter Board did not make them sufficiently informed to play a positive or critical role. That suited Sir Roderick Jones very well. He had no intention of sharing his control. He might have to go through the motions of democratic government. He might have to give his fellow-directors the impression of participating in the control of Reuters—and this he

A mysterious resignation

could do well for he was capable of great charm and courtesy. But what he gave them was the illusion; he retained the reality.

Roderick Jones was an autocrat who lived and ran his business autocratically. He had a grand, vice-regal manner. When, every two or three years, he made his extensive tours abroad, it was not in the style of a mere businessman, however successful and important. For him there were never any moments of unseemly haste, none of the fatigues of airline travel and overnight stops. His was a stately and dignified progress by ship or, if overland, by decorous private railway coach. Rarely did he suffer the impersonalities of hotel life. Wherever he went, it was either to friends with yachts or country houses or as the guest of the British ambassador or governor; receptions and dinner parties were held in Jones's honour. In London he had an impressive house at Hyde Park Gate where he and his wife—Enid Bagnold, the writer—entertained people who were somebody. Jones was an accepted figure in political and diplomatic circles, in good Society and among the mighty and sometimes bold barons of Fleet Street.

Roderick Jones was a small man. It was a P.A. man who said of him, 'He was very nearly a great man—all he lacked was a few inches in height.' He had a spare, trim body, straight back and he was good on a horse. He had been a master of hounds in the Cape. His taste in clubs was inoffensively catholic: Brooks's, Travellers', Beefsteak, Garrick and Hurlingham. He even became chairman of the governing council of Roedean. The clothes, of course, were all that one would expect of such a man and on formal occasions he could deck himself out in some exotic orders and decorations: the Legion of Honour; Knight Commander of the Order of the Saviour from Greece; First Class of the Order of the Brilliant Jade from China; a grand officer of the Order of the Crown of Italy. Sir Roderick Jones played to distinction the role of the head of a great world news agency, both in his presence and in his talents, a consummate negotiator, a formidably persuasive charm, a safe repository for high-level indiscretions.

At Reuters he expected and received reverence and awe from his staff. He cared for his staff and praised their work as from a royal height; any who caused displeasure to come to the sovereign's eye was wise to seek other employment. Jones's entrances and exits were attended with suitable ceremonial. There was, for instance, a set plan which was put into action the moment

Reporter Anonymous

he said to his secretary, 'I am ready to go.' A call went to his chauffeur to bring the car, which was garaged round the corner from the office, to the front entrance. A boy was sent out to jump up and down on the pneumatic pad controlling the traffic lights so that Sir Roderick's car should be unimpeded and he should not be kept waiting. In the entrance hall the commissionaires lined up ready to salute him as he left. At the moment he walked out through the door the car drew up.

Jones lorded it over his fellow-directors on the Reuter Board. There is no doubt that he considered these men from the provinces his inferiors and that he would have preferred the company around that table of the peers of Fleet Street, of Kemsley, Rothermere, Riddell, Beaverbrook, Burnham, Camrose and Major John Jacob Astor of *The Times*. As it was, he treated the P.A. directors with charming condescension. He made them feel how fortunate were they, whose experience was so confined and whose reputations were so parochial or, at best, insular, to be with him, the man of the big world, the friend of the mighty and powerful. When it came to the skilful art of name-dropping, there were few who could compete with Roderick Jones—or, to be fair, who had such a globally distinguished acquaintance to call upon. Jones was too clever a man to give his colleagues direct offence. So long as it did not interfere with his own plans or run contrary to his own ideas, he appeared only too happy to adopt the occasional suggestion they put to him. But he kept secret from them the kind of basic information about what the company was doing, how it was being organised, what he intended for the future, which is the right of any Board of Directors.

During the five years immediately following the first purchase of Reuter shares, when the P.A. members of the Reuter Board had only a bare majority, there seems to have been little disposition to question or criticise Jones. This may have been due, partly at least, to the permissive wording of his contract, which authorised him 'to act in such manner as shall be in the best interests of the company', although it also provided that 'he shall comply with the instructions of the board'. The Board did not know enough about the workings of the company to be able to issue instructions. Successive P.A. Chairmen did try to impress on Sir Roderick the need for remedying this state of affairs but generally with little success. Whenever he was approached, Jones always assured the

A mysterious resignation

Board he was only too willing to give all the information asked for. He welcomed the indications that his fellow-directors were becoming more interested in Reuter affairs, for that could only be to the good of the company. But in practice he went on much as before and the Board remained largely as ignorant as before. As one P.A. Chairman observed, 'Reuter affairs always gave me the impression of intangible influences operating behind the scenes because R.J. seemed to be possessed of an Oriental mind which exhibited a most disarming blandness.'

This 'blandness', this seeming willingness, even eagerness, to fall in with suggestions made to him, disarmed his colleagues on the Board and carried him through successfully. But even before the final rupture of his association with Reuters there had been occasions when he went too far and his colleagues, suffering gladly for the most part, rebelled. The first and most important of these concerned the relationship between Reuters—and hence the P.A.—and the Associated Press under Kent Cooper.

When the cartelisation of news was at its height, with Havas and Reuter having successfully arranged world news-agency activities to their own rich convenience, the Associated Press, as a Reuter client, had been subject to restrictions on the sale of its own news outside North America. This, as we have seen, was unacceptable to Kent Cooper. Persistently, while maintaining superficially friendly relations with Jones, Cooper campaigned against these restrictions, gaining one small concession after another. The conflict was brought to a climax, however, by Cooper's ambitions to operate freely in the Far East. Japan and China were, traditionally, Reuter territory, where Reuters had exclusive rights in the buying and selling of news. In 1932 Roderick Jones did concede that the Associated Press might enter the international news market in China and Japan but when, in the following year, Cooper went to Japan and made a contract with a Japanese news agency which placed the A.P. on an equal footing with Reuters, Jones blew up. Cooper had done nothing which he was not permitted to do under the 1932 concession but he had done it without first telling Sir Roderick. This, from an agency still allied to Reuters and one which Sir Roderick obviously regarded as still in some way subject to his imperial throne, was intolerable.

Jones called a special meeting of the Reuter Board and denounced the long-standing Reuter-A.P. agreement. The other

Reporter Anonymous

members of the Board cannot have understood fully at the time quite what it was all about, what they were agreeing to and what the implications were for the P.A. Through Reuters, the Press Association and the Associated Press, which were very similar in constitution, had exchanged their news. Both enjoyed the arrangement. Kent Cooper had in the past visited the P.A. and liked what he saw and the people he met. Jones's denunciation of the alliance between A.P. and Reuters would have meant that the Press Association would have had to get its North American news from elsewhere, presumably from the United Press, A.P.'s chief rival. Whatever the quality of the U.P. coverage, it was not what the Press Association wanted—which was, simply, a continuation of the old arrangement with A.P. Kent Cooper wrote to the General Manager of the Press Association, Harry Robbins, telling him what had happened. Robbins was horrified and put his own views strongly to the P.A. Board that the connection with the A.P. was a valuable one and their own interests would be damaged if it were severed.

The P.A. Board, convinced, went into action. To Kent Cooper they sent a message suggesting further conversations. To Roderick Jones they expressed their opinions with unusual vigour. Jones saw that they meant to get their way and, wisely, submitted with grace. He went to New York where he negotiated a new agreement. This liberated both agencies from the old restrictions. (In the past, Reuters' service in the United States had been strictly confined to the A.P.; this had been part of the pre-war Four-Party Treaty, to which Reuter, Havas, A.P. and the German agency, Wolff, had put their signatures.) Now Reuters and A.P. could sell their news services anywhere they liked in the world without the other's agreement. The restrictive arrangements between Havas and Reuter and the European agencies in the Continent of Europe lingered on but the New York deal meant a major break with the past. So far as the Press Association was concerned, the outcome was wholly satisfactory. A direct contract was signed between the Press Association and the Associated Press by which the A.P. received the P.A. service by direct teleprinter at its London office, while, on behalf of the P.A., Reuters, in New York, received the A.P. teleprinter service. This contract gave the P.A. an independent voice in the event of any future crisis in the relationship between Reuters and the Associated Press.

A mysterious resignation

Another cause of friction between Sir Roderick and the P.A. was the project to put up the new building to house both Reuters and the P.A. At the beginning of 1935, the Reuter Board made the rather strange proposal that Reuters should erect the building on the basis of a ninety-nine-year lease granted by the P.A. as owners of the freeholds. When the P.A. Board met they rejected this idea and decided to go ahead with the business entirely as a direct P.A. investment, though under the control of a joint P.A.-Reuter building committee. This incident illustrates the curious ambivalence of P.A. directors who were also, of course, the same men, plus Jones, who constituted the Reuter Board. In 1936 it was discovered that notices to owners of neighbouring buildings about rights of light were being issued by the architects in the name of Reuters—though the P.A.'s name was included as well. The P.A. Board promptly laid it down that all future documents should be solely in the name of the P.A.

Sir Roderick Jones was, until 1938, the only member of the building committee who was always in London. He bore the brunt of much of the work connected with it. He thought of the building as the Reuter building and in his book assigns the P.A. interest in it to a subordinate role and talks of the P.A. being backed by the substantial resources of Reuters—which, as the P.A. owned Reuters, was another way of saying the P.A. had its own resources behind it. When it came to announcing the move into the new building, each organisation sent out its own publicity. The Reuter material made only the most casual reference to the P.A. share in the venture. There was also irritation at the way he tried to qualify the responsibility of the P.A. General Manager for administering the building. These latter incidents occurred just before the war started. They annoyed the P.A. directors but, had they known it, there were much more serious things to worry about.

During the 1930s Reuters began to lose more and more money on its news services and to rely upon the profitable commercial services to finance them. Competition from the American agencies and from European agencies, many State-subsidised, cut into traditional Reuter markets. The quality and quantity of the news services fell off. Economies affected their efficiency and their growing inadequacy resulted in further loss of custom. One consequence was a paucity of British news in foreign countries. The propaganda churned out by the Axis powers went virtually unchallenged by the British. This was particularly true of South America and the situation concerned many people. Reuters came in for criticism. Yet it could not afford to increase its supplies of British news sent abroad, unless the British papers paid substantially more to Reuters or the Government made it possible for Reuters to send our more news without its costing the agency any more. That was the background to the events which led to Sir Roderick Jones's ultimate resignation.

During the crisis period which preceded the Munich agreement of September 1938 the British Government gave Reuters the facilities it needed to increase the flow of British news overseas. Much of Reuters' normal news services was sent out by wireless. What the Government now offered was free transmission facilities at Rugby for expanding those services. No money passed between Government and news agency. There was no official interference with the content of the services, only an understanding that the world would be getting more British news through Reuters. The arrangement appealed to Roderick Jones. He was able to improve his news services. At the same time the news agency was once again, as it had been in the first world war, performing a patriotic service.

In the summer of 1939 Jones mentioned to the Reuter Board that negotiations were going on between him and Government representatives to expand the Reuter wireless services still further. He added that pressure was being put on him to agree to conditions which he believed were not compatible with the independence of Reuters. But, he said, the Board could rely on him to defend and maintain the integrity of the company.

At the September 1939 Board meeting Sir Roderick reported that he had signed an agreement with the Ministry of Information. He believed, he said, it was a very good one from Reuters' point of view and he asked his colleagues to give their approval. He had provided them with a long memorandum about the agreement. He seemed to have done a straightforward business deal with the Government. Reuters, he had agreed, would enlarge its news services to Europe and to the rest of the world outside the western hemisphere, by means of free wireless transmissions from Rugby and Leafield. The Government recognised that to collect and prepare this extra news would involve Reuters in additional expendi-

A mysterious resignation

ture it could not hope to recoup. So the Ministry would pay Reuters just under £20,000 a year. The only condition attached, said Jones in his memorandum, was that because these payments might swell the Reuter profits, the Government should have a share in any benefit. Reuters would be subject, in effect, to a 60 per cent excess profits tax and, in order to assess the agency's liability, Government auditors were to have access to Reuter accounts.

Jones assured the Board meeting there were no further, undisclosed obligations except that the Government would expect Reuters to 'take heed' of any suggestions about these additional services. The P.A. directors were uneasy about the meaning of those two words. There was a long discussion about the dangers of Government intrusion. Roderick Jones gave them an assurance that if the Government were ever to interpret those words as giving them the right to influence the content of Reuter news services he would be the first to resist them and to repudiate the contract. With that, the contract having been signed by Jones, the Board gave their approval.

The directors still felt uneasy, however. They were anxious, as their predecessors twenty years before had been, about the possible injury to Reuters' reputation by any close association with Government. But the Government contract was not the only cause of their anxiety. That was just one more example of the way Sir Roderick Jones acted without informing or consulting his colleagues as they believed he should. Jones had been given his head for so long that he had developed a Gaullist presumption about his status. I am Reuters, he seemed to say, and Reuters is me.

There had been another example, earlier in 1939, of his presenting his Board with an accomplished fact. Present, by Jones's invitation, at three Board meetings was Christopher Chancellor, Reuters' Far East General Manager. At the last of these meetings, the Board were somewhat surprised when, after the minutes had been read, Sir Roderick announced that he had appointed Chancellor as a third General Manager of the company to be permanently resident in London.

The P.A. directors got together after the meeting and Alexander McLean Ewing, of the *Glasgow Herald*, who had become Deputy Chairman of Reuters when John Buchan left, was deputed to talk to Jones. He told him that in future, before making appointments of this importance, the Board should be consulted. The Board, said Ewing, had to look ahead to the time when they might need to find a successor to Jones and they would not like to think that Chancellor had been brought to London to be foisted on them some day as Sir Roderick's nominee for the post. Jones assured the Board at a later meeting he had no such intention, although he looked upon Chancellor as one of Reuters' best men. The only reason he had brought Chancellor to London, said Jones, was so that he and the Board would have a chance of assessing his merits. (As the Board were to discover, Christopher Chancellor was a young man of outstanding ability—but that was not the point of their objection.) The other members of the Board had good reason to remember these meetings and Jones's words at a later stage.

The men with whom Sir Roderick was dealing now were not the kind to play indefinitely a passive role, merely giving their approval after the event to his unilateral decisions. McLean Ewing, for example, had been on the P.A. Board—and therefore on the Reuter Board—since 1930, and he had been Deputy Chairman of Reuters since 1935. He was very familiar with Jones's imperious behaviour. Ewing was a very canny Scottish accountant, a man who was opposed to impetuous action and who sought his objectives by long, patient, reasonable negotiation. If Jones respected any of his P.A. colleagues it was McLean Ewing, and Ewing, for all his growing doubts about Roderick Jones, appreciated what he had done for Reuters in the past and recognised his value. James Henderson, of the *Belfast News-Letter*, could trace his family membership of the P.A. back to its earliest days and he had an aggressive pride in the provincial press. Herbert Staines, of the *Sheffield Telegraph*, and F. C. Whittaker, of the *Scarborough Evening News*, were men with a similar sense of tradition, and Raymond Derwent, of the *Bradford Telegraph and Argus*, was especially jealous of Reuters' independent reputation. But the two men who were most resolved to make Jones change his ways were Samuel Storey, M.P., of the *Sunderland Echo*, as energetic a director of the P.A. and Reuters as he was a newspaper proprietor, and William Haley, of the *Manchester Evening News*, who could find some detached amusement in watching Roderick Jones in action but had no intention of being his tractable courtier.

A mysterious resignation

It was McLean Ewing's inclination to avoid trouble whenever possible, to find a compromise course of action when parties were in dispute. But he was certainly not a weak man and, after the Board meeting at which Jones announced the contract with the Ministry of Information, he shared his colleagues' view that the time had come for positive action. They resolved that Roderick Jones must either agree to reforms in the way he was running Reuters or they would give him notice.[1]

During the next two months they had a number of meetings with Jones and before the end of the year he submitted to the Board a programme of reforms which the directors—and the Consultative Committee, which included John Scott, of the *Manchester Guardian*, and Arthur Mann, of the *Yorkshire Post*—considered satisfactory. They saw the first practical result in an administrative report which Sir Roderick presented to the Board at the end of January 1940; it contained just the kind of information which he should have been supplying from the day the P.A. became majority shareholders in Reuters. Everyone was pleased and relieved to feel the major cause of friction had been removed and a new phase in their relationship with Jones had begun.

Soon afterwards, however, the P.A. directors became aware that senior members of the Reuters' staff were acutely concerned about Jones's conduct of the company's affairs. No men, it seemed, dare offer the slightest criticism of him and it had become impossible for them to discharge their own responsibilities efficiently. The P.A. Board decided that Roderick Jones must go at the end of the following year, 1941. To spare Sir Roderick's dignity, they agreed not to serve the notice in a cold, legal fashion, but by an exchange of letters between him and the Chairman of the P.A. Other developments were to prevent such a leisurely and seemly end to Jones's long and distinguished career at Reuters.

In October 1940, and again in November, Sir Roderick reported to the Reuter Board on meetings he had had with Frank Pick, the Director General of the Ministry of Information. Pick was pressing Jones to allow the Ministry some positive control over Reuters. Jones told the Board he was opposing any suggestion of interference with Reuters' independence. The other directors were not satisfied. They asked Samuel Storey to investigate

[1] Sir Roderick's contract was due to expire at the end of 1940 but he had to receive twelve clear months' notice of termination.

the relations between the Government and Reuters and authorised him to take any steps he thought fit. He went to work and, although his information was incomplete, he quickly learned enough to justify the apprehension he and his colleagues felt. At Storey's suggestion, he, James Henderson, the P.A. Chairman, and McLean Ewing met together in Glasgow. Henderson and Ewing asked Storey to see Pick and try to get a full account of the situation.

Pick told Storey that he had finished his negotiations with Sir Roderick Jones and that Jones was going to circulate a draft agreement to his fellow-directors before the next meeting of the Reuter Board in December—at which he, Frank Pick, was to be present. When Jones sent out the draft to his colleagues, with verbal alterations suggested by himself, he urged them to give their approval to the agreement in writing, without waiting for a Board meeting. Pick was pressing for signature, he told them, but he assured them that, as amended, the document was innocuous. Once it had been signed, he added, nothing more would ever be heard of it.

Not a single member of the Board gave his assent. Far from finding the document harmless, it seemed to them to give the Ministry such powers to interfere in Reuters that the company's independence would be grievously impaired.

While this was going on, under pressure from the Board to let them get into closer touch with the organisation and get to know the General Managers better, Sir Roderick held a dinner party for his fellow-directors and his top executives. Even by Jones's standards of entertaining, this party was staged with a style of astounding magnificence—'with just about one butler to each chair', as one of the guests has recalled. Nothing that could be calculated to impress and intimidate was missing. But if Jones had hoped to induce in his colleagues such a feeling of awe that they would thereafter stifle their criticisms, he was to be disappointed. They came away the more determined to find out what was going on.

The P.A. Board held an emergency meeting in Leeds immediately before the December meeting in London of the Reuter Board. Its purpose was to determine their attitude towards the draft agreement. They decided to have nothing to do with the Pick document. The discussions continued in a first-class com-

A mysterious resignation

partment of the train from Leeds to London. McLean Ewing said it would be easier for them to take positive action over Roderick Jones if they could be sure that Samuel Storey was prepared to give all the time necessary to running Reuters. Storey told Ewing, as he had already told Henderson privately, that he would be pleased to tackle the job if the need arose.

Frank Pick came to the Reuter Board meeting to expound his ideas but no decision had been taken on them a week later when he resigned from the M.o.I. His successor, Sir Walter Monckton, was invited to the January meeting. Sir Walter said he had not yet seen all the papers relating to the negotiations and he would let them have his views later. The Board appointed a three-man committee—Jones, Haley and Storey—to deal with Monckton and to conclude an agreement with him, provided they were satisfied it did not contain anything which could compromise the integrity of Reuters.

A few days later, Storey and Haley had a meeting with Sir Walter. He asked them a strange question—or it seemed strange to them at first.

'Are the Board of Reuters satisfied,' he asked them, 'that they know of all the agreements between H.M. Government and Reuters?' He laid particular stress on what was known as the '1939 Agreement'—the one by which the Government had paid Reuters to increase its wireless news services. The two directors told Monckton that Jones had submitted the agreement to the Board after signing it. They also mentioned their anxiety about the expression in it—'that Reuters would take heed' of any Government wishes about the Reuter services. But, they added, Sir Roderick had assured them it had little significance. Then came the shock.

The 1939 Agreement, said Monckton, did not stand alone. There was a supplementary agreement, dated August 1939, which Lord Perth, who was dealing with the matter at the time, had sent to Sir Roderick Jones. In that supplementary agreement—which became known as the Perth Letter—it was stated that Reuters bound itself to put into operation certain specific changes in its administration and that the Perth Letter must be regarded as an integral part of the main document. Sir Roderick Jones, added Monckton, had signified his receipt of the Letter and his acceptance of it. The date of that acceptance, as his colleagues were to realise, had been some two weeks before he had submitted the principal agreement to them at the September Board meeting.

Haley and Storey asked Monckton if he could show them the Perth Letter and Jones's acceptance of it. Sir Walter replied that it was not for him to inform any Reuter director of facts relating to their business of which they should have been aware. They should ask Sir Roderick Jones for copies of all correspondence, he said.

The two P.A. men acted immediately. They asked Jones for copies of all correspondence which had passed between himself and the Government representatives during the negotiations. 'I can assure you, gentlemen,' Sir Roderick replied, 'the Agreement stands alone and there are no other letters in existence which have any bearing on it.'

On Monday, the 3rd of February 1941, the seven P.A. members of the Reuter Board met in London. Haley and Storey reported to them. The Board authorised the two men to go back to Jones and tell him they had definite information of the existence of a letter from Lord Perth which accompanied the agreement and of the acceptance of its terms by him. Was he prepared to hand over those documents or must they apply to the Government for them? Thus confronted, Jones produced the Perth Letter from his file.

The two men returned to their colleagues with the letter which Storey read to them before passing it round for inspection. In the preamble it was stated that the Letter was to be regarded as an integral part of the main Agreement; that Sir Roderick would 'forthwith' appoint Christopher Chancellor to be the principal General Manager of the company and to be the medium for communication between H.M. Government and Reuters; that the Board of Reuters would make arrangements to separate the offices of Chairman and Managing Director, and that the Reuter Board would consult the wishes of the Government in making appointments to important positions.

A formal meeting of the Reuter Board was held at which Sir Roderick Jones was questioned about the letter and his acceptance of it. Jones said that so far as he was concerned the Perth Letter had no existence as a valid and effective document because it was only a draft which had never been signed or acknowledged by him

A mysterious resignation

as operative. He was asked how he had come to have acknowledged it to Perth. Jones said that what he was acknowledging was a draft only and that consequently his acceptance must also be regarded as merely a draft. Therefore, he said, he had been justified in saying that no letters had been exchanged when the question was first put to him.

'Is there any colleague of mine on this Board,' asked Jones, 'who believes that I have withheld information or documents from him?'

'I do,' said one member of the Board.

Sir Roderick Jones rose from his chair, picked up his papers, put them under his arm and walked out of the room. His dignity, his bearing, even at that terrible moment, won the admiration of his colleagues. But there was no doubt in their minds about what must happen. Their indignation was great. There was a proposal that he should be summarily dismissed from office and it looked for a while as though that course would be followed. But ultimately it was agreed that McLean Ewing, as an old friend, should see him and suggest to him that he should offer his resignation—though Ewing was to be armed with a copy of a motion for his dismissal if he should resist.

James Henderson, as Chairman of the P.A., went with Ewing to see Roderick Jones. The interview was short but painful. Jones agreed to resign. The terms of the public announcement would be drafted by him. There would be no explanation of his decision. He would receive his full emoluments up to the end of 1941 and a pension of £5000 a year for the rest of his life.

There is no need to go into further detail about the final stages of his departure from Reuters. The attitude taken by the P.A. directors now has its own ample justification. Of Sir Roderick Jones three things should be said. First, that until the latter years of his Reuter career he had been an outstandingly successful head of the company. Second, that he had been encouraged in his autocratic ways by his fellow-directors for a long, long time and if, in 1939, he behaved as though he were a law unto himself, it was scarcely surprising and he was probably unaware of usurping the rights which belonged to the Board. Third, that the agreement he made with the Government was not, in his view, one which could harm the reputation of Reuters. He believed it brought financial help to the company when it was badly needed and also enabled

Reporter Anonymous

Reuters to perform its patriotic duty as he believed it should do. He had always believed that he had managed to perform his dual role in the first world war without compromising his own integrity or that of Reuters; he clearly believed he could do so again. To the last, he was, according to his own lights, an honourable man acting in the best interests of his company and his country.

The Reuter Board was now composed entirely of P.A. directors and they found themselves suddenly loaded with the burden of running Reuters. The capable executives who had looked after day-to-day operations under Sir Roderick were still there but the responsibility for higher policy belonged to the men from the P.A. The first thing they did—Henderson proposing, Ewing seconding—was to elect Samuel Storey as the new Chairman of Reuters. He threw himself into the work with great vigour. He gave up the managing directorship of his own papers. He was conscious of neglecting his political career—he was at that time Parliamentary Private Secretary to Florence Horsbrugh, Parliamentary Secretary, Ministry of Health. He worked long hours at Reuters, making arrangements to sleep on the premises. Aided by the three General Managers he initiated numerous improvements in the Reuter administration and services. But his term of office was to be a short one.

Although, in 1925, the Newspapers Proprietors' Association had rejected the offer of an equal share with the P.A. in the ownership of Reuters, with the going of Roderick Jones, the London papers decided it was time they had a voice in the direction of Reuters. Jones had been close to the Fleet Street proprietors and so long as he was at the head of Reuters they were content to stay outside. But they were shocked by his resignation; they knew nothing of the real reasons for his going—or only as much as he had told one or two of them himself; and they felt that if Reuters was to survive and they were going to take its services they must have a hand in it. Because of the rumours which had been going around they were also suspicious of the relationship between the agency and the Government. Lord Kemsley, in whom Jones had confided some of his anxieties during the months of friction preceding his resignation, played a leading role in the moves to bring the N.P.A. into Reuters.

On 21 March 1941, six weeks after Sir Roderick's resignation,

A mysterious resignation

the N.P.A. made a formal request that the P.A. Board should receive a deputation. A meeting was arranged for 8 April, when Lord Rothermere, as Chairman of the N.P.A., tabled a long memorandum. It reviewed past history, stressed the need for Reuters' independence and efficiency, referred to the increasing activities of the American news agencies, and proposed joint working between the provincial and national newspapers. Under this proposal the P.A. would sell half of its Reuter shareholding to the N.P.A. The memorandum stressed that the joint working would not depreciate the position of the provincial press and that the London newspapers were making their request in a spirit of collaboration. It also said:

'If common agreement cannot be found we would have to ask Reuters to disclose to us what steps are being taken to organise the collection of news in the present German-controlled countries and elsewhere. Agencies that are now mere puppets of their governments must be suspect for many years and we should have to know the sources of foreign news so that we could determine whether we should remain as subscribers or organise our own news collecting and distributing agency, or make other arrangements. We doubt if the provincial newspapers have the experience necessary to satisfy us who have our own representatives in all parts of the world.'

At their first meeting with the N.P.A., the P.A. Board merely told Lord Rothermere that they already had been considering the possibility of broadening the Reuter ownership and they would consider the proposal. Two special Board meetings followed and one of the Consultative Committee. There was a split both among the directors and the members of the Committee, but a majority voted in favour of negotiations with the N.P.A.

The minority did not object to the London papers having an interest in Reuters but did not see why they should have an equal share. Having carried Reuters alone for sixteen years they felt that to offer the N.P.A. an equal partnership would be altogether too generous. There has never been any love lost between the provincial press and the national papers and there is no doubt the minority feared that, with an equal shareholding, the N.P.A. would dominate Reuters. The effect of this, they felt, apart from any blow to provincial pride, would be a Reuters run in the interests of the London papers, its services geared to their needs rather than those of the provincial press. This minority did not like what they took to be the threat in Rothermere's memorandum that if the P.A. did not agree to the N.P.A. proposals, the London papers would start their own agency or deal with Reuters' rivals. Nor did they like being told that they, unlike the London papers, were incapable of running a worldwide news agency. They recognised that Reuters would need substantial financial backing in the years ahead but they held that, if the worst came to the worst, the provincial papers had the resources to continue on their own.

The majority argued that arrangements could be made to avoid any possibility of the N.P.A. dominating Reuters. They did not take Rothermere's 'threat' seriously. Above all, they believed it would be to the advantage of all for Reuters to be owned by the whole British press, that N.P.A. experience and finance would be of great value in sustaining and developing the agency and in relieving the P.A. of what might well become a very onerous financial burden.

The negotiations went ahead but the split remained and eventually spread to the whole P.A. membership. It was to prove the sharpest and most serious difference of opinion in the whole history of the P.A. to this day. At the time of the first meeting with the London papers, James Henderson was Chairman of the P.A. He was one of those who opposed the idea of equal partnership but, within a month, his year of office had ended and he was succeeded as Chairman by Alexander McLean Ewing. (This was Ewing's second spell in the chair.) During the next six months McLean Ewing's equable temperament and talent for conciliation were to be fully extended. His contribution to the ultimate success of the negotiations was a most positive one.

For nearly five months a sub-committee of the P.A. Board—McLean Ewing, William Haley and Raymond Derwent—negotiated with the N.P.A. Finally, it was agreed that the London newspapers, through the N.P.A., should buy one half of the issued capital of Reuters at £4 10s. a share, the price paid by the P.A. in 1930. This meant a total payment of just under £170,000. The *Daily Express*, as represented by Leslie (Dick) Plummer, thought this price too high and observed with detached admiration that the P.A. negotiators had struck a very good bargain. At first sight, the plans for the future composition of the Reuter Board

A mysterious resignation

were surprising. It was to consist of six directors, three appointed by each party. Even if one or two directors were absent, each party was to retain its power to cast three votes. There was to be no Chairman; one of the directors would preside at meetings but without any additional or casting vote. A Reuter Trust was to be set up which would declare the intention of the proprietors to carry on the agency efficiently and not for profit—there were not to be any dividends—and to maintain its integrity and independence. Each party was to appoint four trustees to ensure that the ideals of the Trust were upheld and also to settle any matter upon which the Board failed to agree. Some considered this a formula for deadlock and indecisive management. Others, including William Haley who had a big hand in the drafting, argued that if a proposed line of action was so contentious that fourteen men could divide equally for and against it then it could not be the kind of action that ought to be taken. The argument about the merits and demerits of the arrangement have continued to this day.

One unfortunate consequence was that Samuel Storey's Chairmanship must end. Storey had opposed from the start the idea of the N.P.A. taking half the Reuter shares. He argued against it on the P.A. Board. When, by rotation, he retired from the Board in May 1941 his place was taken by Malcolm Graham, of the *Express and Star,* Wolverhampton, who also joined James Henderson in opposition. Having left the Board, Storey had no direct knowledge of the progress of negotiations except where they concerned himself. He felt particularly aggrieved about the agreement made with the N.P.A. which meant his laying down the Chairmanship of Reuters. He had neglected his own interests to get Reuters back into shape and it seemed to him and a good many others that he was receiving a poor reward for his efforts and his sacrifice; he took no money from Reuters.

But the deal went ahead.[1] On 8th September 1941 the P.A.

---

[1] The *Daily Express* did not buy shares with the rest of the N.P.A. Apart from any question of the price being asked, the *Express* felt that Reuters should stand on its own commercial feet. The *Express* would and did continue to buy the Reuter services but, rather than buy shares in it, preferred to spend money on developing its own news coverage. The *Express* did take a shareholding, however, after the death of the *News Chronicle* in 1960.

Reporter Anonymous

Board approved the arrangements by a vote of five to two and the Consultative Committee by the narrower majority of seven to five. (Those members of the Consultative Committee who were not also directors—these now included Storey—voted against the proposal by three to two.) The P.A. Boards of earlier days had made their purchases of Reuter shares without first consulting with the whole body of shareholders, although there had been no secret about their intentions. In 1941 the Board again decided to go through with the sale without putting the proposal to an extraordinary general meeting of the Association. This course of action was unquestionably within the Board's powers but the decision to act in that way was, at least, a tactical error. The negotiations had been confidential but the news that something was going on had leaked out—not surprisingly, perhaps, considering the resolute opposition within the P.A. itself. Some members of the P.A., on the strength of what little information they had been able to get, became uneasy and decided to act together to find out exactly what was being done in their name. There were enough of them to cause the General Manager to tell his Board that, constitutionally, an extraordinary general meeting must be called.

The meeting was held in the conference room at 85 Fleet Street, and lasted all day. It revealed just how irreconcilable the two sides were. It also showed how strong was the conviction on the part of those in favour of the deal that they were acting in the best interest of Reuters and the P.A. Their opponents were no less convinced of the contrary. There were many comments on the wording and meaning of the original Rothermere memorandum. McLean Ewing called it a 'remarkably reasonable statement'. James Henderson certainly did not share that opinion. William Haley thought it merely contained 'statements of fact'. R. A. Gibbs, of the Luton *Evening Telegraph*, saw the N.P.A. as wielding 'the big stick'. The argument was tough, blunt, occasionally passionate, occasionally personal. But for the most part it was conducted in good temper and for this, again, McLean Ewing, who chaired the meeting, was to be thanked. It was Gibbs of Luton who proposed that the sale should not go through and that the co-operation of the London newspapers should be sought on a basis that would still leave the P.A. in control of Reuters. On a show of hands, the resolution was rejected by forty-three to seventeen. James Henderson, fighting to the last, called for a poll,

A mysterious resignation

which was taken immediately. The resolution was again defeated —by 5024 to 2272.[1]

But even now the controversy was not over and the opposition was not dead. A few days later, on 22nd October, the future of Reuters was debated in the House of Commons as a matter of 'extreme public importance and urgency'. Some M.P.s were highly suspicious of any development which could put still more power in the hands of the London newspapers. Samuel Storey had argued at the P.A. meeting for a 'genuine Reuter Trust which would hold all the Reuter shares . . . really to appoint the directors, and the trustees and the directors to be representative of national interests and of Reuters' spheres of action'. In the House of Commons he put forward this view again. Replying to the debate, the Minister of Information, Brendan Bracken, a former newspaperman, said it was for the newspapers, not the Government, to settle the future of Reuters. He thought that the P.A. and the N.P.A. could put the Reuter house in order. He promised another debate if necessary.

It did not prove to be necessary because the P.A. and N.P.A. negotiators 'dreamed up' new provisions for the Reuter Trust which satisfied some of the critics (but not Samuel Storey) although they themselves were dubious about their virtues except as a political expedient. They proposed, when they met Brendan Bracken and Kingsley Wood, the Chancellor of the Exchequer, the next day, that an independent Chairman of Trustees, nominated by the Lord Chief Justice, should be appointed. They also suggested that any future amendments of the Trust should first be submitted to the Lord Chief Justice and that the Trust should be

[1] Some time afterwards, it was suggested that the majority against the resolution was 'more than made up by the votes of the provincial editions of the London newspapers, and of the provincial newspapers allied to London newspapers'—in other words that those papers which might be suspected, by their ties with London, to have a vested interest in the sale to the N.P.A. had swung the decision. In fact, even if their votes had been eliminated, there would still have been a majority against the resolution. Lord Buckton (formerly Samuel Storey) maintains that if the votes of the *Yorkshire Post* (which took the lead in requisitioning the meeting but withdrew its opposition to the N.P.A. deal shortly before the meeting began) were eliminated, this statement would no longer be true. His claim rests upon a different interpretation of which votes could be termed 'independent' and which might be held to have been influenced by 'ties with London'.

irrevocable for a minimum of twenty-one years and thereafter was not to be dissolved unless the Lord Chief Justice was satisfied that its continuance in any form was impracticable.

Now, at last, the sale was completed. Sir Lynden Macassey, K.C., was appointed as the first independent Chairman of Trustees. The new Reuters immediately demonstrated its purity to the world by cancelling the arrangements by which the Government had given the agency specially favourable terms for the transmission of news overseas by wireless. The new Board wanted to dispel once and for all any suspicion that Reuters was aided by Government subsidy and therefore that its independence might be tainted. Reuters told the Government that whatever transmission facilities were available should be granted to all news agencies without discrimination.

This is not the place to tell the story of Reuters in any detail and a few notes must serve as a postscript to the dramatic events of 1941. Possibly with a feeling that he had been let down by his colleagues and understandably disappointed at the new arrangements for running Reuters, Samuel Storey resigned all his P.A. appointments. Of the three Reuter General Managers, William Turner retired almost at once and William Moloney in 1944, leaving Christopher Chancellor in sole charge. The office of independent Chairman of Trustees was, with the consent of the Lord Chief Justice, abolished in 1950. Experience had shown it was not essential and by then, too, the ownership of Reuters had been broadened. The Australian Associated Press and the New Zealand Press Association (both owned by the newspapers of their countries) had joined the P.A. and the N.P.A. as partner-proprietors of Reuters, appointing jointly one Reuter director and two Trustees.[1]

In 1959 the Reuter directors thought that, after all, it would be an advantage to have a Chairman, though he could be given neither a vote nor a casting vote. What he could do, however, was to give aid and counsel to the General Manager between Board meetings, watch matters of policy, and represent Reuters on appropriate occasions both at home and abroad. John L.

---

[1] In 1949, after long negotiations, the Press Trust of India also became a Reuter shareholder, appointing a director and a Trustee. Both parties recognised this was in the nature of an experiment and after four years the arrangement ended amicably.

A mysterious resignation

Burgess, of the *Cumberland Evening News*, Carlisle, a past-Chairman of the P.A., was elected Chairman of Reuters in 1959 for a term of three years. He was re-elected in 1962 and again in 1965.

Fourteen / In war as in peace

On the evening of March the 13th, 1940, a P.A. reporter, Philip Bloomberg, was sent to cover what looked like a routine job at the Caxton Hall, Westminster, where the East India Association was holding a meeting. A former Governor of the Punjab, Sir Michael O'Dwyer, was to address the Association. Bloomberg listened to Sir Michael, made the necessary notes for his report and could have left, although the meeting had not yet finished. He decided, however, to wait until the end to check a few points with O'Dwyer. He never had the chance. As the meeting closed, an Indian in the audience shot Sir Michael dead. Bloomberg quickly verified such facts as he could and then hurried in search of a telephone. But the police had locked the doors of the lecture room. Bloomberg pleaded but neither he nor anyone else was allowed to leave. For two and a half hours he waited in that room, fretting lest, somehow, the story would leak out before he could put it over to the P.A. However, when he did get away he found he still had his scoop.

By coincidence, that incident happened on the same night that Sir Kenneth Lee, the then Director General of the Ministry of Information, and Sir Walter Monckton, the Director General of the Press and Censorship Bureau, were being taken on a tour of the P.A. editorial and telegraphic departments. As the P.A. Chairman was to report, they 'expressed surprise at the education they had received.'

They, and even more particularly their departments, were in need of education. As in the first world war, the press faced, at the beginning of the second world war, an ignorance of journalistic practices—and democratic values—which was bound to lead

In war as in peace

to frustration and ill-feeling. Just what the press had to endure at the start was characterised succinctly in 1940 by the P.A. Chairman, Herbert Staines:

'In the negotiations with the officials of the shadow Ministry of Information,' he said, 'there was disclosed a tendency, born of a complete lack of knowledge of press methods, to cabin and confine press facilities; and the agencies found it necessary to carve a polite but insistent way through a jungle of red tape as well as to dispel an atmosphere that the press must be content with small concessions. If from the first,' he added, 'a wider view of the world-wide responsibilities of the press had been adopted, if it had been appreciated that the facilities asked for were essential in the national interests, the storm that later blew up over the newly born Ministry might have been considerably moderated.'

But the authorities did respond to pressure and tuition more quickly than in the 1914-18 war. Henry Martin, the Editor-in-Chief, was just the man, with his fervent, almost evangelical belief in the role of the Press Association, to instruct them and to keep them up to the mark. It was not long before the P.A. had come to occupy a unique position in the eyes of the authorities and to be regarded, very properly, as an invaluable channel to the press as a whole.

What the P.A. was seeking from the Government was not, of course, an unqualified freedom to report the news. As in the first world war, it was asking for a positive approach to the question of press liberty and national security. It wanted the authorities to ask, in effect, 'Is there any reason why we should not allow this news to be published?', rather than 'Why should we allow this news to be published?' But in those two questions is contrasted the attitudes of journalists and officialdom over the centuries.

Between the censors and the P.A., however, a particularly cordial and sympathetic relationship evolved. This, again, owed much to Henry Martin's efforts. It seemed to be the genuine wish of the censors to interpret their responsibilities benevolently and they found in Martin a man to whom, despite his primary interest, they could turn for sensible and objective advice.

Causes of serious friction remained, however, between the Press Association and the Ministry of Information. In the autumn of 1941 the P.A.'s Editor-in-Chief became justifiably apprehensive about what he regarded as a growing encroachment by the

Reporter Anonymous

Ministry's news division upon the P.A.'s traditional field of activity. The news division had been created to supply the press with official and semi-official news but it became over-ambitious. More and more, the service supplied by the division began to contain items of a more general kind. In the P.A. view the Ministry's pretexts for doing so were of the flimsiest. Henry Martin smelt competition of the most undesirable kind. What was more, he became aware of a more blatant interference with news agency enterprise. Visitors from abroad, for instance, were being intercepted so that they could not be interviewed on the day they arrived but were kept back for a Ministry press conference the following day.

Shortly before Christmas, 1941, Henry Martin was attending a Newspaper Society lunch at which Brendan Bracken, the Minister of Information, was the guest. Martin asked the Minister bluntly whether it was his policy to allow the news division, either then or after the war, to become a subsidised news agency in competition with the recognised, independent agencies. Bracken said he had no such intention and agreed that a subsidised agency must be suspect. From that time on, there was little further cause for complaint.[1]

Henry Martin strenuously corrected an official concept of the P.A. as a mere tube through which hand-outs could be distributed to the British press. The authorities imagined it would be the function of the news agency to pass on, undiluted, all the 'copy' that came to it from Whitehall. They were quite shocked to discover that the P.A. had a positive responsibility to select, to edit, to gut and even—outrageous thought—to translate the richer modes of officialese into plain English.

While Whitehall initially misconceived the role of the P.A., however, it was right in seeing the agency as the essential means of communication with the press, especially the provincial press. This role was enhanced in wartime when there was greater need for and a greater dependence on a central news-gathering machine. In conjunction with Reuters, the P.A. fed a regular supply of war correspondence to the provincial papers, so that the humblest of sheets could carry first-hand accounts of the fighting to match the

[1] With Cyril (later Lord) Radcliffe as Director General in the later years of the war a much better understanding grew up between the press and the Ministry.

In war as in peace

coverage which the big papers received from their own reporters. The service was made the more personal and humane by the inclusion of 'home town' stories—reports with an emphatic parochial slant. The P.A. Court Correspondent put on uniform to follow the King wherever he might go, whether it be to inspect troops in training or to the Normandy beach-head.

When Churchill made a major speech in Parliament, the P.A.'s customers received a verbatim report, perhaps eight thousand words long, say, as well as forty 'snaps'—highlights of the speech —transmitted within minutes of their being delivered in the Commons. This was the P.A. Parliamentary team performing, in war as in peace, the task expected of it. Only the quality of the speech or the gravity of the occasion distinguished it from a normal day's work. Yet it needs no dramatisation to perceive how vital a function those men in the gallery of the House of Commons were performing.

Much of all this was taken for granted. It was generally assumed that nothing would stop the P.A. service, whatever the difficulties. As Walter Hawkins, of the *Bristol Evening Post*, said, 'When our buildings and plant were threatened by enemy raids, the one thing we did not worry about was the Press Association service, because we knew it would get through somehow, and it did.' That was partly the result of good luck in that 85 Fleet Street, the new headquarters into which the P.A. had moved only two months before the outbreak of war, never received a direct hit. It had one very close shave during the great fire raid of 29th December 1940. That night the lovely church of St. Bride's, Fleet Street's 'own' church, was burned out. The tower of St. Bride's was only eleven feet from the east wall of the P.A. building, but the wind blew away the flames and sparks. That same night all the P.A.'s provincial telegraph channels were out of action for a short time. The Manchester newspapers and *The Times*, whose own circuits out of London were still working, came to the rescue. Press Association 'traffic' to the Manchester centre was passed from there round all the other centres and circuits. The Post Office did good work on the repairs and the P.A.'s normal transmission system was soon in service again. The Post Office showed the same speed in repairing the circuits after a raid on Bristol had cut off the P.A. centre from the local post office.

Plans had been made to meet any foreseeable disaster. The

basement at 85 Fleet Street was equipped for editorial work and transmission over both the provincial telegraph system and the London teleprinter system. It also had an emergency canteen and sleeping quarters so that work could have been carried on there indefinitely in the event of the upper floors being out of use. The P.A. staffs did take to the basement frequently during the night raids of 1940-1 and early 1944, although they worked normally during day raids by aircraft and later during the V_1 and V_2 day and night attacks. It was in the basement that the night editor, Frank Turner, received what was to become a familiar telephone warning from the P.A. man at Dover that 'London is going to have a packet tonight by the way they're coming over here.'

There was a second line of defence to cope with the situation if work at 85 Fleet Street were to become completely impossible. Arrangements were made with Kemsley Newspapers to equip a big room in Kemsley House in Gray's Inn Road for use by the P.A. in emergency and similarly with the Exchange Telegraph in Cannon Street. This plan was put into action for a few hours in April 1941, when, late on a Sunday night, a land-mine landed on the other side of Fleet Street and the P.A. building had to be evacuated. The day staffs began their Monday morning's work in Gray's Inn Road and Cannon Street but the land-mine did not explode and was soon removed.

Finally, if London itself had become untenable, it was planned to carry on at Manchester (in the offices of the *Guardian* and *Evening News*) and at Birmingham. These arrangements were never needed. As another means of overcoming widespread breakdowns of communications—and, after the fall of France, of trying to deal with a situation in which some parts of the country might be cut off by an invasion—the P.A. intended to send out news messages by wireless. The P.A. installed wireless transmitters and the provincial papers equipped themselves with the special receiving sets needed. On a wavelength allocated by the Ministry of Information, the P.A. conducted a number of successful rehearsals—but, again, the plan never had to go into action in earnest.

Like every other private organisation, the P.A. suffered from shortages of all kinds, of staff, of mechanical spare parts, of the special telegraph slip used for 'punching' the messages. But the maintenance of the P.A. news services was regarded as of national importance and no source of an essential supply ever dried up completely.

From the men at the top of the Press Association the war demanded resourcefulness, innovation, ingenuity and stamina. The man who bore much of the load was, inevitably, the General Manager, Edward Davies. Davies had been in executive command of the P.A. for little more than a year when the war started and he had had no previous experience of news agency work. Nor had he ever before carried such a large responsibility. He had been Secretary of the Newspaper Society for twelve years where the staff was a very small one. Now he had to administer an organisation employing hundreds and with an income of around £350,000. Edward Davies was still only thirty-six when he came to the Press Association and he was understandably slightly apprehensive about his new job. But it is most unlikely that anyone else ever knew it. Davies was a slightly built man with a quiet, unassuming manner which a stranger could easily misinterpret. In fact, as successive P.A. Boards were to discover, he was a tough, determined man, an excellent chess player who brought to negotiations and to administration the qualities of calculation and cool appraisal. Davies has said himself he was 'always most constitutional' in his dealings with his directors. 'If, and it did happen sometimes,' he said, 'they have been in agreement with my view on some question, all right, the matter was settled. If they have disagreed with me, I have always tried to see to it that they had a second chance to consider the question.' A man of dry, glancing wit, Edward Davies, unlike so many credited with that kind of talent, could really be described as a gifted, impromptu speaker. According to Laurence Scott of the *Guardian*, who joined the P.A. Board in 1948, when he first knew Edward Davies he had 'two gimmicks'. He wore gaudy ties which he put on immediately before a Board meeting and took off again immediately afterwards; and he drank orange squash. 'He gave up both after his visit to America [in 1953],' said Scott.

From the astonishingly early age of twenty-three when, after a few years as a journalist, he was appointed Secretary of the Newspaper Society, Edward Davies had had a close association with the leading figures in the provincial press. Clearly, the impression he had made on them there had given them the confidence to bring him to the P.A. even though he lacked news agency experience. Coming in from the outside was an advantage to him and to the P.A. Although he had to learn the business at the same time as managing it, he could view the P.A.'s problems pragmatically, unhampered by tradition. Davies soon had for his colleague, as Secretary of the P.A., a man even younger than himself and equally keen to get things done. This was Ernest Harvey, who was only twenty-six when in 1939, along with more than a hundred others, he applied for the job from which Percy Shaw was, at last, at the age of sixty-nine, retiring. Harvey had been working at Reuters. These two men, Davies and Harvey, were of just the right age and quality to carry on the next stage of the P.A.'s development. But they, like everybody else, had to wait until the war was over. Ernest Harvey, indeed, joined the Army himself in 1942, serving for most of the time as an intelligence officer in India and the Far East. For the next four years Edward Davies acted as Secretary as well as General Manager.

For all the anxiety and responsibility of the wartime administration, Davies must have felt a sense of frustration at having to mark time. But he did succeed, with the help of two of his directors in particular—William Haley and Raymond Derwent—in putting one major reform into operation. This was the introduction of what was called a Comprehensive Service, which meant that the P.A., instead of selling numerous individual services, now lumped many of them together and sold the package for an inclusive charge. To someone outside the newspaper industry this might seem merely a change in detail, an administrative convenience. It was certainly the latter but its importance was also very much more than one of detail. This Comprehensive Service provided subscribers with an all-round news service which would satisfy all their general needs and they would have no cause to feel that they were being deprived of certain items, some quite important, because they were classified under a separate heading. Editors were especially pleased to be relieved of the irritation of the P.A.'s 'offered specials'. Too often these had been stories which they felt should have been included in the ordinary news service but for which they were invited to pay a separate charge. In the early thirties, for instance, a visit to Wales by the Prince of Wales could have come into this category.

In the past, all papers, however big or however small, taking the same service, had been charged the same amount. The only

In war as in peace

variation had been that evening papers had paid less than mornings for comparable news supplies. With the introduction of the Comprehensive Service, the P.A. adopted a system of graded charges, operated for many years by news agencies in other countries. Newspapers were now divided into classes according to their daily net sales, the more successful bearing a larger share of the co-operative burden than the less successful. The distinction between mornings and evenings was ended.

A new arrangement was also made with the London papers whereby the separate news services previously supplied to them were now combined into an 'All-in' Service, very similar to the provincial Comprehensive Service. The N.P.A. paid the P.A. a bulk sum and its individual members worked out how the cost should be shared. These significant changes in the structure of the P.A.'s news services and in the manner they were paid for took a surprisingly short time to achieve. But another major alteration which Edward Davies hoped for took very much longer.

From almost his first day at the Press Association, Davies wanted to replace the old system of transmitting the news. The Creed-Wheatstone system had served the P.A. well since its installation after the first world war but it was clear to the new General Manager that the time had come for a further advance. There was no fault to find mechanically with the Creed but it simply could not cope adequately with all the P.A. traffic. It was, in effect, a single-line railway. If there were several stories competing with one another in interest and importance, they could go through only one at a time, which meant, at the receiving end, in the newspaper offices, editions could be missed. On a busy news day, as the afternoon wore on, there was a massacre of news items which had been prepared for the evening newspapers but could not be sent to them in time to be of use. Afterwards there was such an accumulation of morning paper copy that the wire was choked until late in the evening. (Of course, important and urgent messages were expedited and the wires were cleared for copy which had to be sent at fixed times, such as Stock Exchange reports and racing results.) From the practical point of view, the Creed suffered from another shortcoming. Everything it sent out arrived in the form of a tape 'punched' in Morse code and this tape had to be passed through another machine for translation into a printed message. The editorial expansion which followed the appointment of an Editor-in-Chief exposed the deficiencies of the system. As early as 1928 a proposal to duplicate some of the circuits was being considered but the expense was one of the reasons given for not going ahead with it.

In 1934 when Jock Newlands, the chief of the Telegraph Department, retired and was succeeded by his capable deputy, Leonard Warren, it was recognised that the P.A. must go on, as the more progressive private wire newspapers had already done, to use more sophisticated machinery and telegraphic codes which would allow the news to be transmitted faster and over more than one channel—and to be received already printed at the newspaper offices. It was another fourteen years, however, before the new system—known as 'voice-frequency' or v.f.—was in operation. From 1935 to 1939 the P.A. was building its new offices. From 1939 to 1945 the war impeded progress.

At last, by May 1949, the new system was in operation, except to Ireland, for which the British Post Office could not then provide the necessary v.f. circuits. Belfast was added to the teleprinter system in 1953 and Dublin and Cork soon afterwards. The whole scheme had been a tremendous challenge to the P.A.'s telegraph chiefs and mechanics, who had not only had to plan and carry through the re-equipment in London and all the provincial centres but also to give help and advice to many newspapers for whom the idea of multi-channel teleprinter working was a completely new and formidable proposition.

From the beginning, the new scheme was a success. Instead of one Morse channel working at 120 words a minute, six channels, each working at sixty-six words a minute, were available, providing a capacity of about 400 words a minute. That was the most obvious advantage but it was not the only one. All newspapers were now served direct from London and each received the same items of news at precisely the same moment. Racing results and 'special' items could be sent over particular channels without interference with other news. Finally, 'printing-up' of punched tape in the newspaper offices was a thing of the past, for the news was now printed in page form by the teleprinters at the receiving end, ready at once for the sub-editors and the linotype operators.

On the 20th of November 1947 the *Star*, the London evening paper, gave up the whole of its front page to a picture of Princess Elizabeth and Prince Philip leaving Westminster Abbey after their

Princess Elizabeth and Prince Philip leaving Westminster Abbey after their wedding in 1947. P.A. picture by A. E. Creffield

"Psst! Keep that ——— thing out of his reach until we've got our pictures."

A comment by Giles in the Daily Express *on the affair of the Duke and the photographers (see pages 243–4)*

News-gathering in the electronic age. Reporters and photographers crowd round as Lord Moran discusses the progress of his patient Sir Winston Churchill. The P.A. reporter (wearing hat, near centre) takes a note

In war as in peace

wedding. The *Star* described it as 'the picture of the day'. More papers reproduced it than any other single picture of the wedding. It was taken by A. E. ('Bill') Creffield, a photographer employed by P.A.-Reuter Photos, another post-war development. The negative of that picture arrived at the P.A. building at 12.55 p.m. By 1.10 p.m. it had been printed and captioned. A motor-cycle despatch rider left immediately for Croydon airport carrying packets containing copies of that picture and twenty-four earlier ones. At the airport a fleet of chartered aircraft were waiting. They were airborne by 1.47 p.m. Many of the packets were dropped by streamer at prearranged spots near provincial towns to be picked up by local evening papers; others were picked up from aerodromes. From midnight on the Wednesday to midnight the following day—the day of the wedding—P.A.-Reuter Photos turned out 4735 prints: pictures of the Abbey rehearsal, of late-night and early daylight scenes, of the ceremony itself. In Britain they were delivered to newspapers by special messengers, by train, by air. Telephoto prints went to the London offices of provincial papers which had the apparatus for wiring them; radio prints and air packets were sent to customers all over the world.

The royal wedding presented the biggest test up to that time for an organisation that was only two years old and as yet did not possess the equipment for sending out pictures by wire. Nearly twenty years earlier, in 1928, the P.A. directors had looked into the possibility of starting a service for transmitting pictures to a small group of papers which were interested. But in the end those papers decided to act individually and the project fell through. With pictures as with all else, the P.A., as a co-operative, could only move as fast as its members wished and allowed it to go.

The idea of starting a news-photo service cropped up from time to time but it was not until 1944 that a positive decision was taken. The American news agencies, especially the Associated Press, had developed photo supplies as a very useful adjunct to their international news contracts and Reuters thought it might be worth-while to enter the world news-photo field. So P.A. and Reuters joined together to set up a new company, which was generally referred to as 'the photo company'.

The man appointed as its first Manager was William Truby, who had been an executive on the pictorial side of newspapers before the war and, during the war years, ran the photographic sec-

Reporter Anonymous

tion at the Air Ministry. Truby had no illusions about the job he was taking on. He knew that of all the competitive jungles that of the news-photo agencies was one of the toughest. But he was excited by the challenge. When the photo company went into action for the first time on 26th November 1945 Truby had a small staff of six photographers and two editors. He was lucky to have persuaded Leslie Burch to join him as picture editor and to help him with the planning before the new service started. Few men could have known more than Burch about the work of a picture agency. He had been trained as a newsreel cameraman and then became chief staff photographer of the London News Agency. He had covered three royal tours of the Empire as official photographer for the British press.

The initial aim of the photo company was to supply provincial papers with up to thirty pictures a week, delivering them daily either to the London offices or sending them by train to the head office. The accent was always on speed; speed in getting the plates back to 85 Fleet Street, speed in printing the pictures, speed in getting them to subscribers. The new company was fighting other agencies which had been in the business a long time and also the national newspapers with their own staff photographers. The photo company wanted to sell to the London papers, of course, but its first task was to give the provincial papers such a good service that they could compete with the nationals. The daily supply of pictures was to be part of the Comprehensive Service of news.

The photo company was a success right from the start. At the end of the first year's operations Truby was able to report that there had been 12,000 publications of P.A.-Reuter pictures in the provincial press, 5400 in the London papers and magazines and more than 16,000 overseas. Those figures become the more remarkable when it is remembered just how fierce a fight it was to find space for pictures in newspapers harshly emaciated by newsprint rationing.

Truby and Burch waited just as impatiently as Edward Davies and Henry Martin for the expansion of the P.A.'s private wire system. Until they could wire their pictures to all provincial papers they felt that their efforts to achieve speed were being partially wasted. Those efforts did bring some astonishing results, however. An example taken from the first week of the service shows just how fast they could work. Walter Lockeyear, one of

In war as in peace

the staff photographers, took a close-up of Princess Elizabeth arriving at the Albert Hall. The time was 2.30 p.m. That picture was rushed back from Kensington to Fleet Street and twenty-nine minutes after it had been taken prints of it were on their way to the London evening and Sunday papers. But so long as newspapers outside London had to wait for the pictures to arrive by train high-speed operations in London could never demonstrate their true value.

Experiments were being conducted to find out which would be the best type of transmitter for a wired photo service. Once more, as on so many occasions in the past, the *Glasgow Herald* played a part. In May 1948 a portable transmitter was taken to the Worcester county cricket ground and pictures of the match against the Australian touring side were transmitted by wire to 85 Fleet Street.

In October 1948 the photo company began to operate a wired photo service. At the start it was confined to a minority of provincial papers which had the necessary apparatus at the receiving end. But in less than two years there were enough to make it possible to distribute photos in the same way as news, transmitting them simultaneously to papers in all parts of the country. The number of P.A.-Reuter pictures used by provincial papers went up and up. From 12,000 the first year, it grew to over 84,000 in 1956. In 1967 the figure was well over 100,000. On the 3rd of October 1952, by virtue of its arrangement with an Australian newspaper, the photo company scored a big scoop, making the front page of all the national papers, with the first picture of the first British atomic-bomb explosion. The photo company excelled in the coverage of big news stories like the 1953 flood disasters, the Olympic Games in 1948, the death and funeral of George VI and, above all, a great ceremonial occasion like the Coronation, when the staff were on duty continuously for two and a half days, snatching sleep on office tables.

The doings of royalty are the source of some of the more obvious photo-agency activity: posed pictures, formal visits, official openings, overseas tours, weddings and funerals. It was another royal wedding in 1960—Princess Margaret's—which set up another record for the photo company whose laboratories produced more than 14,000 prints in a single day. It was a royal activity of a different kind which momentarily damped the enthusiasm of

243

two P.A.-Reuter staff photographers. They were taking pictures of the Duke of Edinburgh at the Chelsea Flower Show in 1959 when they found themselves in the centre of a series of water jets coming from sprinklers concealed in the lawn. Coincidentally, the Duke was standing beside the button which operated the sprinklers by remote control. Buckingham Palace put out a denial that the Duke had pressed the button.

One of those photographers was Walter Lockeyear who, during the war, accompanied the commandos on the Dieppe raid and, later, attached to Churchill as official photographer, covered the Yalta and Potsdam conferences. It was Lockeyear who, in 1958, had done outstanding work in covering the State Opening of Parliament when he was one of two photographers allowed for the first time into the Chamber of the House of Lords. He and his colleagues managed to do so despite restrictions which overzealous officialdom, in the shape of no less a personage than the Lord Great Chamberlain, the 5th Marquess of Cholmondeley, would have imposed on them. The Marquess gave orders that photographers must take only one picture of the Queen on the throne and that with not too wide an angle. Lockeyear ignored the instruction and produced magnificent black-and-white and colour pictures.

When William Truby retired at the end of 1961 he had every justification for pride in the organisation he had done so much to build. So, too, had Leslie Burch, who retired two years later. Many times, photographs taken by P.A.-Reuter photographers won top prizes in the *Encyclopaedia Britannica* competition. A picture library was created which now ranks as one of the largest and most valuable in Britain, housing more than a million negatives. It has been enriched by the acquisition of other picture collections and includes such rarities as Dr. Crippen and Ethel Le Neve standing in the dock; Winston Churchill at the Sidney Street Siege; family portraits of the last of the Tsars and Captain Hurley's pictures of Sir Ernest Shackleton at the South Pole.

Despite its success, the photo company was still living in the same premises where it had been set up in 1945. They had been the best the P.A. could get at the time but they became less and less adequate. The staff deserved a better home. They also deserved better equipment than that which had been bought in 1945; much of it, even at that time, had been second-hand.

In war as in peace

It was sixteen years later, towards the end of 1961, that the photo company moved into its new home, with laboratories claimed to be the most modern and comprehensive in Fleet Street.[1] The P.A. found the space needed by taking the lease of a pub called The White Swan. This pub, which was part of the structure of the P.A. building, was being closed. It offered the photo company the extra living room it needed. With much more elaborate equipment and with more staff, the organisation was ready for new ventures into colour and into commercial and industrial photography.

Its chief executive after Truby's retirement was Derrick Knight, another man whose professional talents had been employed during the war. He ended as a lieutenant-colonel in charge of the Army film and photographic unit in South East Asia. Before that he had been anything but an armchair soldier. With both still and newsreel cameras he had covered the war on many fronts and received the M.B.E. for his work at the Salerno landing. After the war he worked for the Shell Organisation, becoming head of the Shell Photographic Unit before joining P.A.-Reuter Photos.

The photo company owed its new home and its modernisation largely to one man—William Young, of the *Eastern Daily Press*, Norwich. It was in 1960 that, for the first time, a P.A. director was appointed to the Board of the photo company. (Previously the Board had been composed only of the P.A. and Reuter executives.) Young brought a new and positive drive to the company and he played an outstanding part in its development over the next five years, serving it as Chairman for four of them. Although the company still operated under the P.A.-Reuter label, photos had become more and more the sole concern of the P.A. It was the P.A. which took the entire responsibility for rehousing the photo company and for providing the new equipment. The initial hope that, with Reuters participating, the photo company would become an international picture agency was never realised.

In 1965 Reuters dropped out altogether. Young carried on as

[1] In performing the opening ceremony, Lord Brabazon of Tara told how, in 1940, he had broken the strict rule of the House of Commons forbidding photography in the Chamber. Using a little Minox camera he took a time exposure from under the gallery. Neville Chamberlain was making his last speech in the Commons.

Reporter Anonymous

Chairman until the end of that year when the photo company was liquidated and the organisation, now with a staff of over eighty, became a department of the P.A. The service it gave to subscribers was unaffected. The speed at which the photographic department can send out wired photos by automatic transmission gives some idea of the value of that service. A picture can be ready to take off the receiver in a provincial newspaper office within half an hour of the negative being received at the P.A.

At the same time as William Young joined the Board of the photo company, another P.A. director, Reginald Gleave, of the *Southern Evening Echo*, Southampton, was appointed a director of P.A. Features. This company had been another post-war joint enterprise between the Press Association and Reuters, venturing into the field of news features, marketing feature articles, cartoons and comic-strips. By the time Gleave joined its Board in 1960, the P.A. was running the business alone. With nearly forty years' experience as a working journalist, first as a reporter and then an editor, the help Gleave brought to the company was of a very practical kind. It was soon recognised, however, that there was no point any longer in running the features operation as a separate company and no need to bear the extra administrative costs of doing so. In 1963 the company was liquidated and, in becoming an integral part of the P.A., the business was actually strengthened. Today, its features and strips are sold mainly in Britain and a large number of provincial papers carry them.

In 1946 Edward Davies, with Henry Martin's agreement, initiated the creation of a separate section of the editorial department with the title of Special Reporting Service. Its object was to cater for the more particular and parochial interests of individual newspapers in a way that was not possible within the confines of the general news service. It would amplify reports from the Law Courts or from Parliament; it would keep an eye open for stories whose interest was too localised to be included in the general service or, at best, very briefly; it would undertake, when commissioned, to supply special reports of court cases, meetings, inquiries, and the like. This service was strikingly successful, under the direction of two experienced P.A. men, first that of W. T. ('Tommy') Tomlinson and then of L. C. J. ('Mick') McNae— who is also a recognised authority among newspapermen on the law as it affects journalists.

In war as in peace

All this growth and innovation was still directed to the unchanging aim of the Press Association to provide for its members and subscribers the kind of service that would help them to produce better newspapers. It cost a lot of money. Between 1926 and 1946 the P.A. borrowed, mostly from members, nearly £700,000. At almost any time during that twenty years it might have answered to the description given by Alfred Burchill of the *Liverpool Courier*—when he was Chairman—that the Association was in the happy position of the man who said he had borrowed enough to pay all his debts.

Many years later, in 1955, Malcolm Graham, of the *Express and Star*, Wolverhampton, gave two interesting statistics about the economics of his own newspaper to illustrate how cheap the P.A. service really was. What he was paying for the service was, he said, only 1.7 per cent of his paper's total costs and less than 11 per cent of the editorial costs. 'When one thinks,' he added, 'of the large proportion of our papers which are filled with the news which comes from the P.A., including Reuters and the Joint Service with the Exchange Telegraph, that is marvellous value.'

An explanation of just how the Press Association provided its service was made public in 1948 when its structure—its finances, its administration, its editorial organisation—was anatomised for the benefit of the Royal Commission on the Press which sat from 1947 to 1949. The P.A. submitted written evidence and its Chairman, General Manager and Editor-in-Chief also appeared before the Commission to answer oral questions. In his impromptu replies, Henry Martin illuminated most revealingly his own tastes, prejudices, beliefs and, perhaps, his ultimate inability to accept the necessary limitations upon the Editor-in-Chief of a news agency. There was, for instance, a series of questions about how the Press Association decided what news to send out and what to 'spike'. When Martin was asked whether there was any real clash between his sense of what was important and that of individual newspaper editors, he replied:

'. . . Two or three years ago the Archbishop of York sent me a speech he was to make on Saturday afternoon on sex and the abuse of sex by young people, and drawing the Christian moral. I decided that I could not issue fewer than 800 words of that speech. I issued that all over the country, and I should say that every evening newspaper on that Saturday afternoon published those 800 words as we had sent it, so that anyone of intelligence and of a religious turn of mind could see exactly what the Archbishop of York was trying to inculcate: the Christian ideal of sex and marriage. The London newspapers cut that considerably and one Sunday newspaper just picked out the reference to sex, without printing anything of the moral attached to it, and that, I think, may be typical of the difference between the London and the provincial newspapers.' Henry Martin was riding a favourite hobbyhorse.

A little later he was asked: 'To what extent are your own ideals of what is a balanced account affected by the reception your accounts get from the Press? Have you modified your own ideas of what should go out as a result of the reception accorded to your material?'

'I am afraid,' said Martin, 'I have refused to modify my ideas. I have a sense of responsibility (and I think it is a very strong stewardship) towards the reading public, and, whatever newspapers may or may not publish, particularly in London, that does not influence me in the least. I know that, for instance, in the last two or three years there has been a greater stream of co-ordinated religious news passed through the Press Association than ever before and it is welcomed by the bulk of the provincial newspapers, who are closely in touch with the public.' Then Martin added an even more contentious comment which was to provoke a vigorous professional reaction.

'I would also say that on cultural matters generally the Press Association is years ahead of the newspapers . . . excepting perhaps *The Times* and the *Manchester Guardian*. I send out news on archaeology, on music, and on a range of subjects in which I happen to be interested, and because I am interested in them I think there must be a large section of the population interested in them; and we prepare factual reports very carefully, it may be on art, or on music, it may be an antiquarian lecture, but in effect one is just dumping them into a quagmire.'

Lastly, there was Martin's expression of respect for the provincial editor compared with his counterpart in London.

'The provincial editor,' he said, 'is in so much closer touch with his readers. If he goes off the rails he has only to walk down to his club for luncheon and half a dozen people will be there to put him back; therefore he has a sense of civic responsibility, which

In war as in peace

breeds national responsibility. But in London there is such a remoteness between the editor and his reader.'

All this was too much for Arthur Christiansen, the great editor of the *Daily Express*. Christiansen directed the main strength of his protest against Martin's remarks about culture but he may well have felt the more personal outrage at the assertion of 'remoteness' between the London editor and his readers. Arthur Christiansen's evaluation of any story in his own paper was whether it would interest and be understood by the man in a back street in Derby, or Wigan, or Wallasey, and he never returned from a visit to the provinces without delivering a rebuke to his staff for their obsession with all things metropolitan.

Christiansen sent a letter to the Chairman of the Press Association and a copy of it to the Chairman of the Royal Commission. In the letter he enquired whether Henry Martin's views in relation to the national press had the support of the Chairman and Board of the P.A. He went on:

'I also write on behalf of my staff to protest against Mr. Martin's outrageous comments on the standards of education and cultural values among journalists on the *Daily Express*, for my staff must, of course, be included in Mr. Martin's generalised and unsubstantiated strictures.' Henry Martin had also criticised the educational standards of journalistic recruits and had added, '... there is practically no cultural standard among reporters or subeditors (as a whole) in news agencies and on newspapers ...'

'The *Daily Express*,' wrote its editor, 'far from employing reporters and sub-editors with "practically no cultural standards", takes the utmost care to see that its employees are not only thoroughly trained in the craft of journalism, but are men of wide culture and learning. A good proportion are, in addition, university men with high academic honours. Mr. Martin, taking no account of the difficulties under which newspapers have been produced since 1939, declares that the P.A. might just as well "dump" its cultural coverage "into a quagmire". He neglects to record that the *Daily Express* (and, I am sure, other national newspapers) employs its own specialists in music, the arts and the sciences, to whom space is given in preference to P.A. copy. He contrasts the national press most unfavourably with the provincial press, and ignores the fact that each has its function—one to stress local news and the other national and international news. He criticises the national press most unjustly of ignoring spiritual issues, taking no account of the coverage of these issues which does not emanate from the P.A. Mr. Martin's right to speak the things that are in his mind is not challenged. But it is his duty to substantiate his charges, or else to hold his tongue . . . Mr. Martin should prove his allegations in detail or withdraw them unreservedly for the sake of the honour of those employed by the national press.'

It was Walter Hawkins, of the *Bristol Evening Post*, who, as Chairman of the P.A., sent this judicious reply to the editor of the *Express*.

'The Board,' he wrote, 'fully accepts responsibility for the factual evidence given to the Royal Commission on the press about the Association's services and organisation, but the Association does not deal in opinions, and it was clear from the phrasing of some of the questions put to Mr. Henry Martin (our Editor-in-Chief) by the members of the Royal Commission that it was his personal opinion which was sought, which he gave, and to which you have taken exception. While you may not agree with the opinions he expressed, your letter shows that you would be among the first to defend his right freely to speak his views . . .'

Those were days in which allegations about the deficiencies of the press were being flung about with abandon and men like Christiansen were hypersensitive to criticism, the more so, no doubt, when it came from inside the profession. Certainly, Martin's highly idiosyncratic opinions could have been expressed with more prudence and restraint but, in retrospect, there is something rather pleasing about such a full-blooded break with the anonymity and impersonality in which the Editor-in-Chief of the Press Association is normally shrouded.

Fifteen / 'A monopoly news service'

The Press Association has never failed, for a single day, to supply a service of news. There was a most serious threat in 1952, however, when the P.A. faced a situation in which it risked a total stoppage for the sake of standing by what it regarded as a fundamental principle.

The danger arose out of a dispute between a union—the National Society of Operative Printers and Assistants (Natsopa) —and a Scottish newspaper management—D. C. Thomson of Dundee. The rights and wrongs of that dispute are not relevant to this story but the action proposed by the unions to increase the pressure on Thomsons certainly is. They wanted to cut off the *Sunday Post* in Glasgow—one of the D. C. Thomson group— from P.A. news services. This could have been a damaging blow to the paper. Some of the P.A. telegraphists were called upon by their union to refuse to transmit services on Saturdays to the *Sunday Post*. There was a further threat. If, said the unions, the P.A. nullified this action and supplied the *Sunday Post* by some other means then all P.A. employees who were members either of Natsopa or of the National Union of Journalists would stop work.

The P.A.'s own relations with the unions over the years had been good although there had been some hard negotiating, particularly over wages, from time to time. In this instance, the dispute was one with which the Press Association, as a news agency, had no direct concern. But the directors of the P.A. felt that if they acquiesced in the action proposed by the union they would be creating or helping to create a most dangerous precedent.

The initial risk was avoided by the General Manager's prompt action. The first notice of trouble came on the Friday. The Board

Reporter Anonymous

had no time to consider fully what ought to be done. Edward Davies saw the union men and put to them the argument, among others, that the P.A. had a contract with D. C. Thomson and must fulfil it. The unions, while appreciating the P.A.'s problems, did not accept this argument. But, because of efforts the Ministry of Labour was making to bring about a settlement, they agreed not to do anything that weekend to aggravate the situation.

What Davies had helped to achieve was a breathing-space and that, as so often in industrial affairs, was most valuable. It gave time for the P.A. Board to hold a special meeting and then for a conference with representatives of the Printing and Kindred Trades Federation (P.K.T.F.) for consultation with the newspaper organisations, and for a further discussion by the Board. During these moves, which were spread over a fortnight, the P.K.T.F. had still not accepted the P.A.'s definition of its responsibility, which had been first asserted by the General Manager and later confirmed and elaborated by the Board. So the threat of strike action against the Press Association remained, action which could have affected every newspaper in the land—and the B.B.C. The unions, however, did undertake not to instruct their members to withdraw their labour without a further conference with the P.A. Board. Fortunately, the possibility of a head-on collision between the P.A. and the unions—which neither could have wished for but which the P.A. was ready, if necessary, to suffer—never became more than that. The Minister of Labour set up a court of inquiry into the Thomson dispute and so far as the Press Association was concerned the danger of a strike was never renewed. Although there were moments of tension during the two stoppages in the newspaper industry during the 1950s—the London stoppage in 1954 and the provincial one in 1959—the P.A. again maintained the position it had taken up in 1952 and its services were never interrupted.

The basic principle upon which the P.A. based its attitude during the 1952 dispute, said Hawkins, who was in the chair for the second time in three years, was that 'it is the Association's duty to make every effort in all circumstances to see that news supplies reach every one of its subscribers. We fully recognised,' he went on, 'that in coming to that decision we ran the risk, in this dispute or any future similar dispute, that the Association's services to all its subscribers might be seriously reduced or perhaps stopped

'A monopoly news service'

altogether. We none the less felt that we were doing the right thing and indeed the only thing possible.' He then analysed the reasoning behind the decision.

'In the first place,' he said, 'we are sufficiently old-fashioned to think that having made a contract it is our duty to try to fulfil it. Our relationship with our subscribers is much closer than that of a supplier of a commodity. The P.A. is part of every subscribing newspaper and every subscribing newspaper is part of the P.A. What touches one must touch the other. We did not feel, therefore, that we could take the very simple line of saying that if some trade union instructed members of our staff not to supply a particular subscriber we could just stand by and do nothing except make ineffectual protests.

'We are of the opinion also that in our case something more is involved than the legal aspect of a contract. Freedom of access to news supplies is part of the freedom of the press.... If it is accepted that news supplies can be interfered with for this purpose, it will be more difficult later—should the case arise again—to maintain that they shall not be cut off for some other reason.' Walter Hawkins then mentioned a third argument which the Board had 'pressed strongly' upon the unions, and which people outside the newspaper industry might find the most persuasive of all.

This third point, said Hawkins, was that 'the Press Association is in a unique position as being the only news agency in this country with a completely nation-wide organisation for the distribution of news, that its news service is available without restriction to everyone, and that it should therefore never be interfered with as a result of any industrial dispute, or of any other dispute, either inside or outside the newspaper industry'. Obviously, such a declaration could not be defended without qualification. There are no absolutes in industrial affairs which would permit the upholding of one abstract ideal of freedom at the ultimate expense of another, the freedom of men and women to band together to forward their interests and prevent their exploitation. But it can stand as a clear statement of the importance of the Press Association as a national institution and as a definition of the public interest in its operations which any trade unionist can accept—and which the trade unions, to this day, have appreciated and weighed carefully in times of trouble.

Reporter Anonymous

In the years following the second world war, as throughout its history, the P.A.'s value has been most obviously demonstrated in its coverage of the great occasion. These are the kinds of occasion which individual provincial newspapers would be wholly incapable of covering for themselves and where even the London newspapers, the B.B.C. and the Independent Television companies still lean heavily upon the P.A.

There had been an editorial plan in existence to deal with the death of Winston Churchill for some years before it happened. Throughout the last stages of his illness, and during the time of the funeral itself, the Press Association led the world's press and news agencies with its coverage.

While Sir Winston lay dying at home at Hyde Park Gate the P.A. kept watch there twenty-four hours a day. Reporters and photographers worked in shifts of eight hours or more. It was a job that had to be done but it had to be done discreetly and often it had to be done under unpleasant conditions. It was winter and bitterly cold. There was no shelter from wind or rain and the nearest public lavatory was nearly three-quarters of a mile away. At their desks in 85 Fleet Street the editorial staff worked shifts of sixteen hours a day or longer. The lying-in-state, which also had demanded round-the-clock coverage, was an even more arduous task than that of watching the Churchill house. On the day of the funeral itself, twenty-three reporters were stationed along the route from Westminster Hall to Waterloo Station. This, too, had been planned in advance. The phonists—the men who accompany reporters and telephone their 'copy' back to Fleet Street—had to force their way through the vast crowds lining the route. P.A. Photos had eighteen photographers out, including one on a roof overlooking St. Paul's. Their first picture was of the scene in the streets at 6 a.m. Their last ones were of the floral tributes on the grave and of people filing by in tribute. During the funeral they took eighty-two black-and-white pictures and by the end of the day more than 6200 prints had gone out and 135 original colour transparencies had been processed. Too many statistics merely numb the mind, but these few can convey the formidable scope of the operation.

P.A. reporters, who possess what has become an unfashionable journalistic attribute—the ability to take a verbatim shorthand note—are well used to covering police courts. But, even for the

'*A monopoly news service*'

P.A., the Great Train Robbery, which established an entry in the record-books as Britain's longest criminal trial of the century, offered a challenge which went beyond routine. Once again, only a brief accumulation of figures can give any idea of the size of the job, which not a single newspaper or broadcasting organisation would have dreamed of taking on for itself.

The preliminary proceedings took three weeks; at the Aylesbury Assizes the trial spread over twelve weeks. There were more than 600 exhibits and 257 witnesses were called. During the trial, the P.A. had no fewer than fifteen reporters covering it. One of the two men who spent longest on the job, Noel Richley, had fourteen notebooks, weighing nearly four pounds, as a souvenir. Like that of his colleagues, Richley's work remained anonymous. The regular, reliable report of what was said in the court went out day after day, largely taken for granted by the press, B.B.C. and I.T.N., a tacit tribute to the P.A.'s efficiency.

A P.A. reporter who made a rare emergence from anonymity[1] in a sequel to the Great Train Robbery was Alfred Browne. Early in 1966, after several newspapers had approached the Home Office to allow reporters to go inside Durham Prison to interview the jailed train robbers there, the authorities agreed to give facilities to one journalist. The Newspaper Proprietors' Association and the Newspaper Society had no difficulty in agreeing that it must be a P.A. man. Alfred Browne was given the job because, as the P.A. said, 'he just happened to be the senior reporter who was available'. By that accident, the name of Alfred Browne—and that of the Press Association which he joined as a phonist at the age of sixteen—appeared on the front pages of London and provincial papers all over Britain.

In the early days of the P.A. a team of reporters covering a major assignment would send their copy direct to subscribers from the nearest point of transmission—the local post office. In 1958, to achieve the quickest possible service from the Empire Games at Cardiff, the P.A. set up its own 'post office', a self-contained transmission unit from which news could be sent direct

---

[1] Another instance which should be recorded is the interview given by Aneurin Bevan to Arthur Booth, the P.A.'s chief reporter, in March 1960. It was the first interview Bevan had given since his major abdominal operation. (The P.A. also had exclusive pictures.) As it turned out, Booth was the last reporter to see him before his death.

Reporter Anonymous

to subscribers and the normal, intermediate process of phoning copy to London was cut out. In effect a miniature P.A. was established only a few hundred yards from the arena and within seconds of the finish of an event, the result and description of it were going straight to the newspapers.

The supreme, recurrent test of the P.A.'s organisation, and perhaps its outstanding achievement, is its coverage of General Election results.[1] The broadcasting services, the newspapers and the political parties are wholly dependent upon the Press Association. Of course it is theoretically feasible for each individual newspaper and the broadcasting authorities to arrange for telephone calls from each of the 630 constituencies to tell them the results; but in practice there would be comprehensive chaos. As it is, they confine themselves to sending individual reporters to 'key' constituencies to try to beat the P.A. to a result and to provide a 'colour' piece about the atmosphere and the reactions of winner and losers. A General Election is one time when they acknowledge ungrudgingly the superlative service provided by the P.A.

The present highly sophisticated operation has been evolved since the second world war, starting with the 1950 General Election. It was then that Ernest Harvey, the Association's Secretary, became actively involved for the first time in organising the P.A. coverage of election results. He and Charles Jervis, then day assistant editor, concentrated efforts on improving some of the procedures to ensure that messages about the state of the parties—the party scores at any stage of the election—were both fast and infallible. Until then, that section of the election service had been unrefined and less than efficient. Its revamping in 1950 proved particularly worthwhile because of the photo-finish with the Labour majority of only five. The P.A. minute-by-minute service was acclaimed by newspapers for its 'machine-like precision'.

From that time Harvey's interest in every part of the results service was intensified. No detail of organisation escaped scrutiny. Trial runs were timed with a stopwatch to cut seconds off some of the procedures. From 1911 until 1964, General Election results were collected jointly by the P.A. and Extel. The scope for com-

---

[1] The nation-wide coverage of municipal elections is, in a way, a more painstaking one because the machinery for collecting and collating the results is more hazardous and the parties can rarely agree on the gains and losses. But a General Election is a more concentrated, exposed challenge.

The P.A. serves radio and television

ABOVE: *P.A. copy being received in the reporting organiser's room at Broadcasting House where B.B.C. reporters and correspondents are given their assignments*

BELOW: *In studio 3b, radio's main news and current affairs studio, the author, George Scott, holding a P.A. news flash, conducts an interview for the* Ten O'Clock *programme*

The old and new methods of communication

ABOVE: *A Wheatstone morse set showing the operator punching a message on to tape*

BELOW: *Receiving the news and picture services on present-day equipment at a member-newspaper's office*

'*A monopoly news service*'

petition between the two agencies was limited to the speed at which the results could be processed and transmitted and to supplying a cumulative tally of seats won and of gains and losses, as well as other material with which the bare results could be clothed.

With the 1951 General Election the P.A. established a firm ascendancy over Extel both in speed and in the volume of material sent out. Thereafter the P.A. kept abreast of new techniques of electoral analysis. In a foreword to *British Parliamentary General Election Results in 1950-64*, David Butler, unofficial psephologist-royal, wrote: 'One of the main developments in electoral commentary since 1945 has been the appreciation that percentages are more revealing than plain figures. It was a great breakthrough when, in the 1950s, the Press Association started after every by-election to flash the turnout and the party percentages along its wires within a minute or two of sending out the crude result.'

The efficiency of the P.A. General Election service depends initially upon its reporters. There is one at the count in each constituency. The instant the result has been announced, he rushes to a telephone. At the P.A. a completely automatic telephone system connects him with any one of ten men or women ready to take his result. In less than half a minute teleprinters are repeating the result, with a mass of additional detail, in newspaper and foreign news-agency offices and in radio and television news rooms throughout the world.

It is difficult to imagine how a computer could take over the jobs of these reporters telephoning results from the constituencies. But a computer could and eventually will carry out the purely mechanical operations previously done by men and women. It was on Ernest Harvey's suggestion that, in the 1964 General Election, an NCR 315 computer was put to work for the first time. Into it, before the poll, was fed the mass of factual information about candidates, parties, previous results, majorities and so on which forms the starting-point of any election commentary and which it could disgorge again to order. In addition it was able to produce analyses of 'swing', nationally and regionally, calculations of the percentage poll, forecasts of the final state of the parties and all those other piquant ingredients of a modern election.

Unfortunately, the computer could not be housed in 85 Fleet

Reporter Anonymous

Street and figures of the results had to be telephoned to the computer team a mile away. In turn, the information provided by the computer had to be telephoned back to P.A. headquarters. Consequently, it took a minute and a half to get the swing on a particular result. This delay was reckoned too long by the P.A. itself although the overall operation brought great credit to the agency. So, too, did the 1966 General Election when there was a direct teleprinter link between the P.A. and the computer. The gap between teleprinting the result into the computer and transmission of the 'swing' was cut to about half a minute. The service now included a running forecast of the ultimate result. It is now possible to foresee a future in which, suitably programmed in the weeks before an election and fed on polling day with the results in the form of votes cast in each constituency, the computer will do the rest. It will punch tape at very high speed which, fed into P.A. transmitters, will produce a complete service of full and detailed results and analyses on P.A. printers all over Britain. For thirty-six hours P.A. subscribers will be receiving their service direct from the computer.

Fewer and fewer men and women will be needed to carry out the operation. But at the 1966 election nearly a thousand contributed to the service; reporters, copy-takers, sub-editors, accountants, mathematicians, typists, telephonists, telegraphists—and computer experts. That General Election was the first one for more than fifty years at which the P.A. had collected the results on its own. The reason was that, the previous autumn, Extel had decided to close down its general home news and Parliamentary services to newspapers. These services had become, according to the company, 'completely uneconomic'.

With the Extel closures, the Press Association, which had done its fair share of monopoly-fighting in its time, found itself the subject of Parliamentary and public debate as 'a monopoly news service'. The Liberal Party called for action by the Monopolies Commission 'to ensure the continuance of a competitive service'. Hugh Jenkins, a Labour M.P., asked the President of the Board of Trade to intervene. The printing unions, too, demanded action. An Exchange Telegraph defence committee, set up to fight the closures, sent a letter to George Brown, then Minister for Economic Affairs, appealing to him. The letter stated:

'The obvious dangers—the danger to press freedom, the danger

'A monopoly news service'

of restricted channels for the dissemination of news, the danger of sheer commercial self-interest obliterating the national interests—have been sharply underlined . . . The deprivation of newspapers of an alternative news service (the value of which was recognised by the Royal Commission on the Press) is a further step towards the contraction of ownership and a further contraction of outlet. We are convinced that such a move is inimical to good public policy and that a thorough investigation is vitally necessary...'

The central London branch committee of the National Union of Journalists also issued a statement:

'The committee deplores the proposed closures and particularly the resulting monopoly in the home news agency field with attendant professional, social and political dangers. The committee is especially concerned at the apparent undervaluation by national and provincial newspaper managements of the Exchange Telegraph services concerned....'

The Press Council expressed its regrets 'because the decision reduces the sources of information available to all newspapers'.

The issue generated a fair amount of heat for about three weeks. But Douglas Jay, the President of the Board of Trade, said, first, he was satisfied that the case was not an appropriate one for the Monopolies Commission and, later, that he was satisfied the 'alternative news-gathering services which are available are adequate to protect the public from any possible detriment'.

Any journalist must sympathise with the instincts of those who sense danger when any channel for collecting or disseminating news is closed. He must share, too, the concern of the unions over the fate of men losing their jobs—seventy out of a total Extel staff of 2000 in this instance. But what was to be done? The Board of Trade inquiries showed that the Extel closures could not be avoided. A subsidy—the company needed an extra £150,000—was surely out of the question. Furthermore, on the 'monopoly' question, the critics, however admirable their motives, were exaggerating the dangers. The *Guardian* is not a paper to suspect of being soft towards monopolies but it commented in a leading article:

'... the M.P.s and trade unionists who want the Government to intervene are barking up the wrong tree. Though the Press Association will now be the only major news agency supplying domestic and parliamentary news, this does not mean it will enjoy a monopoly in any real sense. Most newspapers have access to parallel and alternative news services through their own London offices or through links with other newspapers or groups.

'In any case it is hard to see what the Liberal Party means when it calls on the Monopolies Commission to "ensure the continuance of a competitive service." If the P.A. finds itself alone, that is not its fault. Extel is giving up the reporting of parliamentary and general news of its own choice and for commercial reasons. The company cannot be required to continue a service which it finds unprofitable in order that some newspapers shall continue to enjoy a multiplicity of news sources.'

The Times, too, restored a sense of proportion to the argument:

'... even in the reporting of home and parliamentary news the fears of monopoly are largely irrelevant to this particular issue. So far as major newspapers are concerned no press agency can have a monopoly: its role is to supplement, not to replace their own competitive services. The position is different for the smaller papers, but then Exchange Telegraph has only five provincial subscribers to its general news service. It does not have a telegraphic service throughout the country, which means that a provincial newspaper has to take Exchange Telegraph news in its London office and relay on its own wire network. This is an expense which only the more prosperous could contemplate, and in any case it may be doubted how many provincial newspapers could afford a second national news agency. The Press Association is bound to be the first because it is owned collectively by the provincial newspapers...'

The amount of competition between the P.A. and Extel was, by this time, as *The Times* demonstrated, limited. It was chiefly confined to London. Nevertheless, where it existed it was beneficial. This was recognised by the Press Association, directors, management and staff, as by anyone else. The last of their old rivals had gone, first the London News, then the Central News, and now Extel, all of them confirming the lesson of other countries that no big general news agency can survive without either Government aid or the assured support of a substantial section of the newspaper press.

What remained of the Extel operations were the profitable ser-

'A monopoly news service'

vices, its financial and sporting services and its special news service supplied mainly to clubs and hotels. The P.A. took over the Joint Service from the Law Courts and from the beginning of 1966 it became known as the Press Association Law Service; the Extel staff at the Law Courts joined the P.A. Among the other Extel men who came to the P.A. were their diplomatic and lobby correspondents.

Another famous agency ended its independent existence in 1965, when Pardons, the famous cricket and football reporting agency, was merged with the Press Association. This time, however, there were no protests. The merger was no more than a rational development. Ever since its foundation in 1880 by Charles Pardon, a senior P.A. sub-editor, the firm had had a close alliance with the P.A. It had been providing the P.A., under contract, with its cricket and football services. The two had grown closer and closer together until a merging of identities became the most logical and efficient final step. Although the P.A.'s racing service carried on as a separate department, it was now possible—at last, it could be said—to form a really comprehensive sports department. Its first editor was Harry Gee, one of the three partners in Pardons. All the partners and all the full-time staff came on to the P.A. pay-roll. The only sadness could have been the disappearance of the name of Pardons, a name deservedly acclaimed throughout sporting journalism. In fact, the Press Association has kept it alive, using it particularly in the traditional task of editing *Wisden*, the cricketer's bible.

If to certain insensitive and underprivileged people the graces and pleasures of cricket are a mystery, the jargon and technicalities—let alone the fascination—of racing to a non-racing man are even more incomprehensible. But there was one episode in the 1950s whose importance to the P.A. is immediately apparent.

After its troubles during the second world war the Joint Service quickly regained its prosperity and, at their half-yearly meetings, the members of the joint committee had little to do but congratulate the joint managers on yet another 'record'. There was, however, one source of occasional trouble. Most racecourse managements did not find it easy to run at a reasonable profit and at the same time maintain and improve their properties. Understandably, from their point of view, the more people who paid to come and watch the racing and the more bookmakers who paid

Reporter Anonymous

for stands on the courses the better. This was why in earlier days they had resented the activities of news agency men who managed to communicate so quickly to the public and the off-course bookmakers the results and starting-prices. In time, the agencies had broken down this hostility to the point where they were able to abandon the picturesque but ultimately inefficient practice of ticktacking. The racecourses allowed them and the newspapers to rent telephones on the spot. The courses appreciated the publicity given to racing—as well they might—but they still felt resentful of the off-course bookmaker making his profit out of the programmes they staged and paying nothing in return.[1]

In 1956 the Racecourse Association, representing most of the courses, proposed enormous increases in the fees the Joint Service was paying for on-course telephones. The racecourses hoped that these extra charges would be passed on to the off-course bookmakers who subscribed to the Joint Service. Sympathetic though they were to the feelings of the Racecourse Association, the P.A. and Extel could not fall in with the proposal. The agencies pointed out that they were in business to collect and sell news and their newspaper and non-newspaper customers would object strongly and justifiably if they were to act as tax-collectors for racecourse managements.

The Racecourse Association withdrew, though still unsatisfied, but in 1957 the managements of Aintree (not then a member of the Association) and of Manchester decided to see what they could achieve by independent action. They demanded £500 a day from the Joint Service and other racing agencies for telephone facilities. That was a fantastic demand and the Joint Service rejected it. The Joint Service succeeded in covering meetings at both places without using on-course telephones and both Aintree and Manchester quickly restored the old arrangements.

For many years the racing public depended upon the P.A. to tell them which horses were going to run and which jockeys were to ride them. This service of 'Probables' was as good a guide as was possible but it was far from infallible. Owners or trainers could be reticent or change their minds at the last moment be-

[1] Government legislation has since established a fund, partly provided by bookmakers who now have to pay a levy to be used for the benefit of racing, but the proportion received by racecourse managements is still much less than they would like.

'*A monopoly news service*'

cause, for example, the 'going' had altered and no longer suited their horse. People laid their bets on the basis of these Probables and when one of them did not run they were annoyed. It was even worse when a horse not listed as a probable runner did run and win the race; a remarkable number of punters then claimed they would have had their money on the winner if only they had known he would be running.

In 1959, after years of consideration, the Jockey Club and National Hunt Committee made a decision which meant a big change for the better in the racing world. They decided that the owner of a horse which had been entered for a race must notify Messrs. Weatherby's (acting for the Jockey Club) by noon on the day before the race whether the horse would run or not. If it were nominated to run and failed to do so, the owner must pay a forfeit. Compiling these 'overnight declarations', as they are called, meant much more work and expense for Weatherby's and it was suggested that anyone who wanted the lists of declared runners should pay for them. After discussion, however, it was agreed the lists should be supplied free of charge for newspaper publication. Because the declarations did not include the names of jockeys, the P.A. still had to collect those as before.

For all that the Joint Service was highly successful and the relations between the two agencies were now extremely amicable, the feeling remained at the P.A. that, because of the over-hasty agreement of 1922, the Extel was getting an unfair share of the fruits. Any new agreement, it was felt, should provide for an equal sharing of the surplus earned by the supply of Joint Service news throughout the whole of the United Kingdom. The old agreement had been extended twice but it had to be considered again in 1961. In 1958 the P.A. gave the necessary three years' notice to end the agreement.

During the following year the two agencies failed to find a meeting-point. Extel was ready to make some concessions but they would not have amounted to anything like the radical changes the P.A. was seeking. When the initial decision to give notice had been taken the Chairman of the P.A. was Laurence Scott, of the *Manchester Guardian*, who continued to be closely involved in the discussions about the Joint Service even after he retired from the Board in 1960. Another director, who contributed significantly to the ultimately successful outcome, was Pat Winfrey, of the East

Reporter Anonymous

Midland Allied Press. Winfrey was a warm and friendly personality, a gusty character, with little regard for the niceties of protocol (which proved embarrassing, occasionally, for the P.A. officers). He held that in its attitude to the Joint Service the P.A. 'must think big'. By this he meant that, unless the Extel agreed to a Joint Service on the basis of complete and equal sharing, the P.A. should be prepared to go it alone. This would mean competing with Extel in providing services to newspapers and, more importantly, to bookmakers, previously supplied jointly by the two agencies.

This was the audacious line adopted by the P.A. in April 1960, when there was still no sign of a favourable response from Extel. The P.A. told Extel that a complete and truly Joint Service was the only acceptable basis for negotiations. The threat of what would happen if Extel did not agree was expressed in the most delicate and sensitive manner but the P.A.'s intentions were unmistakable. There was no question of bluff. The P.A. Board initiated research into the cost of going it alone and was ready, if necessary, to sustain a substantial investment to compete successfully with Extel.

At the time that crucial decision was taken Pat Winfrey was Chairman-designate. In June 1960 he became Chairman. In September of the same year, when Extel had still failed to reply to the proposal made six months earlier, Winfrey faced the real possibility of a break. He set out his views, in a six-page memorandum, on the action the P.A. should take if the Joint Service agreement were not renewed. Not all the P.A. directors—nor all the senior members of the Consultative Committee whose opinions were sought—faced such a prospect without misgiving. But they supported the decision of the September Board meeting to stand firm. The Managing Director of Extel, Thomas F. Watson, was to be told of the P.A.'s disappointment at not having received a reply to its proposals.

It is not surprising that Extel should have hesitated long and have hoped that the P.A. would weaken. It was being asked, after all, to make big concessions. But following the clear message from that September Board meeting, Extel moved quickly. It accepted the P.A. demands in principle.

Then the real negotiations began. The broad agreement had to be fleshed with detail but there were no insuperable obstacles and

'*A monopoly news service*'

the new arrangements for the partnership came into effect on 1st January 1962, to run for forty years. The form and terms of the ultimate agreement—which provided for equalisation to be achieved over a number of years and gave Extel the management of all the provincial centres—were perhaps not all that Pat Winfrey would have liked to have secured for the P.A. But it was a fair agreement and by asking for a great deal the P.A. had achieved much. It also meant that a partnership, valuable to both sides, had been saved. It said a lot for both that a new agreement did prove possible. During the negotiations, although it in no way affected them, there was, by most helpful coincidence, a new development. The Government licensed cash betting shops which were set up in large numbers. These shops became Joint Service customers with the result that, although it was relatively worse off under the new agreement, Extel (as well as the P.A.) actually received more from the Pool. The partnership's survival, however, owed much to the two chief executives, Thomas Watson, who became Chairman of Extel as well as Managing Director in 1961, and to Edward Davies, whose negotiating skill and cool head had again proved their value. (Laurence Scott said that any success in the negotiations 'had depended to a large extent on the work done on behalf of the Board' by Davies and 'to only a slightly lesser extent' by Ernest Harvey, the Secretary.)

It was Davies's last—and, in the view of many, his most important—achievement on behalf of the Press Association. On the day it came into effect, he retired as General Manager. He had served for twenty-four years, second only in length of time to Edmund Robbins. Remembering his earlier years at the Newspaper Society, he had every reason to say that he had spent his career in the service of the provincial press. He had spanned arduous and eventful years, as he himself recalled at the time of his retirement.

'Since my arrival,' he said, speaking at a Savoy luncheon in his honour, 'we have occupied and developed a pretty good new building. By guess and by God we managed to get through the war without suffering undue trouble. We put in a complete new telegraph system to our subscribers outside London, including wired pictures, and extended our London system as well. With my friend Sir Christopher Chancellor (among many other things we did together) we founded P.A.-Reuter Photos and the

Reporter Anonymous

Features company . . . The Special Reporting section was established and has flourished exceedingly . . . We founded the noblest work of man, the Comprehensive Service, which so much facilitates the task of the members in finding out what they pay the P.A. and possibly facilitates the P.A. task in making sure the money comes in. We founded the all-in service to our London subscribers . . . In 1941, with the N.P.A. we founded the "new Reuters" . . . We put our relations with the B.B.C. on to a satisfactory basis, not without some difficulty, and that helped us to get on to a satisfactory basis with the new television news company.[1] We co-operated very much with the other British news agencies in labour matters and for my sins I was chairman of their negotiating committee from 1938 until a couple of months ago . . . I had the pleasure of negotiating with Mr. Watson what we call the new Joint Service. . . .'

Like his predecessors, Edward Davies came to identify himself with the Press Association and it was without humbug that he could say, when awarded the C.B.E., 'It is really an honour for the Press Association and as such I shall be proud to wear it.'

In contrast to Edward Davies, the man who took over from him had been a news agency man all his working life. George Cromarty Bloom, a trim, athletic, friendly man, moved over to the P.A. from Reuters, where he was an Assistant General Manager. His background was suitably exotic. His father a Queenslander, his mother from Orkney, George Bloom himself was born in Manchuria; but his parents soon went back to Australia and his boyhood was spent on a farm near Brisbane. He went to Oxford to read forestry, an unlikely preparation for a news agency career but there have been many stranger ones. It was chance that directed him into Reuters. A meeting with a friend, the mention of a job, and off he went to Shanghai, to work with Reuters' commercial services. Shanghai, the Philippines, North China and then back to Shanghai to be commercial services manager for the Far East, working throughout these years under Christopher Chancellor, then Reuter's Far East General Manager. George Bloom was taken prisoner by the Japanese on the same day they bombed Pearl Harbour, 7th December 1941. After ten months he was one of a

[1] The price paid for P.A. services by the B.B.C. and I.T.N. is settled by negotiation—or 'horse-trading', as the present General Manager calls it.

'A monopoly news service'

group of Allied prisoners freed in an exchange deal with the Japanese. Much of the rest of his time with Reuters was spent in Central and South America, where he was concerned with the general as well as commercial news services.

When George Bloom came to the P.A. he was largely ignorant of its affairs and of the ways and needs of the provincial press. But he quickly sensed and appreciated the peculiar 'family' feeling which lingers inside the P.A. even now. He came, also, to respect the historical roots of the men sitting around the boardroom table at 85 Fleet Street, most of them now representing newspaper groups, nearly all of them professional managers like himself, but still reaching back to those provincial traditions and values upon which the Press Association itself has been built.

The coming of George Bloom, with Ernest Harvey taking on the role of Assistant General Manager as well as that of Secretary, heralded a phase of major developments in the Press Association. The P.A. had to adapt and equip itself rapidly for the era ahead, the era of communications satellites, of instantaneous transmission of television pictures across the globe. The pace of change inside the P.A. has reflected what has been happening in a much more dramatic and conspicuous way in the newspaper industry as a whole.

George Bloom brought to the P.A. an intimate knowledge of the techniques and activities of the world's news agencies. He also brought a modern managerial mind with which to shape the agency for the future. He set to work to rationalise the P.A., to eliminate from the organisation any kinks which might impede efficiency. Many of the achievements of good management are hidden from the outside observer; they do not make for colourful narrative: so it is with much that has been done at the Press Association since George Bloom took over in 1962.

The administration was completely reorganised. Management consultants were brought in to assist with the modernisation of the editorial floor. Several positive and practical steps were taken to foster a much closer working relationship and a better understanding between management and staff. The new General Manager paid a lot of attention to the news services. The Associated Press world news service which, previously, had been supplied separately, was now brought into the Comprehensive Service. A.P. world pictures were offered to members and they, too, were later incorporated into the Comprehensive Service. Parliamentary coverage was rationalised with the merger of the Central News Parliamentary Service and, as we have already seen, the Photos and Features companies were liquidated and their operations improved by being integrated into the P.A.

In the field of telecommunications, a start was made in 1967, after years of research and preparation, with teletypesetting. By means of TTS, as it is known, certain kinds of news, transmitted from the P.A. in Fleet Street in the form of punched tape, are translated by automatic process, in provincial newspaper offices, into columns of type ready for insertion in the page. This service was introduced, by agreement with the unions, as a two-year experiment. It was confined at the beginning to the transmission of the daily race card—a form of news chosen deliberately for its complexity; one newspaper reckoned it had saved two and a half hours in the setting of each card. When the experiment began only a few newspapers were equipped to take the TTS service but it was expected that, as the service became more ambitious, more and more newspapers would join in and the use of teletypesetting would move on to a permanent basis. It was also under George Bloom that plans were laid for the modernisation of the whole of the Press Association's networks with transistorised equipment and new fast teleprinters.

In the boardroom, too, there has been that same feeling of drive and urgency which has characterised George Bloom's management of P.A. affairs. The men who were to occupy the chair during 1968, the P.A.'s centenary year, were chosen for their conspicuous abilities. W. D. ('Bill') Barneston, Chairman of United Newspapers, had been a most successful journalist and broadcaster in Scotland before joining his company's Board; his approach combined shrewdness and imagination. His successor as P.A. Chairman was to be Kenneth A. Searle, Managing Director of The Manchester Guardian and Evening News Ltd, who not only brought his distinctive talents but also provided, through the *Guardian*, a pleasingly symbolic link with the father of the P.A., John Edward Taylor. With men like these on the Board—and, in particular, among their predecessors in the chair, Leslie Stallard, of the *Wolverhampton Express and Star*—the P.A. was sure of progressive direction. Institutional status—formally acknowledged by lustrous centenary ceremonials—has been accompanied not by

'*A monopoly news service*'

ossification but by radical and wide-ranging preparations to meet the future on its own terms.

Those changes which the directors and chief executives have initiated and carried through may not lend themselves easily to picturesque illustration but they have helped to invest the Press Association with a new vigour and a rediscovered sense of purpose and identity. Certainly, those who work for it and those who take its services recognise the value and significance of the innovations.

When George Bloom arrived at the P.A., the Editor-in-Chief was Charles Jervis, who had succeeded Henry Martin several years earlier, in 1954. The character of the new man is fairly indicated by what he said when he himself retired eleven years later. 'My one object,' said Jervis, a man with a quiet, gentle face, 'was to humanise the organisation; to recognise that every man is a human being with feelings; and I have done all I could to make a man feel he is someone worthwhile.' He praised the achievements of his staff and was compassionate about their inevitable shortcomings. Charles Jervis was well based in provincial journalism, moving from the *Liverpool Express* to the *Westmorland Gazette* and to the *Croydon Times* before joining the P.A. in 1937. He had an early association with Arthur Christiansen, the *Daily Express* editor with whom Henry Martin had clashed. Recalling memories of Southport, Christiansen wrote,[1] 'Every year I had to cover its famous flower show for the Liverpool *Evening Express*. In my last year on the paper, 1924, I took along a young messenger named Jervis to telephone my copy. He told me he had applied for a reporter's job in the Lake District but hadn't got the rail fare for the crucial personal interview. I loaned it to him and he got the job.'

Charles Jervis's qualities and virtues were different from those of his predecessor but he shared with Henry Martin a jealous concern for the good name of the P.A. While recognising that it was the agency's job, as always, to serve the newspapers with the kind of material they wanted, he insisted on maintaining its objective standards, collecting the facts, checking the facts, but not speculating upon them. He was concerned, too, with preserving the reputation of the P.A. during a period when the press was under heavy attack for its intrusive practices. In serving the news-

[1] In *World's Press News*, 6th September 1963.

papers, the P.A. did not have to imitate all that the newspapers were prepared to do. There were places a P.A. reporter need not go, there were things he should not do. Jervis's definition of news was a wide one, attuned to contemporary tastes, but it imposed important limits. Nevertheless, Charles Jervis had his share of trouble with authority. The most serious incident occurred when he himself was ill and away from the office. In reporting a murder trial at Exeter City Assizes in 1957, a local correspondent, who had served the P.A. for four or five years, slipped up badly. He had not been in court himself and had based his report to the P.A. on notes taken by two of his colleagues. One of these had with him reports of the earlier proceedings in the magistrates' court. In reporting the assize court case, the P.A. correspondent attributed to counsel for the Crown, as part of his opening speech, certain remarks which had been made in the lower court but were not repeated at the assize trial. There was no way by which the P.A. sub-editor who handled the story in London could know of the error and the report was sent out including the inaccuracy. Newspapers published it while the trial was still going on and the defence objected that their client's case had been prejudiced. The judge had to stop the trial, discharge the jury and set the case down for rehearing. As was to be expected, he was exceedingly displeased. At the P.A. the Day Assistant Editor, Leslie Inglis, received a telephone message warning him of impending trouble. Jervis, the absent Editor-in-Chief, faced the prospect of a jail sentence for contempt of court.

The General Manager moved quickly. He consulted the P.A.'s solicitors who had agents in Exeter, where the assizes were being held. The Day Assistant Editor was sent to the city where he was able to arrange for a leading Q.C. to make an explanation and apology on behalf of the P.A. to the judge in court the next day. (Three national newspapers which had published the P.A. report, the *Telegraph*, the *Express* and the *Sketch*, made similar arrangements to express their 'humblest apologies'.)

The judge, Mr. Justice Salmon, said he took the view that 'this is an extremely grave matter'. He granted that the offenders had adopted the right attitude in expressing their regrets at the earliest possible moment but he indicated that they might not have heard the last of it. In fact, not long afterwards, a very courteous chief inspector from Scotland Yard visited 85 Fleet Street, to discuss the case with the P.A. General Manager and Charles Jervis, who had now recovered. He left with the intention of talking to the local correspondent who had made the initial error. The two P.A. executives had not revealed his name but, for all their good intentions, it was fairly obvious the chief inspector knew it anyway. The P.A. heard no more and Jervis remained a free man. But the danger of his committal had been very real and the risk of running foul of the law is a chronic one for the editor of a news agency as for a newspaper editor. When it is remembered the vast quantities of news the P.A. sends out,[1] the speed of the operations with the possibilities of error at every stage, it is remarkable how few serious errors occur.

Some of the biggest news stories of the post-war years happened during Charles Jervis's editorship. The man who succeeded him, John Williamson, had played an important part, as chief news editor, in organising their coverage. Williamson, an easy-mannered, unpretentious man, an unashamed romantic about the men who have built the P.A. and the deeds they performed, had a very similar background to Jervis. He, too, was born in Lancashire, where he spent his first years in journalism before moving to a London suburban paper. He joined the P.A. in 1938, only a year after Jervis. John Williamson's uncomplicated concept of the Press Association's responsibilities was characterised by his attitude to the reporting of the Moors murder case in 1966. Much of the evidence in that case was about sadism, horrifying and sensational. Each newspaper editor had to make a judgement of taste about how much of it he should publish. But Williamson, at the head of a national news agency, had no such decision to make. 'It is not our job to act as censors,' he said. 'We had to send it all out because it's our job to provide a service to the papers and for them to decide what they want to use of it.' John Williamson added only one qualification: 'Of course, we would not "publish" anything obscene.' Clearly, in the Moors murder case, as in all

---

[1] It has been estimated that during the twenty-four hours of an average weekday, the P.A. transmits about 89,000 words to London subscribers and 128,000 to provincial ones. A breakdown shows that the London output consists of 43,000 words of general news, 18,000 from Parliament and 28,000 of sport. To the provinces go 41,000 words of general news, 18,000 Parliamentary, 19,000 Reuter, 4000 Associated Press, 34,000 sport, 10,000 of City news and 2000 in the form of captions to pictures.

Reporter Anonymous

general news stories, the P.A. would cut and condense the material available, but it would be done on the basis of newsworthiness, not moral censorship.

The fifties and sixties saw the retirement or death of many men who had been with the Press Association from the years after the first world war and before the second when the modern P.A. was being built. Leonard Warren, the chief of the Telegraph Department, who had been in charge of the long-delayed and extremely important technical operation to change over from Creed-Wheatstone to multi-channel transmission, retired at the end of 1953 and died only three weeks later. His successor, Jack Lush, had already been with the P.A. for nearly twenty-five years and he had himself played an outstanding part in the post-war developments. Here was a man whose professional enthusiasm could not be doused by difficulty or set-back and who displayed a humorous indulgence of non-technical colleagues.

On the editorial side, Louis Wulff went to the *Evening News* and R. Gomer Jones took over as the P.A. Court Correspondent, occupying an even more distinctive position when the Extel closures left him as the one and only Court Correspondent. His responsibilities as the trusted link between royalty and press became even greater.

Billy Howells, the general sports editor, was only fifty-three when he died in 1960. Charles Grant, at the Law Courts for more than forty years and chief of the team there for thirteen, retired in 1963. So did Frank Turner, who had been deputy editor for the last five years but had been on night turn, rising to be night editor, for thirty-seven years before that, a benevolent and compassionate man who earned much affection. The following year Frank King, the P.A.'s extremely able Diplomatic Correspondent since before the war, died only two years after his retirement. His close friend at the P.A., Arthur Booth, retired in 1965 after ten years as chief reporter. One of the most popular men ever to work in the Lobby at the House of Commons, Edmond Stacpoole, left there in 1966, having received the C.B.E. five years before. E. Spencer Shew, who joined the P.A. when Extel closed its home news services, took over as the P.A.'s Lobby man.

A book like this could not hope to mention all those who have shared in making the Press Association strong and efficient. A few men have demanded mention because of the outstanding part

'A monopoly news service'

they have played. Most of those, because their work is more conspicuous and more colourful, have been on the editorial side. As they would be the first to point out, however, the achievements of the P.A. are based, always, on team-work. That, of course, is true, and is recognised, but one other name must be recalled—that of Robbins.

In 1955 C. J. Robbins, chief of the P.A.'s Parliamentary reporting staff, retired. When he went it was the first time for eighty-five years that the Association had been without a member of the Robbins family. In two generations six members of the family had contributed more than 190 years' service to the P.A. If indeed the P.A. was a 'family' and a 'team', then it was very much of their doing.

The Press Association, which was born one hundred years ago, and started operations with an editorial staff of three sub-editors and one reporter, today employs on the staff 240 journalists and photographers, 160-odd on the communications side and more than 300 on clerical and other work. It still has forty messengers, the descendants of those perky Cockney boys who first carried the name of the Press Association about the adventurous streets of London.

It is inevitable that just as the annual general meeting of the Association has become a perfunctory affair, compared with the warm, familiar, often protracted, often disputatious, nearly always good-humoured meetings of the nineteenth century, so its administration and operation have become more professional and less personalised. It could not be otherwise. But a few echoes of the past linger. Among the members attending the annual luncheon at the Savoy one may find a Tillotson from Bolton, a Scott from Manchester, a Gleave from Southampton, a Henderson from Belfast, a Grime from Blackpool or a Graham from Wolverhampton, among the provincial executives and the distinguished guests. Similarly, among the P.A.'s regular correspondents all over Britain, up to 1500 of them in all, it was still possible in 1967 to find the rare non-professional, the man who was not a local newspaperman. Such a man was 'Lewis of Hope'. Charles David Lewis, a railway signalman in the Hope Valley of Derbyshire, was appointed a P.A. correspondent in 1934. He had built up quite a reputation already, acting as correspondent for a number of papers in his area, and his news sense and his accurate ob-

Reporter Anonymous

servation enabled him to represent the P.A. over one of the wildest stretches of countryside in Britain, the Peak district. If news broke while he was on railway duty, his wife acted as his deputy. In 1967 he was still the P.A.'s 'Lewis of Hope'.

Sixteen / *The second hundred*

The provincial morning newspapers, which rose so proudly during the latter part of the nineteenth century, have been fighting for life since the second world war. Several have died. Others survive precariously. Few, indeed, can face the future with assurance. Not a single town in England and Wales now has more than one morning newspaper which is published entirely locally. Dublin and Glasgow are the only cities in the British Isles outside London which still have more than one evening paper, although provincial evening papers have endured much more successfully and many enjoy real prosperity; a few new ones have been launched successfully during the 1960s. The concentration of ownership, the absorption of independent newspapers into the big chains, reached a point where, following the second post-war Royal Commission, Parliament introduced legislation to try to check any further takeovers.

The years since 1945 have seen the press of Great Britain under anxious public scrutiny. Its ownership, its ethics, its efficiency and its economics have all been subjected to intimate examination and analysis. Large questions have been posed about the public interest. That is a term subject to versatile interpretation but in this instance it indicates a proper concern about the capacity of Britain's newspapers to discharge their democratic function. Can they still provide an adequate outlet for the expression of public opinion in all its diversity? It is not enough that we should hear the opinions of a metropolitan newspaper baron or the corporate opinions of a commercial chain or those of the major political parties. Minorities and individuals, however irrational or mis-

Reporter Anonymous

guided they may seem to those in office, also have the right, or should have, to be heard, even if not heeded.

There is every reason to be perturbed on this score. In Britain, more than in most other countries, the annihilation of distance as a barrier to communication and the rapid development of mass media have brought particularly acute dangers. Increasingly we are under pressure, sometimes explicit, sometimes tacit, to conform. By their nation-wide projection and reiteration certain modes of speech, thought and behaviour become acceptable and deviations from the norm become suspect.

It is easy enough to over-dramatise these trends but it is much more perilous to shrug one's shoulders at them. Even political criticism is assuming an unhealthy gentility. The politicians themselves, acting, once again, in pursuit of what they construe as the best interests of the country, have managed to enfeeble and emasculate television as they were never able to tame newspapers in the past, hard though some of them have tried. Even today, however pallid they may seem by comparison with their nineteenth-century ancestors, it is to newspapers we must look for the reflection of unpopular views, for that instinctive questioning of authority which protects a democratic society from sliding into acquiescence.

There are still, thank goodness, editors and managers and proprietors who do not place respectability at the top of a list of journalistic virtues. Their willingness to offend against orthodoxy, to risk their reputations, are our continuing safeguard. This is certainly as true at a local level as at a national one. Contrary to what some people think, not everything big and important happens in London and not every abuse of power is perpetrated in Whitehall or Westminster.

But newspapers have to pay their way. The Shawcross Commission rightly rejected the idea of subsidies, however indirect, to keep alive an unsuccessful newspaper. Few indeed are the men or companies prepared to bear a loss indefinitely to ensure a paper's survival.

At first sight, the future seems to present even more formidable threats to the press than those it has met in the past. Colour television will take another bite out of newspapers' advertising revenue. The instantaneous transmission of television pictures by satellite from any part of the world will present the world's news

The second hundred

as it happens. Within the newspaper industry itself local papers must meet intensified competition from London papers which can now flash whole pages to regional centres for facsimile reproduction.

How can the press survive—especially the provincial press—in this new world? First, let it be admitted that newspapers—as we know them today—will not be able to compete, and should not try to compete, with television in providing 'instant news'. But there will be an even greater need to interpret that news, for perceptive reporters who can select the significant fact, who can illuminate the motives behind the action. Secondly, although our sense of community, our close identification with our environment, has been eroded, we are still likely to be much more interested in what happens to the man next door or to a plane-load of tourists from our own town than we are in the politics or calamities of far-off lands.

What is even more important, however, is that newspapers may see new hope in those same scientific and technological developments which seem to threaten them. They, too, must make much more use of colour. They, too, must harness television and the computer to bring about a revolution in the editing, the production and the distribution of their product. Given good, professional management, economic realism and the far-sighted co-operation of the unions, the newspaper industry could move into a new phase of development. We are not concerned here with the precise forms these developments may take. The air is rich with imaginative speculation. All that needs to be emphasised is that we are talking not of fantasy but of real possibilities—and there are men in the industry who are well aware of them. We accept without thought today so many things that would have seemed inconceivable a few decades ago. So will the laborious physical processes by which newspapers and books have been produced for the past century soon be accepted as archaic and intolerable. The corollary to 'instant news' is the 'instant newspaper'. It will come.

Where will a great national news agency like the Press Association fit into this picture? Its job will remain the same—to collect and send out news. Its responsibility to ensure its accuracy and to keep it free of the taint of partiality will not be less than it was at its birth in 1868. It will seek every means to increase the speed at which it can transmit the news.

Reporter Anonymous

For as far ahead as one can see, no matter what form newspapers may assume they will still need a central point where news is gathered in, sifted, edited and sent out again. They will want it well packaged: lucid, ready for use, easy to digest. Newspapers—and radio and television—will continue to take that service for granted most of the time, knowing, if an item of news comes from the P.A., 'then it's safe'. They will continue—as they are entitled—to use long passages from that service without acknowledging the source except in those rare instances when its accuracy is questioned. For most of their working lives the names of the men and women who produce the P.A. 'copy' will remain unknown to the people who read it in their newspapers.

This is what those provincial newspapermen who founded the Press Association meant it to be. They meant the P.A. reporters to be *their* reporters. They meant the P.A. to be *their* news agency. They did a good job.

Appendix 1

CHAIRMEN OF THE PRESS ASSOCIATION
1868 – 1968

1868–69	Mr. John Edward Taylor *Manchester Guardian*	
1869–70 ⎱ 1870–71 ⎰	Mr. John Jaffray *Birmingham Daily Post*	
1871–72 ⎱ 1872–73 ⎰	Mr. Frederick Clifford *Sheffield Daily Telegraph*	See also 1878–79
1873–74	Mr. P. S. Macliver *Western Daily Press*, Bristol	
1874–75	Mr. J. Glover *Leamington Spa Courier*	
1875–76	Mr. J. A. Willox *Liverpool Courier*	See also 1900–01
1876–77	Mr. J. W. Jevons *Nottingham Daily Express*	
1877–78	Mr. W. P. Byles *Bradford Observer*	
1878–79	Mr. Frederick Clifford *Sheffield Daily Telegraph*	See also 1872–73
1879–80	Mr. J. L. Foster *Yorkshire Gazette*, York	
1880–81	Mr. F. R. Spark *Leeds Express*	
1881	Mr. J. Maitland *Liverpool Mercury*	(Died during year of office)
1881–82 ⎱ 1882–83 ⎰	Mr. J. Feeney *Birmingham Post*	
1883–84	Mr. R. Redpath *Newcastle Journal*	See also 1893–94

Appendices

1884–85	Mr. C. Mandall Hartley *Doncaster Chronicle*	See also 1904–05
1885–86	Mr. Wm. Wallace Hargrove *York Daily Herald*	
1886–87	Mr. R. E. Leader *Sheffield Independent*	See also 1891–92
1887–88	Mr. William Lewis *Bristol Mercury and Bath Herald*	
1888–89	Mr. George Harper *Huddersfield Chronicle*	
1889–90	Mr. J. R. Forman *Nottingham Guardian*	
1890–91	Mr. John Duncan *South Wales Daily News*, Cardiff	
1891–92	Mr. R. E. Leader *Sheffield Independent*	See also 1886–87
1892–93	Mr. F. Hewitt *Leicester Daily Post*	
1893–94	Mr. R. Redpath *Newcastle Journal*	See also 1883–84
1894–95	Mr. A. G. Jeans *Liverpool Daily Post*	
1895–96	Mr. James Clegg *Bolton Chronicle*	
1896–97	Mr. T. Bullock *Staffordshire Sentinel*, Hanley	See also 1901–02
1897–98	Mr. J. W. Willans *Leeds Mercury*	
1898–99	Mr. Walter Hawkins *Bristol Times and Mirror*	
1899–1900	Mr. G. Binney Dibblee *Manchester Guardian*	
1900–01	Sir John A. Willox, M.P. *Liverpool Courier*	See also 1875–76
1901–02	Mr. T. Bullock *Staffordshire Sentinel*, Hanley	See also 1896–97
1902–03 } 1903–04 }	Mr. Wm. Brimelow *Bolton Evening News*	See also 1911–12
1904–05	Mr. C. Mandall Hartley *Doncaster Chronicle*	See also 1884–85
1905–06	Dr. Charles Russell *Glasgow Herald*	
1906–07	Mr. David Duncan *South Wales Daily News*, Cardiff	

Appendices

1907–08	Mr. Arthur R. Byles	
	Yorkshire Daily Observer, Bradford	
1908–09	Mr. Charles Clifford	
	Sheffield Daily Telegraph	
1909–10	Mr. George Toulmin, M.P.	See also
	Lancashire Daily Post, Preston	1919–20
1910–11	Mr. George Crosbie	
	Cork Examiner	
1911–12	Mr. Wm. Brimelow	See also
	Bolton Evening News	1903–04
1912–13	Mr. J. S. R. Phillips	
	Yorkshire Post, Leeds	
1913–14	Mr. H. J. Infield	
	Sussex Daily News, Brighton	
1914–15	Mr. Walter Scott	
	Rochdale Observer	
1915–16	Mr. Robert Wilson	
	Edinburgh Evening News	
1916–17	Mr. Meredith T. Whittaker	
	Scarborough Evening News	
1917–18	Mr. A. Edmund Spender	
	Western Morning News, Plymouth	
1918–19	Mr. Allan Jeans	
	Liverpool Daily Post and Mercury	
1919–20	Sir George Toulmin	See also
	Lancashire Daily Post, Preston	1909–10
1920–21	Mr. Charles W. Henderson	
	Belfast News-Letter	
1921–22 ⎫	Col. Sir Joseph Reed	
1922–23 ⎭	*Newcastle Daily Chronicle*	
1923–24	Col. Egbert Lewis	
	Bath Herald	
1924–25 ⎫	Mr. Arthur Pickering	
1925–26 ⎭	*North Eastern Daily Gazette*	
	Middlesbrough	
1926–27 ⎫	Sir Charles Hyde, Bart.	
1927–28 ⎭	*Birmingham Post*	
1928–29	Sir James Owen	
	Express & Echo, Exeter	
1929–30	Mr. A. Burchill	
	Evening Express, Liverpool	
1930–31	Mr. R. N. Burgess	
	Cumberland News, Carlisle	

Appendices

1931–32	Mr. Wm. Will *Daily Dispatch*, Manchester	
1932–33	Mr. Robert J. Webber *Western Mail*, Cardiff	
1933–34	Mr. Edgar Grotrian *Hull Daily Mail*	
1934–35	Mr. Norval B. Graham *Express & Star*, Wolverhampton	
1935–36	Mr. A. McLean Ewing *Glasgow Herald*	See also 1941–42
1936–37	Mr. John R. Scott, *Manchester Guardian*	
1937–38	Mr. Arthur H. Mann *Yorkshire Post*, Leeds	
1938–39	Mr. Samuel Storey, M.P. *Sunderland Echo*	Sir Samuel Storey January 1960 Lord Buckton June 1966
1939–40	Mr. Herbert J. Staines *Sheffield Telegraph*	
1940–41	Mr. James Henderson *Belfast News-Letter*	See also 1944–45
1941–42	Mr. A. McLean Ewing *Glasgow Herald*	See also 1935–36
1942–43	Mr. W. Raymond Derwent *Telegraph & Argus*, Bradford	
1943–44	Mr. F. C. Whittaker *Scarborough Evening News*	
1944–45	Mr. James Henderson, D.L. *Belfast News-Letter*	See also 1940–41
1945–46	Mr. Malcolm Graham *Express & Star*, Wolverhampton	
1946–47	Mr. Harold R. Grime *West Lancashire Evening Gazette*, Blackpool	Sir Harold Grime June 1959
1947–48	Mr. Robert T. Lewis *Daily Mail*, Manchester	
1948–49	Mr. W. A. Hawkins *Evening Post*, Bristol	See also 1951–52
1949–50	Mr. Frank Webber, O.B.E. *Western Mail*, Cardiff	
1950–51	Mr. Clement T. Barton *Leicester Mercury*	

Appendices

1951–52	Mr. W. A. Hawkins *Evening Post*, Bristol	See also 1948–49
1952–53	Mr. Laurence P. Scott *Manchester Guardian*	See also 1957–58
1953–54	Mr. A. G. Jeans *Liverpool Daily Post*	Sir Alick Jeans January 1967
1954–55	Mr. J. L. Burgess, O.B.E. *Cumberland Evening News*, Carlisle	
1955–56	Mr. Harry Lindley *Huddersfield Examiner*	See also 1959–60
1956–57	Mr. John Thomson *Evening Sentinel*, Hanley	
1957–58	Mr. Laurence P. Scott *Manchester Guardian*	See also 1952–53
1958–59	Mr. H. L. Howarth *The Northern Echo*, Darlington	
1959–60	Mr. Harry Lindley *Huddersfield Examiner*	See also 1955–56
1960–61	Mr. R. P. Winfrey *Evening Telegraph*, Kettering	
1961–62	Mr. W. M. Young *Eastern Daily Press*, Norwich	
1962–63	Mr. R. R. Gleave O.B.E. 1964 Southern Newspapers Ltd. (*Southern Evening Echo*, Southampton, and others)	
1963–64	Sir Eric Clayson The Birmingham Post & Mail Ltd.	
1964–65	Mr. Allan G. Stephen George Outram & Co. Ltd., Glasgow (*Glasgow Herald* and *Evening Times*)	
1965–66	Mr. A. M. Burnett-Stuart The Thomson Organisation Ltd.	
1966–67	Mr. Leslie J. Stallard The Midland News Association Ltd. (*Express & Star*, Wolverhampton, and *Shropshire Star*)	
1967–68	Mr. W. D. Barnetson United Newspapers Ltd.	

Appendix 2

Persons present at the meeting of Proprietors of Daily Provincial Newspapers at the United Hotel, Charles Street, Haymarket on June 29, 1868

Mr. John Edward Taylor, *Manchester Guardian* (in the Chair)
Mr. F. D. Finlay, *Belfast Northern Whig*
Mr. Sebastian Evans, *Birmingham Daily Gazette*
Mr. J. Feeny, Jun., *Birmingham Daily Post*
Mr. P. S. Macliver, *Western Daily Press*, Bristol
Mr. Thomas Crosbie, *Cork Examiner*
Mr. David A. Nagle, Cork, *Daily Herald*
Sir John Gray, M.P., *Freeman's Journal*
Mr. J. W. Gray, Dublin, *Freeman's Journal*
Mr. J. Robinson, *Dublin Daily Express*
Mr. Thomas Potts, Dublin, *Saunder's News Letter*
Dr. H. Maunsell, *Dublin Evening Mail*
Mr. Coulter, Dublin, *Saunder's News Letter*
Mr. John Leng, *Dundee Advertiser*
Mr. James Law, Edinburgh, *Scotsman*
Mr. C. Wescomb, *Edinburgh Evening Courant*
Mr. J. H. Stoddart, *Glasgow Daily Herald*
Dr. Cameron, Glasgow, *North British Daily Mail*
Mr. William Hunt, Hull, *Eastern Morning News*
Mr. F. R. Spark, *Leeds Express*
Mr. Charles Tinling, *Liverpool Courier*

Appendices

Mr. John Maitland, *Liverpool Mercury*
Mr. John Sowler, *Manchester Courier*
Mr. Alexander Ireland, *Manchester Examiner and Times*
Mr. Joseph Cowen, *Newcastle Chronicle*
Mr. William Saunders, Newcastle, *Northern Daily Express*
Mr. J. P. Latimer, Plymouth, *Western Daily Mercury*
Mr. Edward Spender, Plymouth, *Western Morning News*
Mr. Frederick Clifford, *Sheffield Daily Telegraph*
Mr. Robert Leader, *Sheffield Independent*

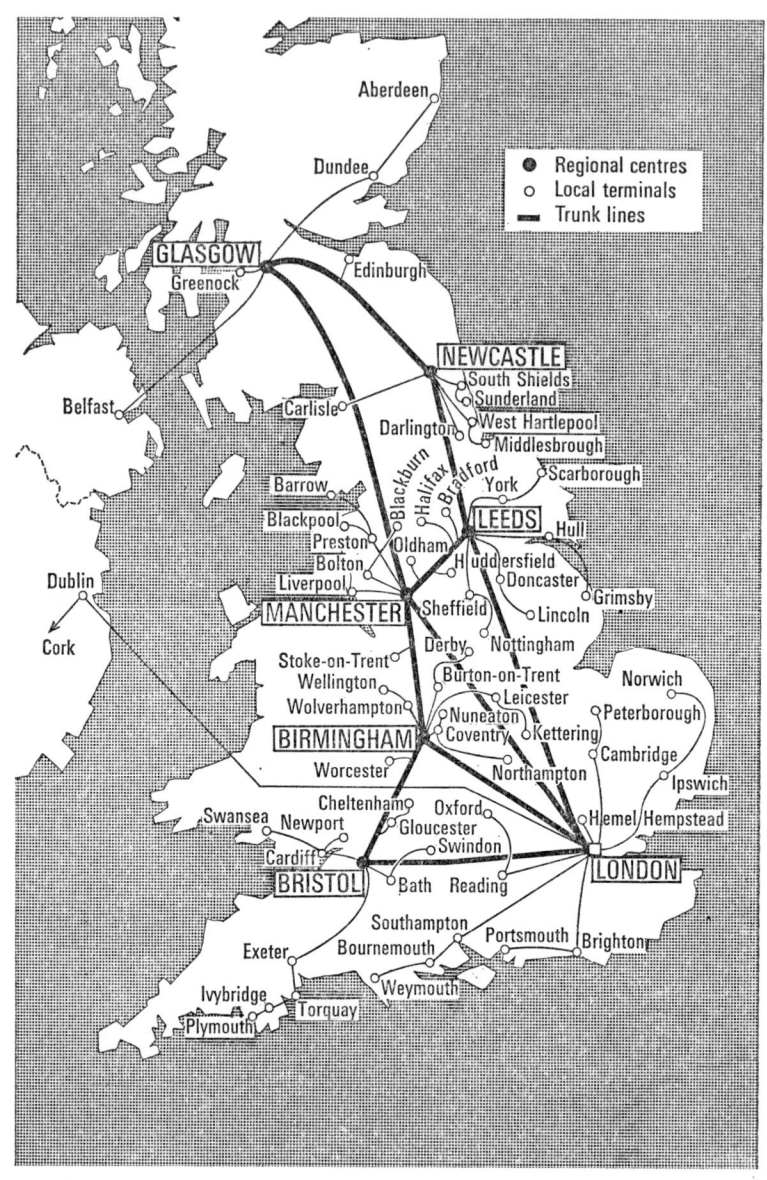

The distribution of newspaper-member subscribers of the Press Association at the beginning of 1968

Appendix 3

Member newspapers receiving Press Association Comprehensive Service October 1967.

Morning

ABERDEEN
Press and Journal

BELFAST
Daily Mirror
Irish News
News-Letter

BIRMINGHAM
Birmingham Post

BRISTOL
Western Daily Press

CARDIFF
Western Mail

CORK
Cork Examiner

DARLINGTON
Northern Echo

DUBLIN
Irish Independent
Irish Press
Irish Times

DUNDEE
Courier and Advertiser

EDINBURGH
Daily Mail
The Scotsman

GLASGOW
Daily Express
Daily Record
Glasgow Herald

IPSWICH
East Anglian Daily Times

LEEDS
Yorkshire Post

LIVERPOOL
Liverpool Daily Post

MANCHESTER
Daily Express
Daily Mail
Daily Mirror
Daily Telegraph
The Guardian
The Sun

NEWCASTLE
The Journal

NORWICH
Eastern Daily Press

Appendices

NOTTINGHAM
Guardian Journal

PLYMOUTH
Western Morning News

SHEFFIELD
Morning Telegraph

Evening

ABERDEEN
Evening Express

BARROW
North-Western Evening Mail

BATH
Bath and Wilts Evening Chronicle

BELFAST
Belfast Telegraph

BIRMINGHAM
Birmingham Evening Mail

BLACKBURN
Lancashire Evening Telegraph

BLACKPOOL
West Lancashire Evening Gazette

BOLTON
Evening News

BOURNEMOUTH
Evening Echo

BRADFORD
Telegraph and Argus

BRIGHTON
Evening Argus

BRISTOL
Bristol Evening Post

BURNLEY
Evening Star

BURTON-ON-TRENT
Burton Daily Mail

CAMBRIDGE
Cambridge News

CARDIFF
South Wales Echo

CARLISLE
Cumberland Evening News

CHELTENHAM
Gloucestershire Echo

CORK
Evening Echo

COVENTRY
Coventry Evening Telegraph

DARLINGTON
Northern Despatch

DERBY
Derby Evening Telegraph

DONCASTER
Evening Post

DUBLIN
Evening Herald
Evening Press

DUNDEE
Evening Telegraph

EDINBURGH
Evening News

EXETER
Express and Echo

GLASGOW
Evening Citizen
Evening Times

GLOUCESTER
The Citizen

Appendices

GREENOCK
Greenock Telegraph

GRIMSBY
Grimsby Evening Telegraph

HALIFAX
Halifax Evening Courier

HUDDERSFIELD
Huddersfield Daily Examiner

HULL
Hull Daily Mail

IPSWICH
Evening Star

KETTERING
Northamptonshire Evening Telegraph

LEEDS
Yorkshire Evening Post

LEICESTER
Leicester Mercury

LINCOLN
Lincolnshire Echo

LIVERPOOL
Liverpool Echo

LUTON
Evening Post (Hemel Hempstead)

MANCHESTER
Manchester Evening News

MIDDLESBROUGH
Evening Gazette

NEWCASTLE
Evening Chronicle

NEWPORT, MON.
South Wales Argus

NORTHAMPTON
Chronicle and Echo

NORWICH
Eastern Evening News

NOTTINGHAM
Evening Post

NUNEATON
Nuneaton Evening Tribune

OLDHAM
Oldham Evening Chronicle

OXFORD
Oxford Mail

PETERBOROUGH
Peterborough Evening Telegraph

PLYMOUTH
Western Evening Herald

PORTSMOUTH
Evening News

PRESTON
Lancashire Evening Post

READING
Evening Post

SCARBOROUGH
Scarborough Evening News

SCUNTHORPE
Scunthorpe Evening Telegraph

SHEFFIELD
The Star

SOUTHAMPTON
Southern Evening Echo

SOUTH SHIELDS
Shields Gazette

STOKE-ON-TRENT
Evening Sentinel

SUNDERLAND
Sunderland Echo

SWANSEA
South Wales Evening Post

Appendices

SWINDON
Evening Advertiser

TORQUAY
Herald Express

WATFORD
Evening Echo (Hemel Hempstead)

WELLINGTON
Shropshire Star

WEST HARTLEPOOL
Northern Daily Mail

WEYMOUTH
Dorset Evening Echo

WIGAN
Evening Post

WOLVERHAMPTON
Express & Star

WORCESTER
Worcester Evening News

YORK
Yorkshire Evening Press

Weekly

BELFAST
Sunday Mirror
Sunday News

BIRMINGHAM
Sunday Mercury

DUBLIN
Sunday Independent
Sunday Press

DUNDEE
Sunday Post

GLASGOW
Sunday Express
Sunday Mail
Sunday Post

MANCHESTER
News of the World
Sunday Express
Sunday Mirror
The People

NEWCASTLE
Sunday Sun

PLYMOUTH
Independent

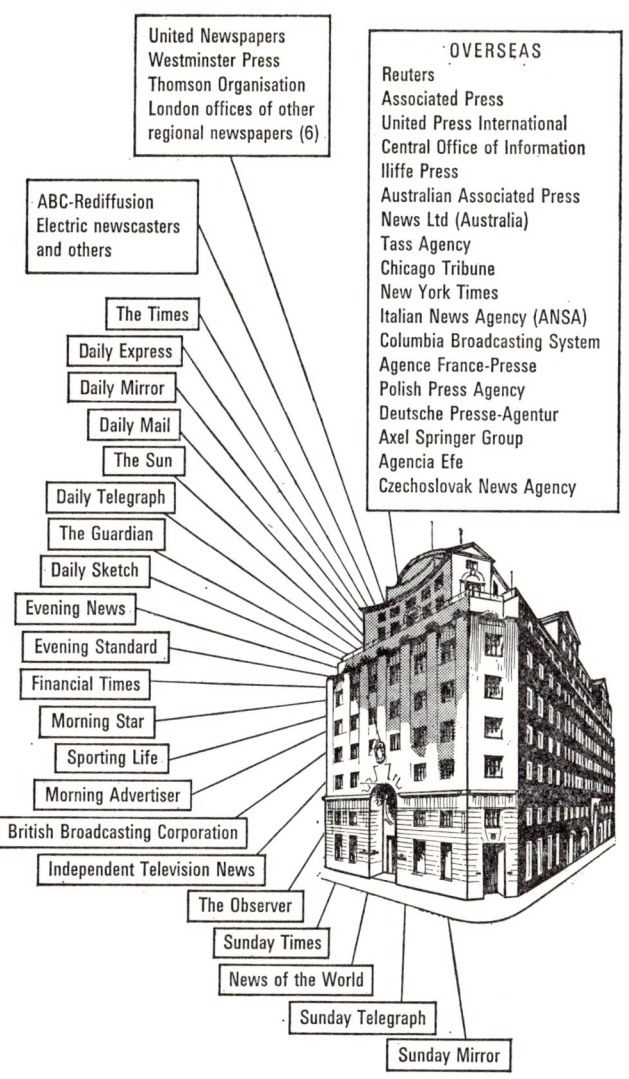

The main London subscribers at the beginning of 1968

Appendix 4

The Times of 20th May 1880 carried this report:[1]

MEETING OF THE CONSERVATIVE PARTY

We have received the following from the Press Association:

A meeting of the more prominent members of the Conservative Party, called by a circular issued by Lord Beaconsfield, was held at Bridgewater-house, Cleveland-square, St. James's, the town residence of the Earl of Ellesmere, at 3 o'clock yesterday afternoon. The circular calling the meeting was as follows:

'Hughenden Manor, May 10, 1880.

'Sir, There will be a meeting of the Conservative Party on the 19th, at 3 o'clock precisely, when the honour of your presence is requested by

'Your faithful servant,

'Beaconsfield.'

The announcement of this meeting was made almost as soon as the result of the late General Election was known, and a good deal of interest was thereby excited in political circles. It had been expected that the meeting would be open to the representatives of the Press, but at the last moment it was decided that it should be held with closed doors and regarded as one of a strictly private character.

The invitations sent out numbered about 550, and the affirmative responses came to within 100 of that number.

Until within half an hour of the time fixed for the meeting, 3 o'clock p.m., there was little to be seen in the neighbourhood of Cleveland-square indicative of the unwonted assembly about to invade the quiet of that secluded neighbourhood, but soon after 1 o'clock there was an

[1] The only parts of the report which have been omitted from this Appendix are further passages describing the arrivals at the house and a long list of names of those who attended the meeting. None of it has any bearing on the accuracy or otherwise of the account of what was said.

unusual number of arrivals at the Carlton-house Club, the principal among these being Sir Stafford Northcote, Sir Richard Assheton Cross, and Mr. E. Stanhope (the late Under Secretary of State for India). About half past 2 o'clock several well known occupants of the Conservative benches of the House of Commons betook themselves to the place of meeting. The first to be recognised were Mr. Fitzwilliam Dick, Col. Dyott, Mr. Bulwer (the late member for Ipswich) and Mr. Raikes (the late Chairman of Committees and late member for Chester), and the two late members for Brighton, General Shute and Mr. Ashbury.

Following almost immediately upon these came the Earl of Beaconsfield, who drove up in his brougham, accompanied by his secretary Lord Rowton. As the ex-Premier passed along the roadway past St. James's Palace he overtook three of the late members of his Administration—viz, Sir Stafford Northcote, Sir R. A. Cross and Mr. Stanhope, who walked together from Carlton-house.

At this time a few spectators had begun to collect in front of the Palace and in the open space facing Earl Sydney's residence and the place of the meeting.

There was, however, an entire absence of anything in the shape of a public demonstration, although several of the lookers-on respectfully raised their hats as the more prominent members of the late Government made their appearance....

The proceedings commenced a few minutes after the hour appointed....

The Earl of Beaconsfield, who was warmly received on rising to address the meeting, expressed the hope that the proceedings would be regarded as of a strictly private, and not of a public character. He referred to the sudden change which had taken place in the position of the party, which, although he admitted it was by no means expected, was not to be altogether regretted. He saw no reason to despair of the fortunes of the party but on the contrary saw already signs of hopefulness and encouragement.

Although they were now on the Opposition side of the House they possessed the power of a united party, which could not fail to exercise considerable influence on the government of the country.

If they were true to themselves and their principles, he looked forward to their return to power at no distant period. He referred to the extraordinary opposition which their policy had encountered, and expressed surprise that Mr. Gladstone, after the repeated expression of his desire to retire from the heat of political controversy, should have been prevailed upon to assume the position of Prime Minister, and associate with it the position of Chancellor of the Exchequer. (Cheers).

It would be unworthy of the Tory party to indulge in vain regrets because they had experienced a vicissitude of fortune which, judged

Appendices

from the experience of the Government, the next election might probably convert into a signal triumph. (Cheers).

It had been rumoured that it was his intention to retire from the position with which he had been so many years intrusted by the party, but he had never given the slightest ground for such a supposition. (Cheers). If those with whom it had been alike his pleasure and honour to be so long associated considered that his retention of the leadership would be of advantage to them, whatever ability he possessed would be devoted to their service in the promotion of those grand constitutional principles to which this country was indebted for the continuity of its national history and the maintenance of its position in the scale of nations. (Cheers).

He was satisfied that the Conservative party would profit by the experience of the late election in one important—not to say essential—particular, and that was as to the necessity for more perfect organisation. The superiority of the organisation enjoyed by the Liberal party was manifest in most of the constituencies during the recent contest, but he hoped that this weak point in the Conservative armour would be strengthened before another appeal was made to the nation. (Hear, hear).

The late Government had given up the seals of office with the consciousness that they had done something to restore the prestige and influence and maintain the honour of the country. They had also the satisfaction of knowing that they had done not a little to promote the welfare of all classes during a period of trade depression without parallel in the annals of the nation.

An enthusiastic admirer of Conservative principles had prophesied that the present Liberal Government would, notwithstanding its denunciations of their policy, be in reality Conservative, and he justified that expectation by the attitude of what had been designated 'Moderate Liberalism.' It must, however, be borne in mind that this view was expressed before the formation of the present Administration and before the advent to exalted positions of gentlemen who prided themselves upon what had recently been characterised as 'destructive Radicalism.' (Cheers).

The present Liberal Ministry was now, apparently, a happy and united family. The lion had lain down with the lamb. Perversity had yielded to acknowledged mildness—the past was to be forgotten and the future made brilliant by a united display of Liberal and Radical fireworks. (Laughter).

The difficulty was not to know what the Liberals intended to do, but what they did not intend to do. Their programme was literally as wide as the poles. The aristocracy was to be taken in hand, the middle classes were to be looked to, and the remaining orders of society were to have boons and blessings showered upon them in an abundance only paralleled in Eastern tales. Whether this remarkable consummation was ever to be obtained was in the secrets of the future; but he must confess to a tendency to scepticism, for he had passed the period of political childhood.

With respect to the future of the Tory Party, he strongly enforced upon all his adherents the need of unity. Although since last he met a gathering of Conservatives the party was not numerically so strong in Parliament, nevertheless by united action they might do much towards the maintenance of principles which were dear to them and which they believed to be the best for the interests of the nation.

He recommended the party to maintain an attitude of dignified opposition. To a certain extent Radicalism was for the present triumphant, but nothing would induce him to believe that its success could be permanent. The entire history of the nation was opposed to such a supposition. (Cheers).

He had with some amount of care endeavoured to trace the cause of the altered feeling which had come over the constituencies, and the conclusion at which he had arrived was that it was the result of a desire for a change of Government, and not the consequence of any dislike to Conservative principles or of any personal antipathy to the men who had been at the helm during the past six years. He would not trouble them with the process of thought by which he had arrived at this conclusion; but he could assure them that it was a conclusion that had not been hastily adopted, and it was important that it should be borne in mind for the future in dealing with the constituencies.

How the discordant elements brought together in the present Government were to retain their cohesion was a problem which he would not attempt to solve. Personally he considered it impossible for such a ministry to be of long duration, and he said that with due regard to the history of past Administrations.

He trusted that in speeches to their constituents Conservative members and those who had unfortunately lost their seats, among whom he was pleased to know that a goodly number were present on that occasion, would lose no opportunity of bringing before the electors the fundamental principles of Conservatism. There was on that subject a great deal of misrepresentation, which it was the duty of every true member of the party to strive to remove.

An impression appeared to prevail in many quarters that Conservatism meant legislation for particular classes and the making of laws in favour of those who were blessed with social advantages of no mean order; whereas it was, in fact, a broad and comprehensive policy which sought to conserve all there was worth preserving in the Constitution of the nation, and to introduce from time to time reforms having for their object the welfare and happiness alike of all classes of the community. (Cheers).

Appendices

They were well aware of what the Conservative Party had accomplished in the interests of the nation, and those triumphs should be steadily kept in view of the people and their influence on the position and welfare of the nation brought prominently forward.

The great characteristic traits of Conservatism should be continually demonstrated. He believed that the principles of Conservatism prevailed largely among all classes of Englishmen. The Conservative working man had been spoken of as a myth, and it was said he was as extinct as the dodo. It had been said that the American caucus system had entirely obliterated the Conservative working man, if he ever had any existence, but he did not believe that Englishmen of any class would long allow their principles to be dictated to them and their political action to be guided by any system of machinery.

He was convinced that strong reason pervaded the working classes, and that the noblest and best of them would be at all times found upholding the principles of that which he had no hesitation in calling the national party. They might not always approve of every detail in the policy of the leaders of the party; but he was satisfied they would always be found stout defenders of its broad principles. They had often given unmistakable evidence of their inherent attachment to Conservative principles.

He urged all who listened to him to assist to the utmost of their power in the organisation of the Conservative working classes.

He was acquainted with several such organisations, which had done much for the promotion of Conservative principles in different parts of the country, and he looked forward to them as one of the most certain means of securing the future triumph of Conservatism. He was persuaded that many of the middle classes of the country had voted against the Conservative candidates through a misconception as to the causes of the depression of trade. No opportunity had been lost in removing this misapprehension, and in showing that the commercial distress did not arise, as was alleged by their opponents, from any lack of prescience or want of administrative capacity on the part of the leaders of the Conservative Party, but from causes beyond the control of any government.

He expressed his satisfaction at seeing that the principles of the foreign policy of the Conservative Government, notwithstanding that they had been so persistently misrepresented and so fiercely denounced, were likely to be carried out by their successors, and he urged them so long as the present Government in its foreign relations continued to maintain the interests and position of the country to abstain from any fractious opposition and to give them an united and patriotic support.

He vindicated the policy of the late Government, as that which was best adapted to the existing state of trade, and stated that the

Appendices

miscalculation of the Indian accounts had taken them by surprise quite as much as anyone else.

He also expressed his pleasure at seeing present at that meeting his noble friend the Earl of Carnarvon, who had rendered signal service to the Conservative cause, and whose readiness to fight again in the ranks of the party with which he had been so long and so honourably connected was an additional assurance of its speedy return to power.

The noble earl, having spoken upwards of an hour, resumed his seat amid prolonged cheering.

The Duke of Buccleuch followed, and in the course of a brief address expressed his conviction that, although Mr. Gladstone had been able to snatch a triumph in Mid Lothian, the victory was only transitory. Lord Dalkeith had been defeated, but the Conservatives of Mid Lothian were wiser now than they were at the time of the election, and had already commenced rectifying the weak points of their organisation. (Cheers).

It afforded him inexpressible pleasure to hear Lord Beaconsfield announce his willingness to continue the leadership of the party, and he had no doubt that under his skilful and prudent guidance it would hold its due position in the state.

The Conservatives had been defeated owing to deficient party organisation and to wholesale misrepresentation, and when the organisation had been corrected and the misrepresentation had been dispelled they would be again victorious.

Sir R. Peel observed that no one had been a greater victim to misrepresentation than he had—misrepresentation not only of the tongue, but also of the pen. However, he was well accustomed to it and instead of being disheartened he found his spirits all the better for it. It roused him to turn upon his assailants, and in exposing their calumnies would be found the best means of aiding the Conservative cause.

He had lately crossed swords with Sir William Harcourt, and he did not think he got the worst of it, for he had the satisfaction of knowing that he had done something to rescue Oxford from being any further misrepresented by the right hon. and learned gentleman, who was now out of the House of Commons begging here and begging there for a seat, and so far with as little chance of finding one as the man in the moon. (Laughter).

The honour of Oxford had been redeemed, and so had that of Sandwich. As the straw showed the direction of the wind those elections showed that the electors found they had already been sold by the leaders of the Liberal party.

Instead of men of moderate means,[1] the Radical element pre-

[1] The sense of this passage seems to indicate that Peel actually said 'men of moderate miens'. The phonetic transcription of 'miens' as

Appendices

dominated in the Ministry, and they were threatened with an avalanche of Radical crochets of the most advanced order. Sir Robert added that he intended to contest Derby against Sir William Harcourt.[1] (Cheers).

The Duke of Richmond and Gordon congratulated the meeting on the announcement of Lord Beaconsfield's intention to remain at the head of the party, and he cordially agreed with what had fallen from the noble earl with reference to its organisation.

Sir Stafford Northcote said that the financial policy of the late Government, considering the great difficulties which had to be encountered, would compare favourably with any of its predecessors.

The Earl of Carnarvon, who was received with enthusiastic cheers, said he regarded with feelings of dismay and doubt the composition of the new Ministry. As one who desired to see the institutions of the country improved in a constitutional manner and in accordance with national precedents, he felt it to be incumbent on him to support the Conservative party to the utmost of his power, and to offer it his most loyal adhesion. (Loud cheers). The times were perilous, and it behoved all who valued the institutions of the land to be on their guard. (Cheers).

The Marquis of Salisbury proposed a vote of thanks to the Earl of Ellesmere for the use of Bridgewater-house. He found encouragement in the knowledge that the Conservative party was thoroughly united and intended to lose no time in seeking to regain the position they had lost.

The motion was carried with acclamation.

The Earl of Beaconsfield thanked those present for the hearty manner in which they had responded to his invitation.

The proceedings, which had occupied over two hours, were then brought to a conclusion.

A considerable number of persons had assembled in Cleveland-square, and by these the prominent members of the party were more or less cheered. The Marquis of Salisbury, who left on foot, received a marked demonstration, which was renewed with even greater vigour as the late Prime Minister drove away in his brougham with Lord Rowton.

'means' supports the view that this was an authentic report and not a fabrication.

[1] At the General Election in April 1880 Liberal candidates—Mr. M. T. Bass and Mr. Samuel Plimsoll—retained both the Derby seats. Shortly afterwards, Mr. Plimsoll accepted the Chiltern Hundreds. On 25th May, six days after Sir Robert Peel (according to the P.A. story) had said he would fight Derby, Sir William Harcourt was returned unopposed for the Liberals.

Index

Abdication, of Edward VIII, 186–7
Adams, P., 75 n.
Advertisement tax, 15
Agency Reuter, 206
Aintree, 262
Aisgill Moor disaster, 97, 98
Allenby, Field Marshal, 143
Appeal of the Wesleyans on Behalf of the Established Church, An, 81
Ark Royal, H.M. aircraft-carrier, 190, 191
Ashanti wars, 121
Ashbury, A., 293
Ashley, C. H., 39, 123, 124
Astor, J. J., 212
Atomic-bomb explosion, picture of, 243
Aylmer, Sir A. P. F., 104
Aylmer, Lady, 104, 105, 106, 107, 108
Aylmer case, 104–9

Bagnold, Enid, 211
Baird, Sir R., 170
Baker, Jack, 94
Balfour, A. J., 78, 81
Barnetson, W. D., 268, 283
Barton, Clement T., 282
Bass, M. T., 298 n.
Bath Herald, 171
Beaconsfield, Earl of, 75, 76, 292, 293, 297, 298
Beaverbrook, Lord, 156, 207
Belfast News Letter, 55, 218
Benn, Sir Ernest, 179
Berry Brothers, 176, 177, 179
Bevan, Aneurin, 255

Bidder, J. T., 65
Birmingham City Art Gallery, 34
Birmingham Corn Market, 66
Birmingham Daily Post, 14, 16, 23, 33, 37, 49, 131, 160, 178, 186
Birmingham Journal, 34
Birmingham Mail, 178
Bloom, George Cromarty, 266, 267, 268, 269
Bloomberg, P., 232
Boat Race broadcast, 174
Boer War, 100, 133, 136
Bolton Evening News, 18, 55, 121, 128, 145
Booth, Arthur, 255, 272
Borthwick, Sir A., 110
Bowskill, J., 92, 94
Brabazon of Tara, Lord, 245 n.
Bracken, Brendan, 229, 234
Brade, Sir R., 135
Bradford, Bishop of, 185
Bradford Observer, 64
Bridewell Royal Hospital Trust, 90, 91
Bright, John, 17
Brimelow, William, 121, 128, 145, 280, 281
Bristol Evening Post, 179, 235, 250
Bristol Evening World, 177
Bristol Mercury, 109
British and Irish Magnetic Telegraph Company, 20
British Broadcasting Company (later Corporation), 170–5
British Parliamentary Election Results in 1950–64, 257
Brown, George, 258

Index

Browne, Alfred, 255
Brownrigg, Sir D., 140
Buccleuch, Duke of, 297
Buchan, John, 207, 210, 217
Buckton, Lord, *see* Storey, Samuel
Bullock, T., 136, 280
Burch, Leslie, 242, 244
Burchill, Alfred, 247, 281
Burgess, John L., 231, 283
Burgess, R. N., 281
Burnett-Stuart, A. M., 283
Bussy, G. M., 43
Butler, David, 257
Buxton, S., 148, 150
Byles, Arthur R., 281
Byles, W. P., 64, 279
Byron House, 160-2, 200

Caine, C. S., 123
Caledonian Mercury, 25
Cambria Daily Leader, 153-4
Cameron, Dr., 56, 284
Campbell-Bannerman, Sir H., 78-9, 102
Camrose, Lord, 176
Candler, E., 140
Canterbury, Archbishop of, 116 n.
Carlist Insurrection, 68, 121
Carnarvon, Earl of, 297, 298
Carr, H. L., 62
Cassell's Magazine, 37
Cattermole, W. J., 93, 95, 102, 103, 130
Caxton Hall, 232
Censorship, 135-46
Central News, 76, 83, 98, 99, 110, 114, 115, 197, 198
    battle with the P.A., 115
Central Press, 22, 33, 52, 114
Central Telegraph Station, 25
Chamberlain, Joseph, 34, 78, 80, 81, 121
Chamberlain, Neville, 190, 191, 197, 245 n.
Chancellor, Christopher (Sir), 217, 218, 222, 230, 265, 266
Chapman, racehorse trainer, 199
Cholmondeley, Marquess of, 244
Christiansen, Arthur, 188, 195, 249, 269
Churchill, Winston S., 132, 235, 244
    death of, 254
Clarke, B., 163

Clayson, Sir Eric, 283
Clegg, James, 280
Clifford, Charles, 128, 281
Clifford, Frederick, 31, 32, 33, 34, 35, 46, 70, 71, 128, 144, 145, 279 285
Cobden, John, 17
Coldwell, Len, 165
Collins, Michael, 163, 164
Column Printing Company, 197, 198
Comic Times, 54
Conservative Party, 75, 292
    P.A. report of 1880 meeting of, 292-8
Cooper, Kent, 208, 213, 214
Cork Examiner, 16, 19, 55, 131
Coulter, at inauguration, 284
Court Correspondent, 101
Cowen, Joseph, 285
Cranfield, A. L., 166, 167, 168, 169, 184, 187
Creed, F. G., 153
Creed system, 153 n., 154, 239
Creffield, A. E. ('Bill'), 241
Cricket Reporting Agency, 123
Crime reporting, 158
Crimean war, 139
Crippen, Dr., 131, 158, 244
Crosbie, George, 131, 281
Crosbie, Thomas, 19, 55, 284
Cross, Sir Richard A., 293
Croydon Times, 269
Cumberland Evening News, 231
Cummins, W. R., 79

Daily Dispatch, 203
Daily Examiner, 35
Daily Express, 137 n., 157, 176, 188, 194, 195, 200, 226, 227 n., 249, 250, 269, 270
Daily Graphic, 95
Daily Herald, 176, 194
Daily Mail, 130, 133, 136, 137, 145, 146, 169 n., 175, 176
Daily Sketch, 187
Daily Telegraph, 36, 141, 194, 270
Dalkeith, Lord, 297
Dalziel's agency, 121, 122
Dardanelles, 138
David Copperfield, 37
Davies, Edward, 201, 237, 238, 239, 242, 246, 252, 265, 266
Dawson of Penn, Lord, 193

Index

Decline and Fall of Lloyd George, The, 156
Defence of the Realm Act, 139, 141
de Reuter, Baron H., 136, 137
de Reuter, 2nd Baron, 206, 208
Derwent, W. Raymond, 218, 226, 238, 282
Dibblee, G. Binney, 280
Dick, Fitzwilliam, 293
Dickens, Charles, 37
Dictionary of National Biography, 54
Dieppe Raid, 244
Disraeli, Benjamin, 75 (*see also* Beaconsfield, Earl of)
'D' notices, 137 n., 138 n, 191
Doncaster Gazette, 29
Douglas-Home, Sir Alec, 75 n.
Dreyfus affair, 120
Druce, T. C., exhumation of, 98–100
Dublin Evening Telegraph, 107
Duncan, David, 280
Duncan, John, 84, 280
Dundee Advertiser, 25
Dundee Courier and Argus, 25
Durham, John, 13 n.
Dyke, Sir W. H., 76
Dyott, Colonel, 293

Eastern Daily Press, 245
Eccleston, Richard, 158, 163, 164, 186, 193, 194
Economist Intelligence Unit report, 163 n.
Eden, Ebenezer, 165
Edinburgh, Duke of, 240, 244
Edinburgh Chamber of Commerce, 27
Edinburgh Courant, 25
Edinburgh Daily Review, 25
Edinburgh Evening Courant, 48, 49
Edinburgh Evening News, 117
Edward VII, coronation of, 101
Edward VIII, 184
Edwards, Sir H., 64
Electric and International Telegraph Company, 20
Electric and Magnetic companies, 24
Elizabeth, H.R.H. Princess, 240, 243
Ellesmere, Earl of, 75, 298
Ellsworth, antarctic explorer, 192
Encyclopaedia Britannica, 182 n., 244
English Social History, 16
Esher, Lord, 111
Evans, Sebastian, 284

Evening Express (Liverpool), 269
Evening News, 166, 176, 272
Evening Standard, 57, 169 n., 187
Evening Telegraph (Luton), 228
Evening World, 177, 179
Ewing, A. McLean, 203, 217, 218, 219, 220, 221, 223, 224, 226, 228, 282,
Exchange Telegraph Co., 110, 122, 125, 126, 127, 197
Exeter Daily Gazette, 133
Exeter Express and Echo, 160
Express and Star (Wolverhampton), 195, 227, 247

Federation of Northern Newspaper Owners, 130
Feeney, J., 279, 284
Feeney, J. F., 34
Ferguson, F., 143
Finch, W., 197
Finlay, F. D., 284
Fisher, Joseph, 29, 30
Fleet Street, in late 1900s, 95
Forman, J. R., 280
Foster, J. L., 71, 72, 110, 279
Franco-Prussian war, 68
Freeman's Journal, 107

Garnett, J., 32
Gee, Harry, 261
General Elections, 75, 256, 257, 258
General Post Office, 13
General Strike, 173
George V, 101
  death of, 192–4
George VI, 243
Gibbs, Philip, 101
Gibbs, R. A., 228
Gladstone, W. E., 27, 41, 75 n., 77, 78, 82 n., 293, 297
Glasgow Daily Mail, 56
Glasgow Herald, 16, 24, 25, 131, 153, 203, 217, 243
Glasgow Morning Journal, 25
Gleave, Reginald, 246, 283
Globe, 57
Glover, J., 71, 279
Glynn, solicitor, 26
Graham, Malcolm, 227, 247, 282
Graham, Norval B., 195, 282
Grant, Charles, 272
Gratwicke, G. F., 133

Index

Gray, Andrew, 100, 158, 196
Gray, E. D., 107, 108, 109
Gray, J. W., 284
Gray, Sir John, 284
Great Train Robbery, 255
Greaves, A., 125
Green, T. W., 44
Greene, Sir G., 135
Grime, Harold R., 282
Grotrian, Edgar, 282
Guardian, Preston, 71
Guild of Literature and Art, 70
Gwynne, H. A., 120, 180

Haley, William (Sir), 182, 203, 218, 221, 222, 226, 227, 228, 238
Hall, Marshall, 158
Hansard, 82
Harcourt, Sir W., 79, 297, 298 n.
Hargrove, W. Wallace, 280
Harker, Ronald, 185
Harmsworth, Alfred, 133, 134, 136, 137, 145, 146 (*see also* Northcliffe, Lord)
Harmsworth, Sir L., 176
Harper, George, 29, 33, 34, 35, 36, 46, 56, 58, 70, 84, 144, 280
Harrington, T., 124
Hartley, C. Mandall, 280
Harvey, Ernest, 238, 256, 257, 265, 267
Hawarden Castle, 116
Hawkins, Walter A., 235, 250, 252, 253, 280, 282, 283
Henderson, Charles W., 281
Henderson, James, 218, 220, 221, 223, 224, 226, 227, 228, 282
Henderson, J. A., 55
Hepburn, Walter, 77, 78, 86, 97
Hewitt, F., 91, 280
Highgate cemetery, exhumation at, 98-100
Hitler, Adolf, 197
Hodgson, G. B., 148, 150, 161, 162, 166
Holmes, A. J., 26
Horsbrugh, Florence, 224
Houchin, H. R., 200
Howarth, H. L., 283
Howe, J., 97, 98
Howells, Billy, 272
Hozier, Clementine, 132
Huddersfield Chronicle, 29, 33, 35, 56

Huddersfield Examiner, 35
Hulton, Sir E., 176
Humphries, H., 165
Hunt, William, 284
Hyde, Sir Charles, 160, 169, 174, 178, 179, 281

Indian Government, and the press, 140
Infield, H. J., 281
Inglis, Leslie, 270
Inky Way Annual, 185
Inveresk Paper Company, 176
Ireland, Alexander, 33, 285
Irish Church Bill, 41
Irish Daily Telegraph, 170
Irish Treaty, 163
Irish University Bill, 82 n.
Irvine, W. A., 36, 38, 65

Jaffray, John, 33, 34, 36, 38, 46, 48, 50, 51, 52, 53, 54, 55, 56, 58, 65, 66, 67, 71, 115, 116, 144, 279
Jay, Douglas, 259
Jeans, A. G. (later Sir Alick), 283
Jeans, Alexander, 78, 108, 280
Jeans, Allan, 203, 281
Jenkins, Hugh, 258
Jervis, Charles, 256, 269, 270, 271
Jevons, J. W., 71, 279
Jockey Club, 199, 263
Joint Law Service, 199
Jones, R. Gomer, 272
Jones, Sir Roderick, 205, 206, 207, 208, 209, 210, 211, 212, 213, 214, 215, 216, 217, 218, 219, 220, 221, 222, 223, 224
Journalist's London, The, 101
Judy, 118

Kemsley, Lord, 176, 224
Kemsley Newspapers, 236
Kidwelly poisoning trial, 158
Kimber, E., 111, 112
King, Frank, 195, 197, 272
King, Wilfred (Sir), 126, 127, 129, 197
Kingsley, Charles, 202
Kipling, Rudyard, 192
Kitchener, Lord, 120
Knight, Derrick, 245
Knollys, Lord, 101

Lamb, Charles, 202

Index

Lancashire Daily Post, 142
Latimer, J. P., 285
Law, Bonar, 156, 157
Law, James, 284
Lawrence, L., 141
Lawson, Hon. H., 128
Leach, C. H., 185
Leader, R. E., 44, 105, 106, 280
Leamington Spa Courier, 71
Lee, Sir K., 232
Leeds Express, 43, 71, 144
Leeds Mercury, 41, 82, 186
Leeke, Admiral Sir H., 15
Leicester Daily Post, 91
Le Neve, Ethel, 244
Leng, John, 284
Lenglen, Mlle, 172
Le Sage, J. M., 36
Lewis, Charles David, 273
Lewis, Colonel E., 171, 281
Lewis, Robert T., 282, 285
Lewis, William, 52, 109, 280
Liberal Party, 75 n.
Liberation Society, 64
Life in Reuters, A., 205 n.
Lindley, Harry, 283
Liverpool Courier, 61, 71, 247
Liverpool Daily Post, 16, 78, 82, 108, 203
Liverpool Express, 269
Liverpool Mercury, 72
Lloyd George, David, 154
Lloyds, 69
L.N.A. Photos Ltd., 130
Lobby correspondents, 196
Lockeyear, Walter, 242, 244
Lombard News Company, 52
London News Agency, 129, 130, 187, 197
London News Service, 129
London Stock Exchange, 67
Lord Mayor's Banquet, 102, 103
Louise, Princess, 57
Lovell, John, 36, 37, 41, 43, 46, 47, 50, 53, 56, 58, 59, 62, 63, 68, 69, 72, 80, 83, 84, 87, 92, 116, 117, 144, 146
Lowing, Elizabeth, 89
Lush, Jack, 272
Lutyens, Sir E., 200, 201

McCallum, J., 98, 100, 115
Macassey, Sir L., 230
Mace, Fred, 89
Macliver, P. S., 71, 279, 284
McNae, L. C. J., 246
Maitland, John, 279, 285
Manchester Evening News, 124, 183, 203, 218, 268
Manchester Examiner, 33
Manchester Guardian, 16, 21, 26, 28, 31, 32, 33, 46, 48, 49, 82, 117, 124, 181, 182, 186, 203, 219, 237, 248, 263, 268
Mann, Arthur H., 186, 203, 219, 282
Manners, Lord J., 60, 61
Manning, solicitor, 105, 106
Margaret, H.R.H. Princess, 185, 243
Martin, Henry, 184, 187, 188, 189, 190, 191, 192, 193, 194, 195, 196, 198, 233, 234, 242, 246, 247, 248, 249, 250, 269
Mason, E. A., 108
Mass-circulation war, 176–83
Maunsell, Dr. H., 284
Midshipmite, The, quoted, 86
Ministry of Information, curb on news, 233–4
Moloney, William, 230
Monckton, Sir Walter, 221, 222, 232
Monopolies Commission, 259, 260
Moore, J., 94, 95
Moors murder case, 271
Morley, J., 79
Morning Post, 110, 120, 141, 180
Morning Star, 44
Mother Seigel's Syrup, 92
Mountbatten, Lord Louis, 190
Munich agreement, 216
Muswell Hill Record, 79

Nagle, David A., 284
Napier, Mark, 206, 207, 208
National Hunt Committee, 263
National Press Agency, 110
National Society of Operative Printers and Assistants, 251
National Union of Journalists, 168, 189, 251, 259
New Bridge Street, 90
Newcastle Daily Chronicle, 159
Newcastle Journal, 64
Newlands, J., 154, 161, 240
News—
  age of, 19
  sporting, 39

303

Index

News Chronicle, 176, 194, 227 n.
News of the World, 135
Newspaper Proprietors Association, 171, 209, 224, 225, 256
Newspaper Society, 15, 171, 237, 255, 265 (see also Provincial Newspaper Society)
Newspaper World, 79, 180
Newsprint, 17
Nickolls, L., 193
North and South Shields Gazette, 22
North Eastern Gazette, 150, 160
North Star (Darlington), 80
Northcliffe, Lord, 130, 131, 133, 175
Northcote, Sir Stafford, 293, 298
Northern Echo, 150, 186
Nottingham Daily Express, 71, 82
Nottingham Journal, 186
Nutter, C. 195

O'Dwyer, Sir M., 232
Owen, Sir James, 160, 281
Oxford Movement, 188

Palatine Hotel, Manchester, 26, 27, 29
Pall Mall Gazette, 57, 130
Palles, Lord Chief Baron, 107
Palmer, H. J., 131
Pardon, C. F., 117, 122, 123, 261
Pardon, S., 123
Paris Commune, 68, 121
Parliamentary news, 41, 43-5, 57, 58
Parliamentary reports, 21, 22
Patey, C. H. B., 63
Peace of Vereeningen, 101
Pearce, F., 95
Pearl Harbour, 266
Pebody, C., 84
Peel, Sir Robert, 297, 298 n.
Perks, S., 97
Perth, Lord, 221, 222
Perth Letter, 221, 222
Phillips, J. S. R., 113, 151, 281
Pick, Frank, 219, 220, 221
Pickering, Arthur, 160, 209, 281
Pigeon, football results by, 19
Pincher, Chapman, 137 n.
Pitman Teacher, 37
Place of Religion in the Post-War Press, The, 188
Plimsoll, Samuel, 298 n.
Plummer, L., 226

Police Budget, 180
Portland, Duke of, 98
Post Office—
tariff revisions, 60-3
telegram deliveries, 148-9
Post Office Rifles, 13
Postal Telegraphs Department, 13
Potts, Thomas, 284
Press, The, 15
Press Association—
administration reorganised, 267-8
advent of the tape machine, 92
and BBC, 170-5
and British Government, 233-5
and Creed system, 153-5
and death of King George V, 192, 193-5
and Exchange Telegraph Co., 122-8
and General Elections, 79-80, 256-8
and Reuters, 38-9, 119-22, 209, 210, 211, 212-13, 215, 230
and the Post Office, 40-1, 48-55, 58-63
during World War II, 141-3, 236
first tariffs, 42-3
founding of, 26
future of, 277-8
Gladstone and the, 75-85
in war, 232-7
insurance and endowment scheme, 89
Irish Treaty scoop, 163-4
messenger boys, 93-5
move to Byron House, 160
photo company, 241-6
private instruction re Mrs Simpson, 184
private wire system, 149
racing results, 164-6
rivalry with other agencies, 114-34
shares, 65 n., 66 n.
sporting news, 122
teletypesetting, 268
voice-frequency system, 240
Preston, H., 123
Printing and Kindred Trades Federation, 252
Provincial Newspaper Society, 15, 28, 29, 35, 62, 65, 92, 110
Punch, 54

Index

Quarterly Review, 170 n.

Race meetings, 39
Racecourse Association, 262
Racing, doping and, 199
Racing Calendar, 199
Radcliffe, Cyril (Lord), 234 n.
Radziwill, Princess, 136
Railways, effect on newspapers, 17–18
Red Lion Court, 129
Redpath, R., 64, 279, 280
Reed, Colonel Sir J., 159, 160, 161, 281
Reed, H. B., 80, 81, 82, 83, 84
Reid, Anna, 104
Reith, Lord, 170, 172, 173, 174
Reuter, Julius, 38, 39
Reuter Trust, 227, 229
Reuters, 118, 119, 120, 121, 132, 205, 234
   and the B.B.C., 172
   and the Government, 216–24
   and P.A. (*see* Press Association and Reuters)
Richley, Noel, 255
Richmond and Gordon, Duke of, 298
Riddell, Sir G. (Lord), 31, 135, 136
Ritchie, A., 41
Robbins, C. J., 197, 273
Robbins, Edmund, 14, 46, 47, 59, 69, 70, 75 n., 79 n., 82 n., 87, 88, 89, 90, 91, 92, 95, 102, 105, 106, 107, 111, 112, 114, 116, 117, 119, 123, 125, 126, 127, 128, 129, 130, 135, 136, 137, 138, 140, 143, 144, 145, 146, 147, 148, 149, 150, 151, 155, 159, 162, 265
Robbins, H. C., 67, 87, 129, 133, 134, 135, 138 n., 143, 158, 159, 161, 162, 166, 174, 195, 198, 201, 202, 207, 214
Robinson, J., 284
Rochdale Observer, 203
R 101, 174
Rosebery, Lord, 78
Rowton, Lord, 76, 293, 298
Royal Berkshire Regiment, 13
Royal Commission on the Press, 178, 247–50
Royal Marine Corps, 15
Royal Naval Film Corporation, 190
Runciman, Walter, 156

Russell, Dr. Charles, 131, 280
Russell, H., 141
Russo-Japanese War, 119

St. Bride's Church, 235
St. Leger, 18
Salerno, 245
Salisbury, Lord, 69, 78, 80, 81, 298
Salisbury Hotel, 54, 110
Salmon, Mr. Justice, 270
Sandringham, 193
Saunders, P.A. reporter, 104, 106, 107, 109
Saunders, William, 22, 33, 46, 114, 115, 285
Savoy Hotel, 31
Scarborough Evening News, 139, 195, 218
Scotsman, 16, 24, 25, 54
Scott, C. P., 32, 181, 182, 203
Scott, John R., 203, 219, 282
Scott, Laurence, 237, 263, 265, 283
Scott, W., 203, 281
Scudamore, F. I., 13, 14, 27, 40, 52, 53, 54, 56, 58, 59
Searle, Kenneth A., 268
Selborne, Lord, 133
Shackleton, Sir Ernest, 244
Shaw, J. D., 82, 83
Shaw, P. A., 159, 169, 202, 238
Shawcross Commission, 276
Sheffield Independent, 44, 105
Sheffield Telegraph, 31, 33, 34, 49, 70, 128, 131, 218
Shew, E. Spencer, 272
Sheffield Times, 37
Shields Daily Gazette, 148
Shrivenham rail disaster, 192
Shute, General, 293
Sidney Street siege, 244
Simpson, Mrs. Ernest, 184
Sims, P.A. messenger, 88
Sino-Japanese War, 119
Sketch, 270
Sketchy Bits, 180
Smith, G., 100–2
South Wales Argus, 154
South Wales Daily News, 84
Southampton Pictorial, 139
Southern Echo (Southampton) 132 n., 246
Southerton, S., 123
Sowler, John, 285

Index

Spark, F. R., 43, 71, 144, 279, 284
Speaking tube, 88
Special Reporting Service, 246
Spectator, 37
Spender, Edward, 22, 114, 281, 285
Sporting Chronicle, 123
Sporting Times, 39
Stacpoole, E. P., 187, 196, 197, 272
Staffordshire Sentinel, 136
Staines, Herbert, 218, 233, 282
Stallard, Leslie J., 268, 283
Stamp duty, abolition of, 15, 16, 17, 19,
Stamp Office, 17
Standard, 54, 180
Stanhope, E., 293
Stanhope, Lord, 190, 191
Stanley, Lord, 27
Star, 99, 169 n., 240, 241
Stead, W. T., 130, 175
Stephen, Allan G., 283
Stockley, Cynthia, 192
Stoddart, J. H., 284
Stone, M. E., 207
Storey, Samuel, 204, 218, 219, 220, 221, 222, 224, 227, 229, 230, 282
Storks, Sir Henry, 14
Submarine cable, first, 18
Sunday Post (Glasgow), 251
Sunderland Echo, 218
Surrey Standard, 37

Tape machine, 153
Taylor, Colonel Du Plat, 13, 14
Taylor, John E., 26, 28, 29, 31, 32, 33, 34, 35, 36, 38, 46, 62, 65, 70, 71, 144, 203, 268, 279, 284
Taylor, R. S., 32
Telegraph—
 effect on newspapers, 17-18
 influence on communication, 20
Telegraph Act, 1869, 23
Telegraph and Argus (Bradford), 185, 218
Telegraph Bill, 27
Telegraph companies, the Press and, 19-22, 23-8
Telegraph Street, London, 13, 25
Telegraph system, nationalisation of, 27
Telegraphs in Victorian London, 13 n.
Telegraphy, speed of, 152-3
Teletypesetting, 268

Television v. newspapers, 266-7
Thaw, Harry, 120
Thomson, D. C., 251, 252
Thomson, John, 283
Thorpe, Jeremy, 75 n.
Tillotson, W. F., 55, 128
Times, The, 15, 19, 22, 69, 70, 76, 119, 121, 122, 133, 134, 137, 138, 141, 176, 182 n., 191, 235, 248, 260
 quoted, 292-8
Tinling, Charles, 284
Tomlinson, W. T., 246
Toulmin, George (Sir), 71, 142, 160, 161, 281
Townsend, Peter, 185
Tranby Croft baccarat case, 112
Trevelyan, G. M., quoted, 16
Truby, William, 241, 242, 244
Turner, Frank, 196, 231, 272
Turner, W., 230
Tweedsmuir, Lord, 210

United Hotel, Haymarket, 28
United Ireland, 84

Victoria, Queen, 116 n.
 Diamond Jubilee, 132
 speech transmission, 20
Voice-frequency system, 240

Wallace, Edgar, 136
War correspondents, 136, 138, 139, 140, 141
Warren, Leonard, 240, 272
Waterford Mail, 29
Watson, Thomas F., 264, 265, 266
Weatherby's, 263
Webber, Frank, 282
Webber, Robert J., 282
Weekly Dispatch, 176
Weekly Examiner, 35
Wescomb, C., 284
West Surrey Times, 37
Western Daily Mail, 62
Western Daily Press, 71
Western Morning News, 22, 33, 114
Wesminster Gazette, 159
Westmorland Gazette, 269
Whates, H. R. G., 23, 178
White Swan, The, 245
Whittaker, F. C., 195, 218, 282

Index

Whittaker, M. T., 139, 281
Whorlow, Henry, 46, 47, 92, 104, 105, 106, 107, 110, 144, 159
Will, William, 203, 282
Willans, J. W., 280
Williamson, John, 271
Willox, J. A., 61, 71, 279, 280
Wilson, Harold, 75 n.
Wilson, Robert, 281
Wine Office Court, 44, 45, 86, 90
Winfrey, R. P., 263, 264, 265, 283
Winn, A., 124, 165
Wisden, 261
Wood, Kingsley, 229
Woodhead, Joseph, 35
Wolverhampton Express and Star, 268
Worcester Evening Post and Echo, 108

World War I, censorship, 135, 137, 138, 139, 140
World War II, censorship, 141
World's Press News, 269 n.
Wright, H., 103
Wright, William, 39
Wulff, Louis, 190, 191, 193, 194, 195, 272
Wynkyn de Worde, 160
Wynne, solicitor, 106

Ye Olde Cheshire Cheese, 44, 86, 87
Yorkshire Gazette, 29, 71, 110
Yorkshire Newspaper Society, 29
Yorkshire Observer, 186
Yorkshire Post, 16, 20, 84, 112, 113, 130, 151, 185, 186, 203, 219,
Young, W. M., 245, 246, 283